AF699734

WITHDRAWN

Ludington Public Library
Founded 1916
Bryn Mawr Pennsylvania

This book presented by

John J. Guinan
in memory of

MARIETTA PATZAU BUSHNELL BOYER

LUDINGTON PUBLIC LIBRARY
BRYN MAWR, PA 19010

JOYCE TREIMAN

JOYCE TREIMAN

LUDINGTON
PUBLIC LIBRARY & INFORMATION CENTER
BRYN MAWR & LANCASTER AVE.
BRYN MAWR, PA 19010-3471

MICHAEL DUNCAN

THEODORE F. WOLFF

HUDSON HILLS PRESS
NEW YORK

First Edition

"Joyce Treiman" © 1997 by Theodore F. Wolff

"Me Me Me Me Me: Joyce Treiman and Self-Portraiture" © 1997 by Michael Duncan

Illustrations © 1997 by the Estate of Joyce Treiman

All rights reserved under International and Pan-American Copyright Conventions.

Published in the United States by Hudson Hills Press, Inc.,
Suite 1308, 230 Fifth Avenue, New York, NY 10001-7704.

Distributed in the United States, its territories and possessions, and Canada
by National Book Network.

Distributed in the United Kingdom, Eire, and Europe
by Art Books International Ltd.

Distributed in Australia by Peribo PTY Limited.

Distributed in New Zealand by Nationwide Book Distributors Ltd.

Exclusive representation in China by Cassidy and Associates, Inc.

Editor and Publisher: **Paul Anbinder**

Assistant Editor: **Faye Chiu**

Copy Editor: **Fronia W. Simpson**

Proofreader: **Lydia Edwards**

Indexer: **Karla J. Knight**

Designer: **Martin Lubin**

Composition: **Angela Taormina**

Manufactured in Japan by Toppan Printing Company.

Library of Congress Cataloguing-in-Publication Data

Duncan, Michael, 1953–
Joyce Treiman / Michael Duncan, Theodore F. Wolff.
p. cm.
Includes bibliographical references and index.
ISBN 1-55595-141-4 (hardcover : alk. paper)
1. Treiman, Joyce—Criticism and interpretation. 2. Treiman, Joyce—Self-portraits 3. Human figure in art. I. Wolff, Theodore F. II. Title.
N6537.T67D86 1997
759.13—dc21 97-20203
CIP

CONTENTS

30043000469704

PLATES

JOYCE TREIMAN

THEODORE F. WOLFF

Artists tend to be specialists. A brilliant sculptor may be little more than adequate as a painter. And a gifted draftsman may have difficulties with color. There have always been exceptions, of course, artists at all levels of accomplishment who are masters of more than one art form. Joyce Treiman belongs to this group. Few recent Americans have been as adept as she with both line and color. Her extraordinary drawings, which run the gamut from miniature studies to complex, large-scale compositions, are the prized possessions of museums and collectors throughout the United States. And her powerful, richly hued canvases have attracted the favorable attention of critics and curators for over five decades.

Even so, true fame has eluded her to date, and for reasons that are not difficult to determine. Her talents were too individualistic and wide ranging, for one thing, to conform to the formal agendas of any of the dozen or so critically acclaimed art movements that sprang up during her lifetime. And her passionate adherence to the European painting tradition of Rembrandt, Velázquez, and Goya precluded her receiving the kind of high-level, quasi-official critical recognition required for art-world fame during a period defined by innovative modernist ideas and dominated by such iconoclastic figures as Jackson Pollock and Andy Warhol.

This is not to say, however, that she was blind to, or unsympathetic toward, modernist ideas and methods. Far from it. No one could speak more eloquently about the modernists she respected—or more devastatingly about those she did not. She loved painting and drawing and accepted anything on canvas or paper she believed to be authentic. Still, she never lowered her standards. Artistic greatness remained the criterion by which she ultimately judged everything, her own work included. If, as a mature painter, she preferred a historically oriented representational mode to one that was abstract, it was because she believed the tradition of Rembrandt and Velázquez was more conducive to the kind of enterprise she had in mind than that of Piet Mondrian and Wassily Kandinsky. On the other hand, if she admired Rembrandt more than Georges Rouault, it was only because Rembrandt's achievements were greater than Rouault's, not because the former represented tradition to her and the latter, revolution.

On the surface, Treiman was a traditionalist. In actuality, she was a fiercely independent, even iconoclastic, artist of great range and abilities. Because of her thorough grounding in her craft and her refusal to conform to any of modernism's numerous dogmas, she was free to do exactly as she pleased. Her work, as a result, had no formal or thematic limitations and ranged from the impishly perverse and humorously paradoxical to the brilliant and profound. She delighted as much in biting characterizations of her fellow humans as in sly art-historical references and affectionate depictions of children and animals. She was as comfortable doing delicate line drawings as attacking large canvases with thick daubs of paint. And when it came to color, no one of her generation was less inhibited than she.

As an artist, Treiman never stopped growing, never rested on her laurels. Following her career was a never-ending challenge and delight. No sooner had one become accustomed to her latest move, or decided that she had exhausted the possibilities of a particular medium or approach, than she would come up with something totally unexpected that was, more often than not, better or more exciting than what had gone before.

That was especially true in 1983, the year in which she produced the paintings that capped her career and established conclusively that she deserves to be ranked among the finest painters of late-twentieth-century American art. In **Thanatopsis, Hercules and the Arcadian Stag, The Parting,** and a number of other extraordinary canvases of that year, she successfully synthesized many of the central but previously divergent elements of her creative vision. All of these paintings are dark, some are grim, but every one represents Treiman at her very best.

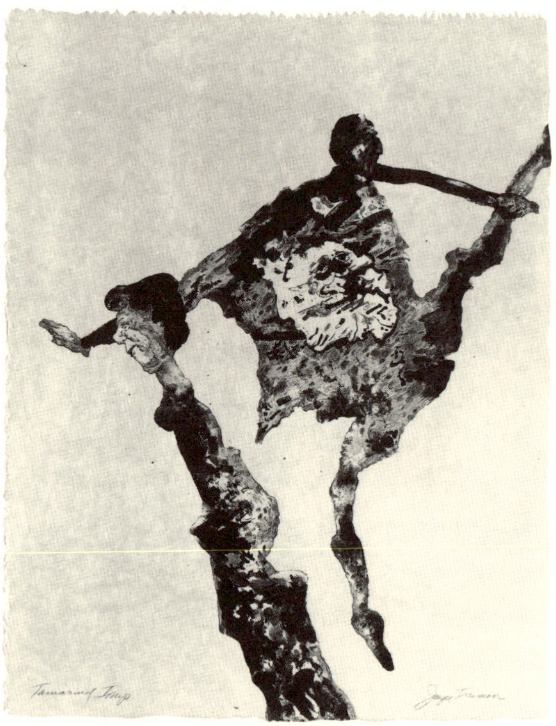

Untitled from the portfolio **The Mirrored Couple**
1961
lithograph, printed in black and green-yellow
$19^{3}/_{16}$ x $15^{1}/_{4}$ inches
The Museum of Modern Art, New York,
Gift of Kleiner, Bell & Co., 963.67.7

While it may be hyperbole to claim that Treiman could draw like an angel and paint like an old master, that statement is not far from the truth. Her drawings—and she made literally thousands of them—may prove to be her best assurance of a lasting reputation, for among them are a number of the finest examples of draftsmanship produced by an American during the past half century. She herself was aware of their quality and upon several occasions expressed pride in her skills with pencil and charcoal. Once, during a discussion on the future of art, she burst out: "I don't know what will happen to my paintings. I think they will be always appreciated, but I **know** my drawings will last."[1]

She was passionate about drawing and practiced it incessantly. If no other model was present she drew herself. Recording what she saw in a mirror was as important to her as it was to her greatest hero, Rembrandt, and like him, she depicted herself in a variety of moods and poses, not all of them serious. At times she dressed herself up in fancy costumes and outlandish hats, at others she was more sedately attired but revealed a mischievous glint in her eye. Best of all were the straightforward, unedited depictions that appeared more and more frequently as she aged, and that not only record her changing physical appearance but give the viewer a clear idea of how she perceived herself both as a woman and as an artist.

Perhaps nothing is more revealing about Treiman's lifelong commitment to art than the opening sentence of an autobiographical essay written in June 1977. Before mentioning anything else about her birth or childhood, she states: "I started drawing at age eight and knew then that what I really wanted was to make art. There was never any doubt although doubts happened along the way."[2]

At the end of the essay, written when she was fifty-five, she expressed herself even more positively. "It goes on, and art and paintings are really my life, and I wouldn't trade it for anything. The paintings as I look back, are an autobiography. I hope they are meaningful. That's all I ask. Keep going, working and painting—that's all there is."[3]

For someone as certain as she about her goals, Treiman was extremely fortunate in her parents. Both René and Rose Wahl, to whom she was born on May 29, 1922, in Evanston, Illinois, recognized her special talent and never questioned her wish to be an artist. Understandably—after all, art did not pay in America during the first half of the twentieth century—they were concerned about her ability to earn a living in her chosen profession. That concern did not prevent them, however, from backing her wholeheartedly in her creative endeavors.

Their support took a practical turn when Mrs. Wahl enrolled Joyce in a children's art class—only to be informed by the teacher after one session that Joyce should be taking an adult art class instead. The family agreed. Mr. Wahl, however, worried about his young daughter's safety in the big city of Chicago. He insisted on accompanying her to her new class on weekends and waiting for her in the hallway until she finished.

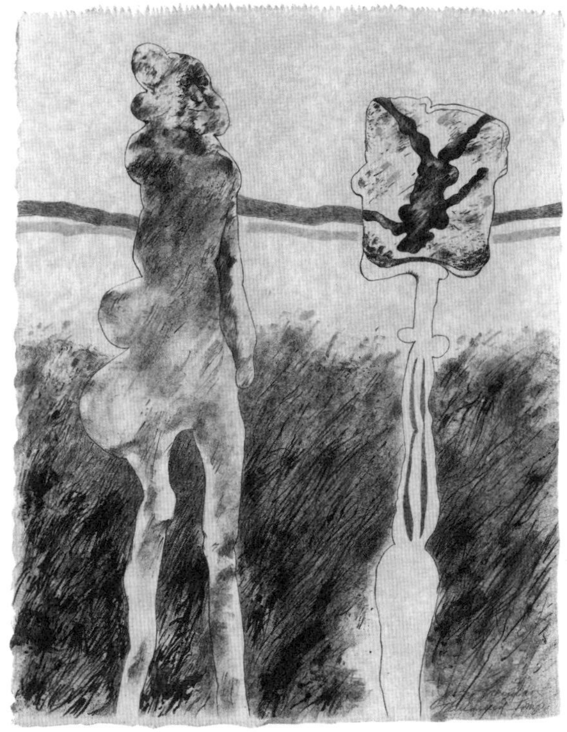

Untitled from the portfolio **The Mirrored Couple**
1961
lithograph, printed in black
$17^{3}/_{8}$ x $14^{3}/_{8}$ inches
The Museum of Modern Art, New York,
Gift of Kleiner, Bell & Co., 963.67.9

By the time Joyce was in high school she was drawing from the model on Saturdays and roaming the galleries of the Art Institute of Chicago. In her words: "I think I must have subconsciously been exercising my eye. The great Impressionist paintings were there and they had a marvelous print and drawing collection. As long as I was in Chicago I used the Art Institute as my training ground for learning about the quality in art from Gothic to contemporary."[4]

After attending Stephens College in Columbia, Missouri, from 1939 to 1941, Joyce Wahl decided to continue her education at the State University of Iowa, at that time one of the few universities that combined studio work with liberal arts and offered a bachelor of fine arts degree. Her decision was a crucial one, for it was there that she met the teacher who would profoundly affect her work. Philip Guston not only introduced her to painting—until then she had made only drawings—he alerted her to the wide range of creative possibilities open to a young artist of talent. Treiman responded enthusiastically, to such a degree that it would be several years before she could completely free herself of Guston's influence.

By 1943 Joyce was back in Chicago painting the unfortunates on the streets of that city and doing layout work for various publications. In 1945 she married the businessman Kenneth Treiman. Two years later she was awarded a Louis Comfort Tiffany Foundation scholarship. With that affirmation of her abilities, she immediately quit her job and began devoting herself exclusively to painting.

Art-world response was swift and gratifying. Galleries in Chicago and New York, and museums around the country, started featuring her work. And she received the first of many awards that would come her way during her career.

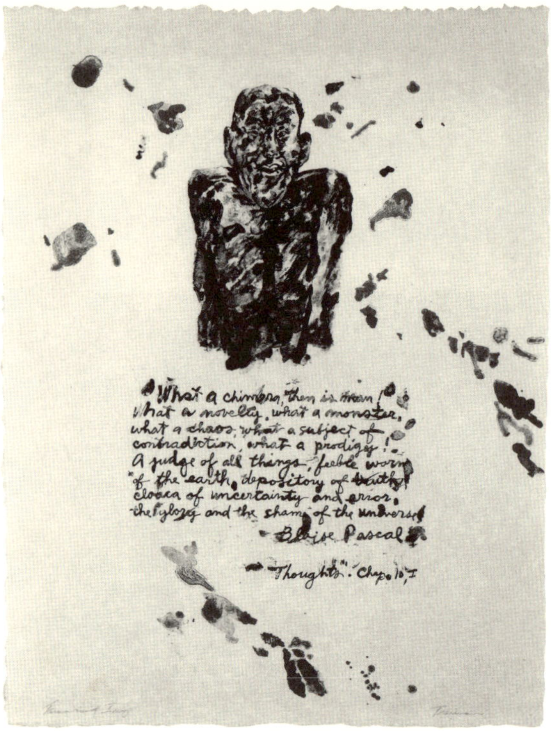

Quotation Page from the portfolio
The Mirrored Couple
1961
lithograph, printed in black and red
20¼ x 15¼ inches
National Gallery of Art, Washington, Rosenwald Collection, 1964.8.2564 (PR)

Treiman took it all in stride. What mattered most was the work, and that was progressing well—so well, in fact, that by the time she, her husband, and their nine-year-old son, Donald, moved to Los Angeles in 1960, she had acquired a solid reputation as one of the Midwest's finest painters and draftsmen.

California came as something of a shock. She explained her reaction to it in her autobiographical essay. "I think it took a while for it to sink in artistically—in terms of the light and color—so different from the inward-looking and soul searching of the Middle West."[5] Before long, however, she was once again painting with a vengeance. Several trips to the Near East and to Europe during the 1960s intensified her interest in color but, more important, deepened her respect for the old masters.

Impressed by the psychological acuity of these artists' paintings, Treiman decided to try her hand at portraiture, not as a career, but as an effective way of probing more deeply into the human psyche. She began with studies of single figures toward the very end of the 1960s but soon expanded her compositions to include several individuals arrayed informally, and often disquietingly, across the canvas. These were followed by her **Artists** series, a number of large, richly detailed paintings in which she depicted herself mingling as an equal with such famous artists of the recent past as John Singer Sargent and Pierre Bonnard.

A diagnosis of lung cancer interrupted her career in November 1983, but an operation and extensive chemotherapy enabled her to resume work in 1984. Except for size and degree of dramatic impact, at first there was little change in the paintings she produced once she returned to her studio. True, her images became more enigmatic, and a new note of poignancy entered her work, but the verve, imagination, and skill that had always characterized her art did not diminish.

This note of poignancy gradually intensified over the next few years and resulted, by the late 1980s, in canvases that were considerably looser in execution and hauntingly, even at times achingly, suggestive of endings and departures. Still, Treiman's positive attitude and sly, self-deprecatory humor—to say nothing of her increasingly exuberant use of color—prevented even a hint of negativity from entering her paintings and drawings.

As 1990 approached, her work decreased even more in size—but not in output. Pastel became a favored medium, and clusters of tiny canvases, each only a few inches in size, left her studio for the Schmidt Bingham Gallery, her dealer in New York.

Joyce Treiman died of a heart attack on June 2, 1991, only four days after her sixty-ninth birthday. In her studio at the time of her death were several unfinished works, indicating that she had been working until the very end.

Two things must be understood if one is to grasp the nature and significance of Treiman's art. First, she began as a draftsman and never denied drawing its central role in her creative vision. Second, she was a fervent advocate of painting that was direct, visceral, and sensuous. Nothing annoyed her more than paint flatly or indifferently applied, especially if the work was nonobjective. "Second-year design-class stuff," she would mutter in front of a canvas executed in this manner, and move on.

Although most painters draw, few produce drawings that exist totally on their own and not primarily as warming-up exercises or preparatory studies for more finished works on canvas. That was not the case with Treiman. She did, of course, produce numerous sketches and studies of this nature, but her major commitment was to the type of draftsmanship that exists as an end in itself. Here she was in excellent company, from Leonardo and Dürer to Degas and Matisse.

As is true of relatively few draftsmen—one need only think of the brilliant but tightly controlled drawings of Holbein and Ingres—Treiman's line could be both precise and free. It could zero in on a face or an inanimate object and record it exactly as it appeared, or it could dash about on a sheet of paper with the same kind of energy displayed by a skater on ice.

It is not surprising, considering that she started to draw at the age of eight and did not begin to paint until she was nineteen, that many of Treiman's drawings have a life and a character of their own quite separate from those of her paintings. It was not until the late 1960s, in fact, when she was already in her mid-forties, that her paintings began to match her drawings in maturity and impact. Outstanding, even extraordinary, as such earlier canvases as **Jacob, Man, Angel** (1956) and **The Poet** (1961–62) may be, they appear somewhat tentative when compared to **The Yellow Lampshade** (1968–69) and **The Adventure** (1970), two of the paintings she produced after her three pivotal European trips at the end of the 1960s.

Her drawings evolved more naturally and effortlessly. "I could draw as easily as I could breathe," is how she explained her early mastery. "Painting I had to learn." One glance at her drawings proves her point. Everything looks incredibly easy. Even highly complex images appear not to have presented problems. And just as important, her touch, which was as light as a feather, was sensitive to every nuance of her subject's individuality and character.

Such linear virtuosity is extremely rare. Only a handful of artists in every generation have it, and even fewer take advantage of it as successfully—or as delightfully—as Treiman. Unlike some draftsmen who remain relatively indifferent to the technical side of their art, Treiman was fascinated by the drawing process itself. Practically every graphic tool or device came under her careful scrutiny at one time or another and could, as a result, be called upon without a moment's hesitation to produce a particular visual effect or to help articulate a difficult form.

In her 1982 drawing **Plumed Helmet: Study for "The Parting,"** for instance, the crisp pencil lines and carefully controlled hatchings and smudges that define the forms and locate them in space are augmented by discrete touches of pastel serving as subtle color accents. And in **The Rock and the Ram** (1984) Treiman utilized a mixture of charcoal, pencil, pastel, and colored pencil to achieve the complex result she desired.

For most of her studies from life, however, and especially for her impressive self-portraits, she worked directly and exclusively in charcoal. False starts and mistakes (if there were any) were either picked off with an eraser or ignored, and the entire drawing was generally completed at one sitting. "I hate to go back and 'match up' where I left off," she explained. "Unless, of course, I feel later that something is missing."

When it came to drawing, Treiman had few if any inhibitions. Nothing was safe from her derisive wit or expansive good humor. She enjoyed thumbing her nose at convention, but no more than she enjoyed poking fun at herself or taking broad swipes at the vagaries of artistic fashion. Since drawing came so easily to her, she used it as casually and intimately as others use speech or letter writing to express feelings or to communicate ideas.

Many of her drawings, as a result, are highly personal statements brought into being primarily to give form to a fleeting impulse, an offhand thought, or possibly a sense of frustration or outrage over a particularly disturbing example of human greed or stupidity. Others—and one must not overlook this more mundane aspect of creativity—obviously are the result of nothing more complicated than curiosity as to how best to capture the effect of sunlight on the rumpled fur of a pet, an urgent need to take advantage of the death of a richly feathered parrot to try out a new pencil technique, or simply a desire to cover a delicately pebbled sheet of paper with a variety of carefully rendered human heads.

In the hands of a less talented and experienced draftsman than Treiman, such drawings would be of little or no interest or value. In hers, however, they exist, more often than not, as gems of creative sensibility and as excellent demonstrations of what the art of drawing is all about.

On the other hand, large numbers of her drawings were as thoughtfully conceived and executed as any of her major paintings. Outstanding among them are the luridly colored pastels of Las Vegas night life she produced in 1980. Brilliantly drawn and pulsating with raucous theatricality, these depictions of grotesque yet oddly appealing denizens of the Nevada nightclub circuit can stand comparison with Toulouse-Lautrec's earlier portrayals of Parisian nightlife characters and events.

Also of exceptional interest and quality are several of her studies for the **Artists** series, especially **Study for Big Bonnard and Me Twice** (1977) and **Study for Turner and Me** (1978), as well as many of her large multifigure compositions, most particularly **The Adventurer II** (1978) and **Plumed Helmet: Study for "The Parting"** (1982).

And, of course, no list of Treiman's finest drawings would be complete without the inclusion of a half-dozen or so of her superb self-portraits and an equal number of her incisive but affectionate depictions of her mother, Rose. Self-portraiture has been practiced for a very long time, but seldom, in this century at least, has an artist succeeded so tellingly and stylishly in transcribing onto paper what appeared in his or her mirror. At times ruthlessly blunt and probing, at others charmingly elusive or delightfully self-deprecating, Treiman's charcoal and mixed-media self-portraits on paper constitute a running autobiographical commentary on where she stood on issues and how she saw herself at various stages during her life and career. Few American artists of this century have been as open and revealing as she. And even fewer have managed it with so much style and grace.

These qualities became even more pronounced toward the end of the 1980s. Increasingly, after 1987, the formal and expressive aspects of her drawings shifted from line to mass, from black-and-white to color, and from a crisply analytical attitude to one that was mellower, less incisive, and even, upon occasion, warmly romantic.

Pastel, applied in a loosely painterly fashion and with a minimum of linear elaboration, played a crucial role in this transformation. Dabs and smudges of deep reds, blues, greens, and browns replaced the lines and dramatic tonal contrasts of her earlier graphic images. And her forms, which previously had moved freely in and out of space, now appeared to float exclusively on or near the surface.

Roses and Vase (1991), one of her very last works on paper, is hardly a drawing at all. Everything about it places it much closer in spirit and execution to such paintings of 1989 as **Much Madness** and **Camouflage** than to any of her drawings of the early 1980s or before. And yet, it is a handsome and moving image and a fitting closure to Treiman's long and distinguished career as a draftsman.

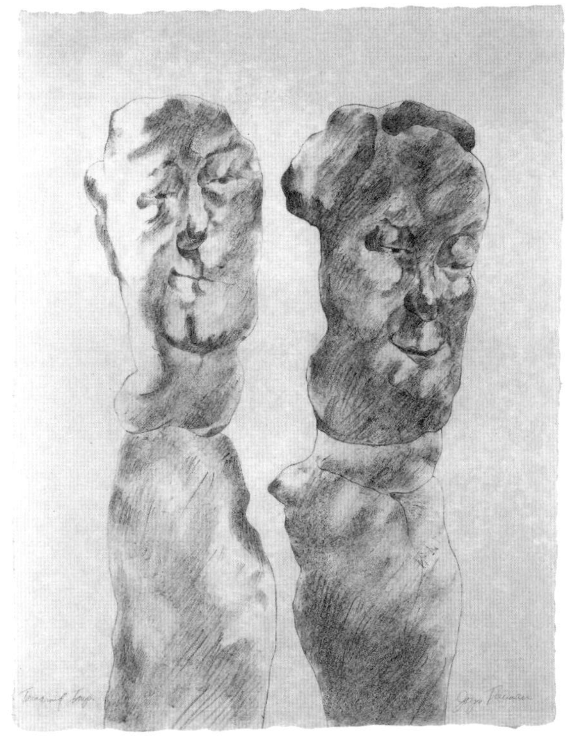

Untitled from the portfolio **The Mirrored Couple**
1961
lithograph, printed in black
20¼ x 15¼ inches
National Gallery of Art, Washington, Rosenwald Collection, 1964.8.2568 (PR)

The evidence of her early work indicates that Treiman was only telling the truth when she claimed that, from the very beginning, she could draw as easily as she could breathe. And that she was being no less than truthful when she insisted, "Painting I had to learn."

The fact that she began to draw at such a young age and to paint when she was nearly twenty says a great deal about her early artistic preferences, but it also helps explain why painting did not come as easily or as "naturally" to her as drawing. After all, at eight, she was free to draw what she wanted, to evolve at her own pace and in accordance with her own talents and inclinations. Even her attendance, shortly thereafter, at an adult art class does not negate this point, since her remarkable skills as a draftsman had already been acknowledged when she enrolled. But that was not so when, as a beginning art student in a prestigious university art class under a highly regarded painter-teacher, she was confronted by the need to master an entirely new way of fashioning visual images as quickly and successfully as possible.

The pressures upon her must have been enormous, especially since, as she admits, "I was in shock about how little I knew about past art—and contemporary art." No matter how well known as an accomplished draftsman she may have been in her circles, in Philip Guston's painting class she was a mere beginner. Furthermore, it was "mind-boggling to be taught by a 'real' professional artist . . . who was already 'involved' and part of the art world."[6] Treiman was impressed and intimidated, not only by Guston's authoritative manner and obvious abilities as a painter, but also by some of the more advanced art students who "mostly came from New York and appeared to be wildly sophisticated about art."[7]

In this environment, mastery had to come swiftly and within a particular technical and formal context. There was not time to evolve at her own pace and in her own manner as she had years before with her drawings. The pressure was on, and even though Guston went out of his way to support what he correctly perceived were her strengths, she soon became confused and vulnerable to the influence of an older and more forceful creative personality. In her words: "I really struggled to learn about painting. . . . Guston was painting in a sort of flat mural style. His color was beautiful and sensitive and his work at that time had mystery. . . . He influenced my work, . . . and fortunately for me his eye was good and his feelings about painting excellent."[8]

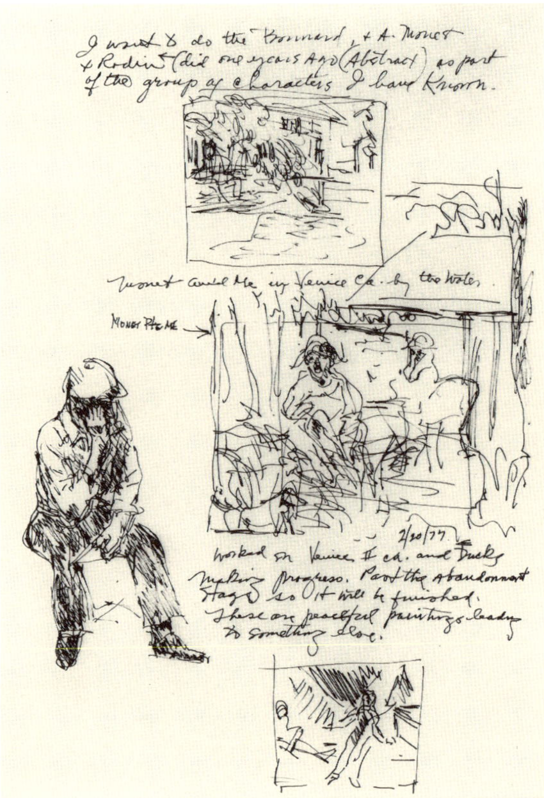

Page from sketchbook
1977
ink on paper
12 x 8 inches
Collection Donald M. Treiman,
Pacific Palisades, California

It was so excellent, in fact, that Guston's influence can still be detected in Treiman's paintings executed almost a decade after she first entered his class. **Street in Motion** (1948) and **Escape** (1950), for example, utilize Guston's style and iconography to such an extent that, at first glance, they could be mistaken for his.

Still, these works are impressive, not only because they were done by one so young, but because they reveal a truly remarkable control over all elements of pictorial construction. Everything in these canvases, whether it plays a significant role or not, was carefully articulated and precisely positioned for its appropriate thematic or aesthetic effect. Confronted by such youthful organizational mastery—especially in a draftsman accustomed to dealing with isolated objects in a linear fashion—it is difficult to object if here and there Treiman took advantage of other artists' technical and formal devices, if she appropriated a bit of Jack Levine here, a touch of Ben Shahn there, and presented it all in a manner reminiscent of the paintings of Philip Guston. Art history argues that one should not object, that it is all part of the process of becoming a mature painter, and that many of the greatest artists of the past and present have done the very same thing. Art history also cautions, however, that this dependency should only be a phase, and once the young artist has successfully passed through such an apprenticeship period, he or she must move on to create independent and original art.

That, of course, was exactly what Treiman attempted and accomplished. The process, however, took somewhat longer than expected, and for reasons that require a brief glance at what was occurring in American art during the decades following World War II.

With the war over, regionalism in all its forms no longer the dominant force in American art, and an entirely new generation of ambitious young artists eager to make up for lost time, New York's art world found itself in a dilemma. Both American-scene and European-inspired modernism had fallen out of fashion; surrealism was dead; the kind of realism practiced by Edward Hopper and Charles Burchfield was suffering an eclipse; and the rugged individualism personified by Thomas Hart Benton was ridiculed and even held in contempt.

The result, not surprisingly, was confusion on the part of America's younger artists. Where should they now look for guidance and inspiration? And even more to the point, what and how should they paint?

The answers came from a small group of New York–based painters of mixed backgrounds and varied talents who shared the conviction that the future of American, indeed of world, art lay in a freely improvised form of painting that combined the best features of abstraction and expressionism. A number of influential critics, dealers, and curators agreed, with the result that almost overnight, abstract expressionism became the dominant mode in American art, and Jackson Pollock, Willem de Kooning, Mark Rothko, and a handful of other artists of similar persuasion became the art world's latest heroes.

Before long, the new movement's influence had become all pervasive and difficult to resist. Treiman, in Chicago, began feeling its impact shortly after 1950. "All around me abstract expressionism was proliferating. I still at that time knew few professional painters—so I tried to figure things out for myself. I saw some of de Kooning's paintings that I liked, and it seemed everywhere you looked all you saw was 'ab ex.' I thought I would try to see what it was about. . . . By 1953 . . . I decided to just move paint around and did a series that was kind of 'ab ex' in form but with figurative overtones. . . . My color was getting higher and I enjoyed my respite from agonizing."[9]

Not surprisingly—Treiman was too much the concerned humanist to abandon figure painting entirely—her experiments with abstract expressionism were soon over. As she admits, "I guess I never did any completely abstract paintings without a 'subject' basis—except for some collages at that time."[10]

Instead, she began to look more closely at nature, and in doing so discovered a strongly lyrical side to her art. Painting in the mid-1950s became for her more a matter of pleasure than of driving social, psychological, or professional concern. She delighted in the world around her and painted it all—but especially gardens, flowers, and birds—simply and directly and in a manner that was increasingly her own.

By the late 1950s, after an inspiring and challenging six-week trip in 1955 to Paris and Italy, where she encountered Monet's paintings of water lilies and Tiepolo's allegorical canvases for the first time, she was ready once again to tackle more psychologically provocative subjects. She started off with a series of laughing men and a large self-portrait, which she subsequently destroyed. These were followed by a group of paintings depicting what she later described as "large heads and torsos of very disturbed men."

The Treimans' move to California in 1960 may have altered her mood and perceptions, but it in no way lessened her commitment to drawing and painting the human figure. That became paramount once again, and it would remain so for the balance of her career, despite the art world's insistence for most of that period that such work was unforgivably regressive.

The 1961–62 **Poet** series, which consisted of several emotionally painted celebrations of poets and poetic inspiration, marked the beginning of the end of her apprenticeship period, as well as of her still lingering doubts as to the relative merits of an exclusively representational approach, or one that also depended heavily on expressionist and nonobjective formal devices for much of its effectiveness.

It is fascinating to watch this final evolutionary process at work throughout the 1960s, to see the last vestiges of abstract-expressionist gestural improvisation gradually disappear in the face of a more pronounced and clearly defined human imagery. In **Dream Sequence (The Couple)** (1962) drips and daubs of paint still more than hold their own in a dazzling display of painterly physicality that threatens to overwhelm the man and the woman depicted. In **A View of Any Arrival** (1964), on the other hand, the human figures begin to dominate, and in **The Birthday Party** (1966–67) representationalism definitely wins out. At this point the process is nearly complete. All that is needed now is acceptance of what has been achieved and the motivation to move ahead aggressively in the new direction.

Her three trips to Europe, in 1967, 1968, and 1969, during which she became more intimately involved than ever with the work of Rembrandt, Velázquez, and Goya, provided her not only with the necessary motivation to delve deeper and more imaginatively into the realist tradition but as well with a clearer insight into how best to accomplish her objectives. She began with portraits of herself and her parents, moved on to full-length single figures, and then began the series of paintings that both established the nature and character of her mature work and informed the world that a new painter of stature and originality had arrived.

Before producing these works, Treiman had been only one of roughly two dozen promising younger American painters working in a vaguely expressionistic representational mode impressive enough to win prizes and praise from museum directors and curators, but not sufficiently individualistic or focused to stamp its practitioners as major American artists. With **Standing Man** (1968–69) and even more emphatically with **The Yellow Lampshade**

(1968–69) and **The Adventure** (1970), that was no longer the case. In them, Treiman found her own voice as a painter and established a clearer and more substantial public image for herself. In addition, their successful execution provided her with a level of self-assurance that, despite moments of doubt and hesitation, would never entirely leave her again.

Standing Man is pure Treiman. Most of the qualities that characterize her mature work—direct, uncompromising representationalism, an old-master and late-nineteenth-century American attitude toward the handling of paint, and a subtle but pervasive undercurrent of both irony and compassion—are present in this canvas. Missing only are the vibrant color, fluid brushwork, and compositional complexities of the majority of her later paintings. Even so, in this simple, stark, crisply defined, and somewhat idiosyncratic study of an old man, Treiman can already be seen at her representative best. She will become richer and more complex as a painter over the years, but never more incisive in her characterization, nor more stylistically economical in her depiction of men and women in purely painterly terms.

Standing Man proves not only that Treiman had looked long and hard at the paintings of Rembrandt and Velázquez but that she had learned how to take what they had to offer and to make it entirely her own. Foreign to the sensibilities of Rembrandt and Velázquez would have been the ironic characterization of her subject and the subtle undercurrent of alienation that permeates this depiction of an elderly bearded gentleman. Both of these typically twentieth-century expressionist devices are even more apparent in **The Yellow Lampshade**, a highly successful painting that advanced Treiman's creative evolution and introduced an entirely new set of formal and technical elements into her artistic vocabulary.

In this fascinating study of a man and a woman standing stiffly apart in a darkened room occupied as well by a large potted fern and several pieces of furniture, Treiman painted a picture of human isolation and alienation that is both exotic and mildly disturbing. Everything in it, from the awkward, self-conscious poses of the couple and the precisely rendered details of the ornamental furniture, to the dramatic contrasts created by its predominantly red, black, and brown color scheme, points to the fact that Treiman had found both something new to say and a new way to say it.

Gone in this painting is any feeling of technical or formal irresolution. Every element is crystal clear and seemingly frozen in time and place. Objects are not only carefully delineated, they are particularized to such a degree that one is certain their exact counterparts exist in the real world. Most unusual of all, however, is the obvious absence of any connection, either physical or emotional, between any person or object depicted and anything else in the composition.

That this effect was intentional was made clear by Treiman in her discussion of **Anomie** (1969–70), an even more complex and perplexing canvas completed roughly a year after **The**

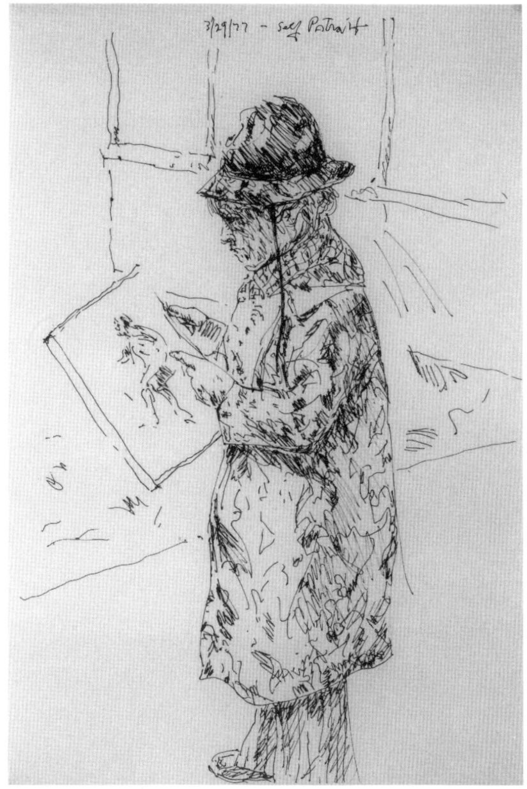

Untitled sketchbook drawing (Self-Portrait)
1977
ink on paper
12 x 8 inches
Collection Donald M. Treiman, Pacific Palisades, California

Yellow Lampshade. "**Anomie** was a kind of culmination of this group of work. I worked a long time on this painting, and it tries to talk about the alienation and neurotic nature of modern man. All the outward trappings are there, but the people who are close together don't really relate to each other."[11]

The eight individuals in **Anomie,** four men and four women, including Treiman herself, who are arrayed in a tight row facing front, bear as little relationship to one another as would eight apples or pears lined up on a table. The only real connection for seven of them (one man in the rear has been distracted by something to his right) is with the viewer, and even such eye contact as exists between them and the person examining the painting is more accidental than significant.

Impressive as **Anomie** may be, one has the suspicion that Treiman's real objective in creating it was to present a rich and varied assortment of powerfully painted men and women in a composition made even more interesting by exotic costuming and dramatic tonal and coloristic effects. If that is so, she succeeded brilliantly, for this work is, in the original meaning of the word, a masterpiece, a work of art produced by an artist to inform the world of her total mastery over a particular form of art.

Having proven herself in **Anomie,** Treiman felt free to move into more difficult and dangerous territory. The beautifully realized and aptly named **Adventure,** which she finished a few months later, represents another major step forward and bears comparison with any of the finest American paintings produced in the 1970s.

It was also the first of her mature paintings to have a clear narrative focus. Something interesting but out of sight of the viewer is occurring, and it has caught the attention of everyone in the picture. Two men and three women, including Treiman once again, respond with a mixture of surprise, disbelief, curiosity, and delight. Their interest triggers the viewer's interest, and one finds oneself caught up in the participants' varied reactions. But there is much more than that to be intrigued and impressed by in this painting. Its color, for one thing, is richer and more luminous, its light gentler and more subtly atmospheric, and its composition more purposeful and fluid, than was the case before. But most significant of all, the people depicted in it no longer appear isolated from one another as they did in **The Yellow Lampshade** and **Anomie.**

The Adventure represents a critical moment in Treiman's evolution as a painter. While it may still reflect something of a draftsman's predilection for crisply defined forms existing independently against flat or neutral backgrounds—thereby creating the effect of objects frozen in place—its greatest emphasis is on painterly and organizational fluidity.

Increasingly, from this point on, the people in Treiman's canvases interrelate dynamically rather than statically. They move about easily in three-dimensional space, speak to, laugh with, and otherwise respond to the individuals near them. Even when, as in **Dear Friends** (1972) and **Thomas Eakins Modeling in California** (1974), they are tightly clustered or very individualistically defined, the overall effect is much more open and "natural" than it was before. For the rest of the decade and into the very early 1980s, Treiman gradually enriched and expanded her painterly vocabulary. Her brushwork became broader and looser, and her color, thanks partly to her love for the paintings of Bonnard, brighter and more freely dispensed.

By 1981 and **Joyeux, Déjeuner,** and **Tiepolo and Me,** Treiman had become an impetuous, even a passionate, painter whose color was as "hot" as anyone's, and whose paint was as freely applied as that of any of her post-impressionist and expressionist favorites. **Joyeux,** in particular, pays tribute to Bonnard in so extravagantly coloristic and free-spirited a manner that one almost forgets what superb control she also had over pure line. And in **Déjeuner,** the paint has been so enthusiastically applied that one is momentarily overwhelmed by its sheer physicality.

By 1983 this note of joyous celebration had run its course, and a darker and more ominous feeling entered Treiman's art. The passion remained, indeed it increased, but the visual excitement and delight that had characterized her work until now were abruptly replaced by a much more somber and tragic vision of art and of life.

It is pointless to speculate about such matters, but one cannot help wondering if Treiman sensed, roughly a year before she was actually diagnosed with the disease in November 1983, that cancer had invaded her body. Yet how else can one explain so abrupt and dramatic a change in her work and, even more important, so great a leap forward in the depth and quality of her art? To this writer, at least, 1983 was the year of Treiman's greatest artistic triumphs. All of her half-dozen or so finest paintings and several of her most magnificent drawings were executed during that year.

Death and the darker side of Greek mythology dominated Treiman's art in 1983. Passionately applied paint and color and profoundly personal imagery fused together on canvas to become powerful and often disturbing metaphors for the meaning of human existence. And at least once, in **The Smoker No. 21,** a partially smoke-obliterated self-portrait, Treiman appears to be making a bitterly prescient comment on the possible source of her as-yet-undiagnosed disease.

Self-Portrait with Skull is another angry, slashing canvas in which Treiman confronts the specter of death, this time with steely-eyed determination. Nothing in her earlier career gave any indication that her art would move in this direction. And nothing she produced previously came even close to projecting a mood of such uncompromising negativism.

It is Treiman at her most vulnerable but also at her most defiant. With the exception of a few similarly grim painted confrontations with death—**The Torso** being the best example—most of her 1983 paintings struck a more positive note owing to her efforts, first to define, and then to reconcile, the best and the worst life had to offer through symbol and metaphor.

In her search for symbols and metaphors, she dipped deeply into Greek mythology. The Labors of Hercules, in particular, struck her as especially appropriate for what she had in mind. In her own words, "Those stories had it all: death-defying challenges; the refusal to accept defeat even against impossible odds; heroic victories; and, of course, pure guts. And what wonderful subjects for all-out, give-'em-hell paintings."

What followed was a veritable catalogue of Hercules' various confrontations, each of them painted more powerfully—and, in this writer's opinion, more brilliantly—than anything she had done before. It is difficult not to apply the word "great" to **Hercules and Cercopes** and **Hercules and the Arcadian Stag,** both of which achieved levels of masterly paint handling unsurpassed by any American artist of her generation. And even such a marginally lesser work as **Hercules and the Nemean Lion** stands as an extraordinary accomplishment at a time when paintings of this nature were considered unworthy of serious recognition by the art world at large.

Of this group, **Hercules and Cercopes** is the finest. In no other painting, not even in **Hercules and the Arcadian Stag,** did Treiman transform idea, emotion, and form into pigment and gesture as completely and successfully as she did in this canvas. She makes her point as much through the textural and coloristic physicality of the paint as through her descriptive references to its four figures. In this work, paint itself "speaks," and it does so as clearly and effectively as in the paintings of such expressionist masters as Oskar Kokoschka and Georges Rouault. No matter how one approaches it, **Hercules and Cercopes** represents painting at its very best. A careful study of its various features should convince any skeptic of Treiman's quality and importance as a painter.

The Parting is darker and more Rembrandtesque than **Hercules and Cercopes,** but no less effective in communicating its "message" through thick, rich applications of paint and color. Based on her 1982 colored drawing, **Plumed Helmut: Study for "The Parting,"** it depicts Treiman and her mother, Rose (whose death in 1976 affected Treiman deeply), looking out rather apprehensively at something immediately to the right but out of sight of the viewer. Various figures, some holding burning torches, surround them, while a length of coiled rope, from which dangle three red roses (and which could well be a hangman's noose) is suspended over Rose's head.

The overall effect is haunting and grim, especially if one compares the painting to its preparatory drawing. The latter is crisply defined, exquisitely rendered, and impish in mood. The former is blunt, boldly, even blatantly, executed, and deadly serious. And yet, comparing the two, it is obvious that the painting, disquieting though it may be, is considerably more compelling and meaningful than its superbly drawn and charming counterpart on paper.

On the other hand, **Self-Portrait in Titus's Hat** (1983), which shows Treiman in costume wearing the hat Rembrandt's young son wore in the great Dutch master's portrait of him, is purely painterly showmanship. In it she celebrates her greatest hero and teacher and informs the world not only that she has learned her lessons well but that she too can paint in a truly old-master fashion. But this amazing painting is also much more than that, for the Treiman who peers out from underneath Titus's extravagant hat is as touchingly alive and human as Rembrandt himself in his most revealing self-portraits.

In many ways, **Thanatopsis** is the culmination of Treiman's 1983 cycle of paintings. It is at once the simplest and the most moving of the lot, for it represents, in a most economical and evocative manner, her serene acceptance of whatever life still has in store for her. Within a barren landscape, and underneath a flaming sky, Treiman sits beside a skeleton. Her left arm encircles its shoulder, and the two appear to be the best of friends. Beneath them the stylized head of a horse looks upward.

It is a simple image but a powerful one and seems to have been painted as casually and effortlessly as one would write a letter. When it was first seen by this writer in 1988 during an exhibition of Treiman's work, it made an unforgettable impression. Later that day, during a walk in the countryside, Treiman spoke of this painting at some length: "It's friendly. That's how I see it. And it has hope. Nothing big or dramatic, but more quiet and restful. In a funny way I made my peace with it." When asked with what she had made her peace, she thought a moment and answered, "Oh, I don't know, with everything, I guess."

Treiman's return to the studio in 1984 after her cancer operation and chemotherapy resulted, after a short period of adjustment, in several major paintings and numerous drawings, including several superb self-portraits. Not surprisingly, she once again changed direction. In **Me and Big Ship** and **Sailing Away**, both from 1985, the viewer is faced, not only by a greater sense of poignancy, but also by a considerably more casual approach to paint handling as well. The tensely dramatic, even at times melodramatic, confrontational undercurrent that characterized her 1983 paintings had been replaced by a new and totally undramatic note of acceptance and quiet expectancy. In addition, a subtle mood of farewell and departure permeates the proceedings. In **Me and Big Ship,** Treiman has depicted herself seated before a large cruise ship about to depart. In **Sailing Away,** the ship has already left.

Despite this change in mood and technique, Treiman's production remained as extensive as ever. Working on a large scale soon became a problem, however. **Wits End and Rose** (1986), **Friends and Strangers** (1987), and **Uphill** (1988) may have been as large as anything she had produced before, but paintings that size were becoming increasingly difficult for her to han-

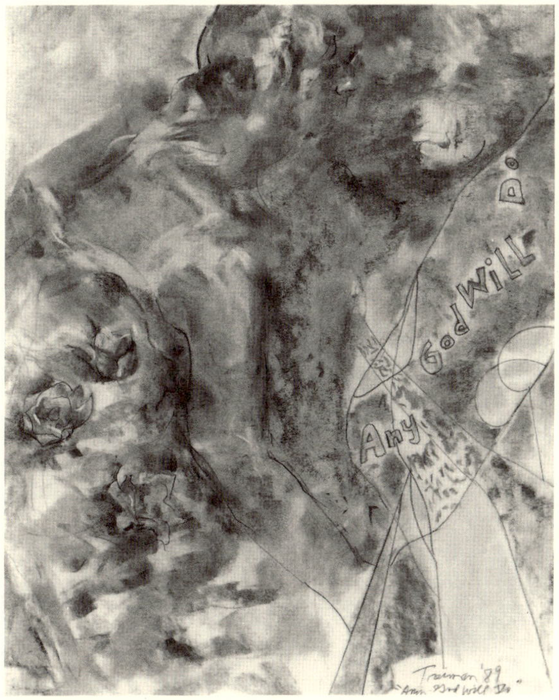

Any God Will Do
1989
charcoal and pastel on paper
14 x 11 inches
Collection Gardner, Carton, Douglas, Chicago

dle. In addition, glaucoma and cataract surgery in 1989 momentarily affected her ability to work, although that did not keep her out of her studio.

As the size of her paintings decreased, her brushwork became more impetuous and improvisational. Many of the tiny canvases she produced from 1987 on are so thinly painted that they could easily be mistaken for spontaneously dashed-off watercolors. Others are so thickly encrusted with pigment that they resemble colored bas-reliefs. Most important, however, her approach to painting itself underwent a significant change toward the end of the 1980s. Simply put, modernist formal devices began to play an ever more crucial role in her later canvases. Evidence of a newfound interest in abstraction, cubism, futurism, as well as in the earlier free-form and geometric works of Wassily Kandinsky, Paul Klee, and Franz Marc can be detected in many of her paintings after 1986. As this occurred, her images became more fractured, her forms more two-dimensional, and her color warmer and more arbitrarily applied. By 1988 the process was well under way, and by the time **Camouflage** was finished toward the end of 1989, the transition had been successfully completed.

An entirely new area of creativity opened up for Treiman, and she took full advantage of it. The softly suggestive and intriguingly enigmatic **Camouflage** and the similarly soft-focused 1991 pastel, **Roses and Vase,** are unlike any of her earlier works and point to worlds of new possibilities. Unfortunately, death overtook her shortly after the completion of **Roses and Vase,** before she was able to utilize this latest development in her art to its fullest. Even so, the paintings and drawings she left from that final period add a touching note to our overall understanding of this richly talented and truly remarkable artist, one who was not afraid, toward the end of a highly successful career, to strike out in a totally new direction.

NOTES

1. All remarks by the artist not otherwise attributed are from conversations with the author.
2. Joyce Treiman, unpublished manuscript, June 1977, notes for Barnsdall retrospective, Los Angeles, under the auspices of the Los Angeles Municipal Art Gallery, in the Treiman estate, 1.
3. Ibid., 17–18.
4. Ibid., 1.
5. Ibid., 10.
6. Ibid., 2–3.
7. Ibid., 2.
8. Ibid., 3.
9. Ibid., 6–8.
10. Ibid., 7.
11. Ibid., 5.

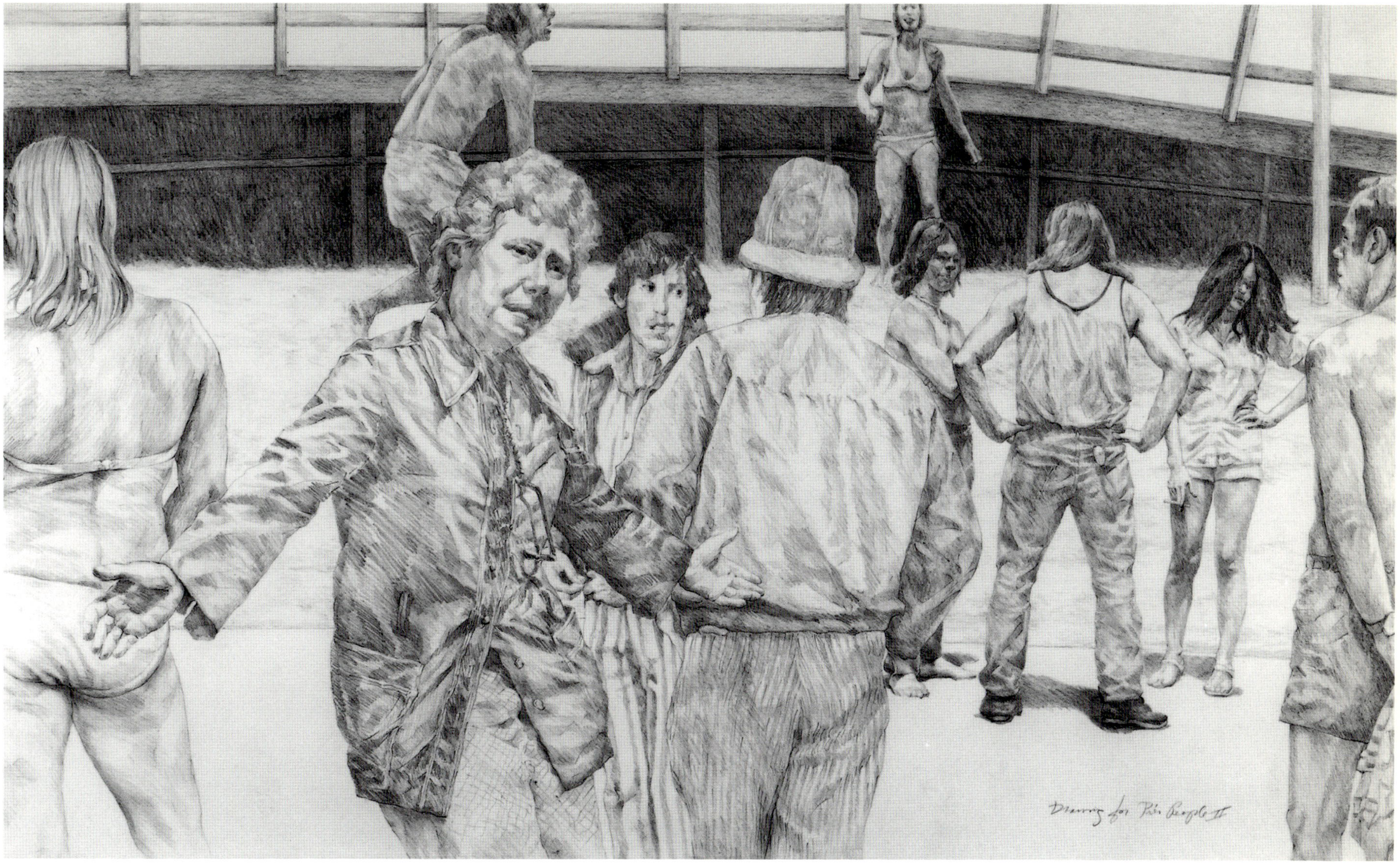

Drawing for Pier People II
1975
pencil on paper
18½ x 29¾ inches
Collection Sally H. Fairweather

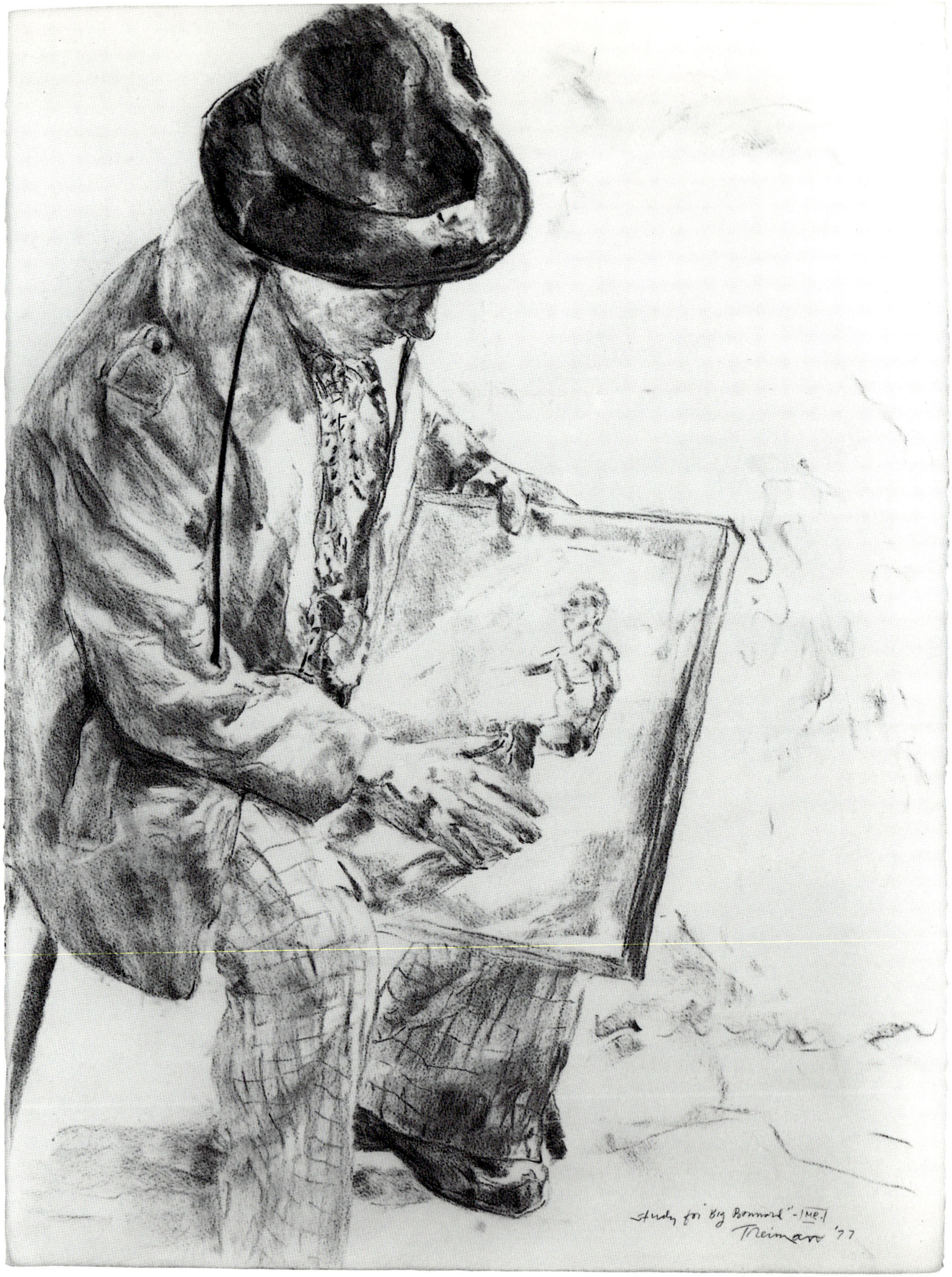

Study for Big Bonnard and Me Twice
1977
charcoal on paper
30 x 22 inches
Abby and Alan D. Levy Collection

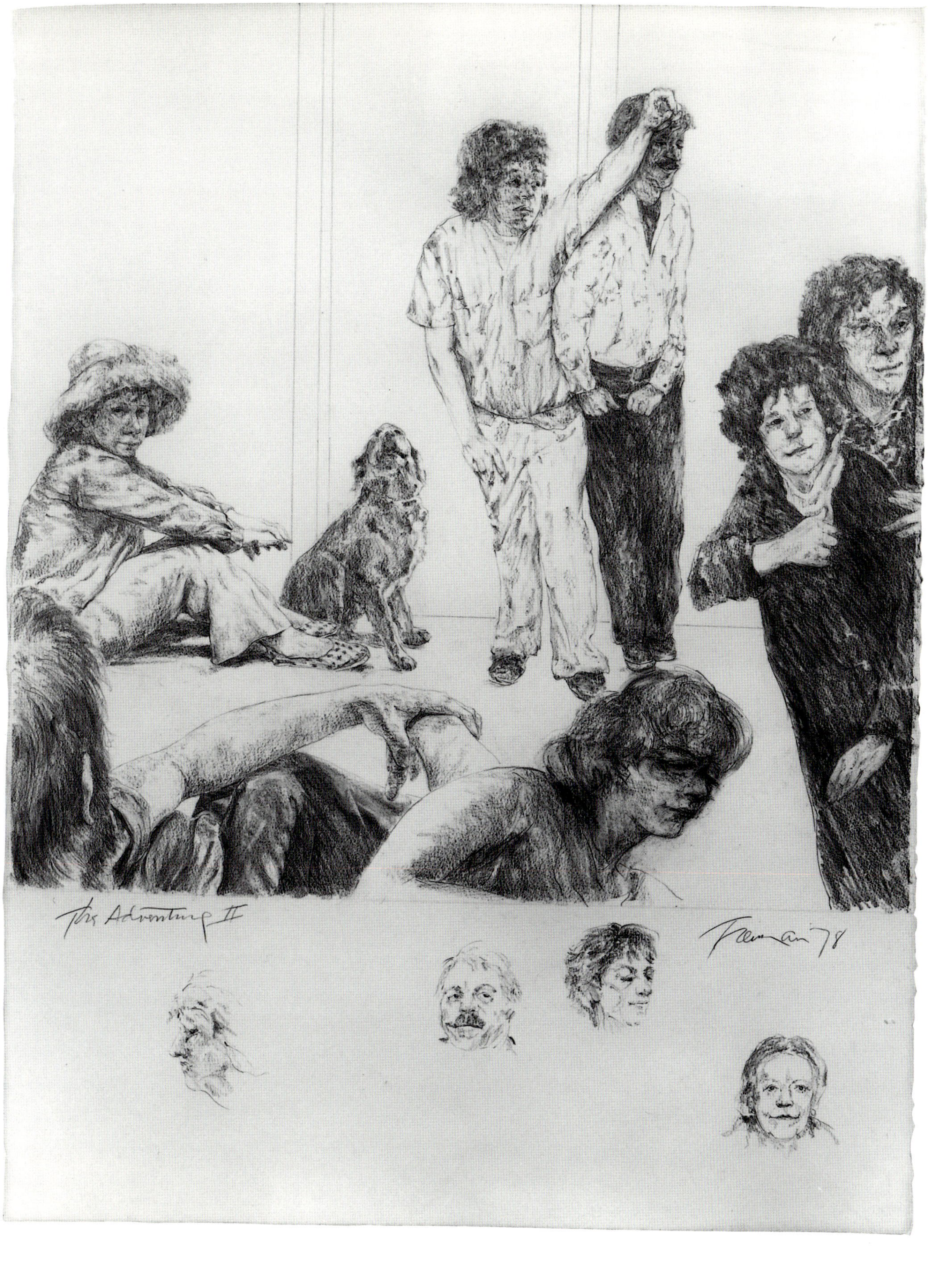

The Adventure II
1978
charcoal on paper
30 × 22 inches
Abby and Alan D. Levy Collection

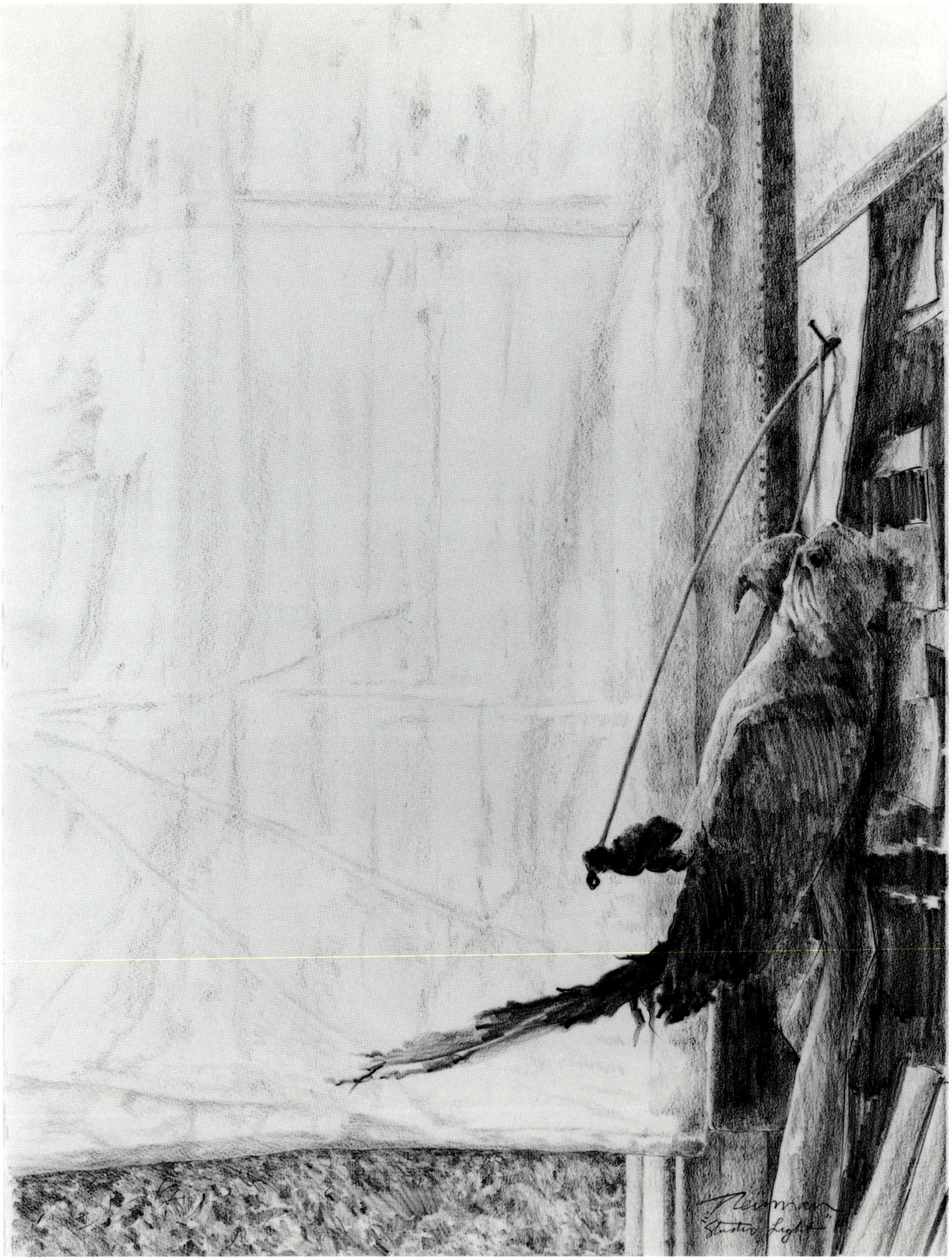

Fallen Parrot
1978
graphite and charcoal on paper
30 x 22 inches
Collection Donald M. Treiman,
Pacific Palisades, California

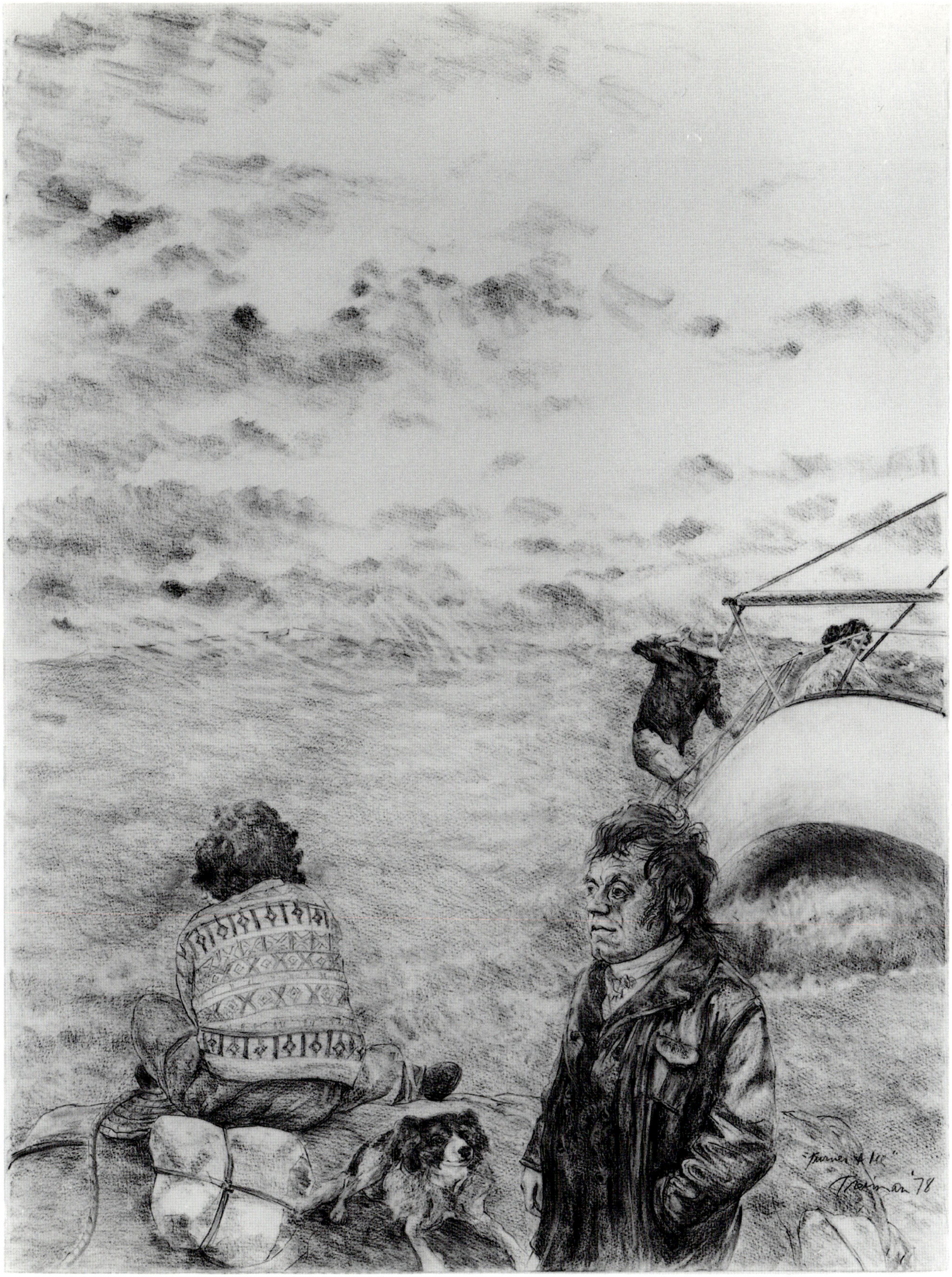

Study for Turner and Me
1978
pencil on paper
30 x 22¼ inches
Darryl and Doris Curran

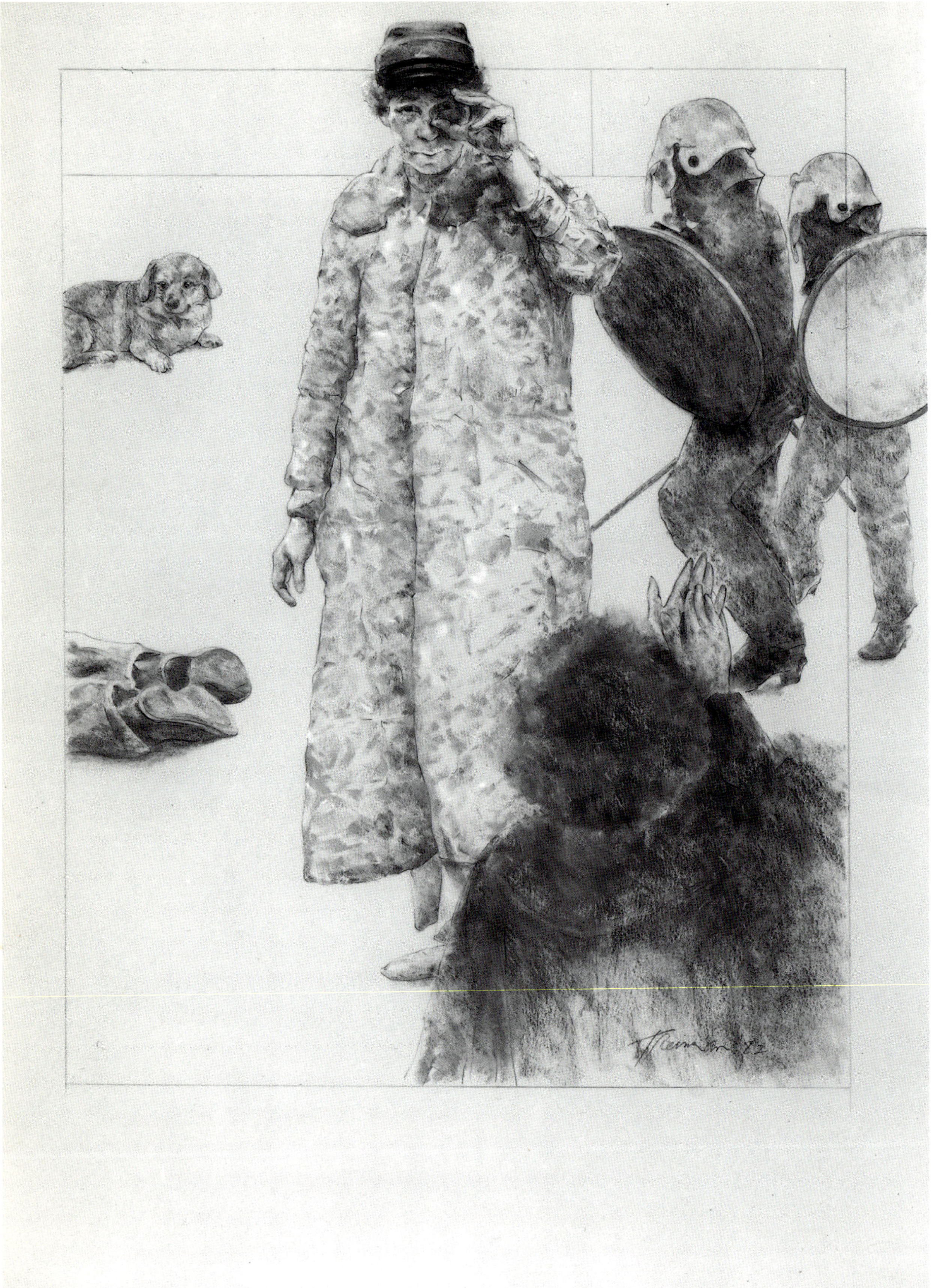

The Measure of All Things Is Man
1982
pastel and pencil on paper
30½ x 22 inches
Esther Sparks

Drawing for "Incident"
1983
charcoal on paper
22 x 22 inches
Abby and Alan D. Levy Collection

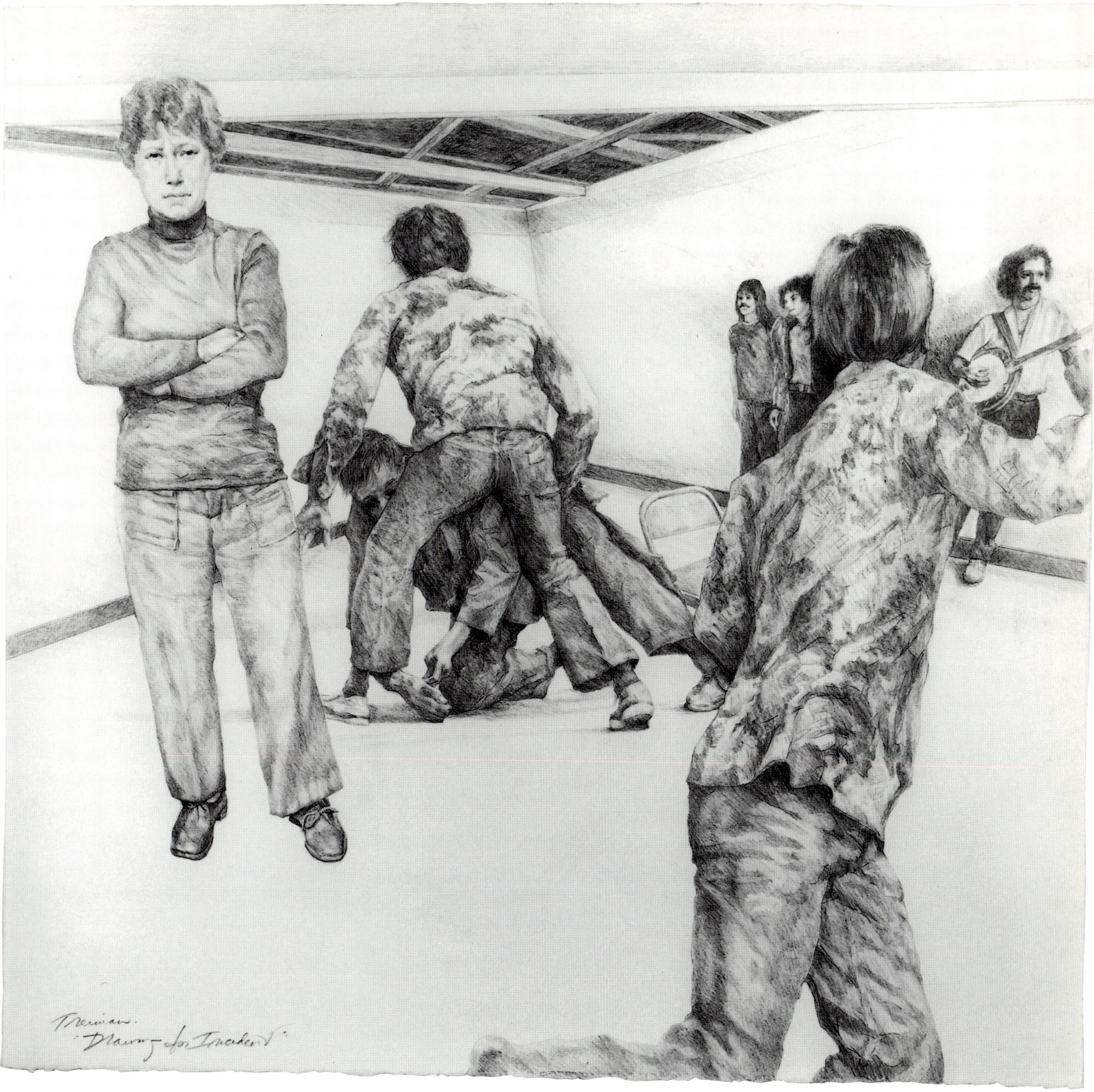
Treiman.
"Drawing for Incident"

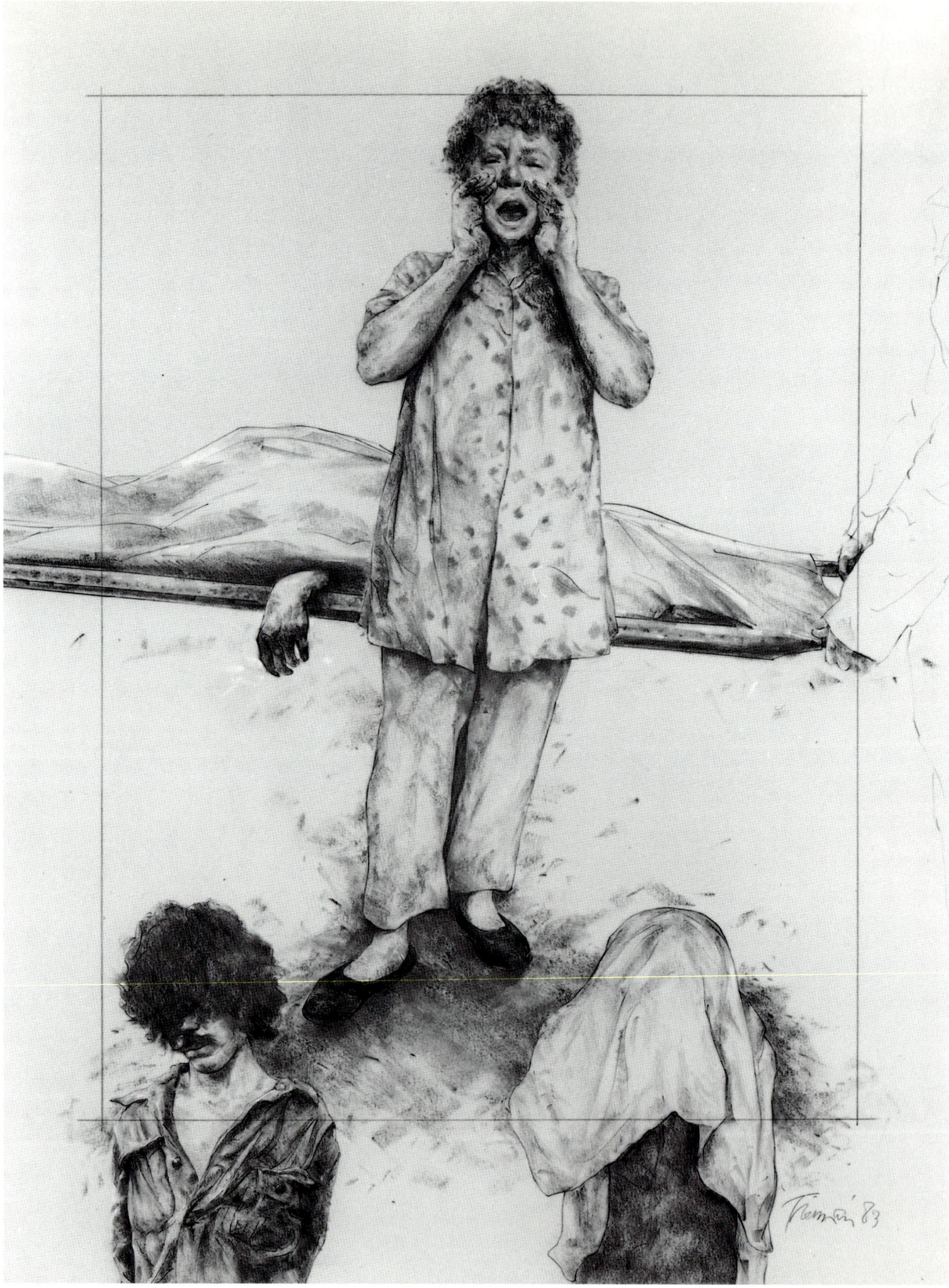

Incident I
1983
pastel and pencil on paper
33 x 25 inches
Darryl and Doris Curran

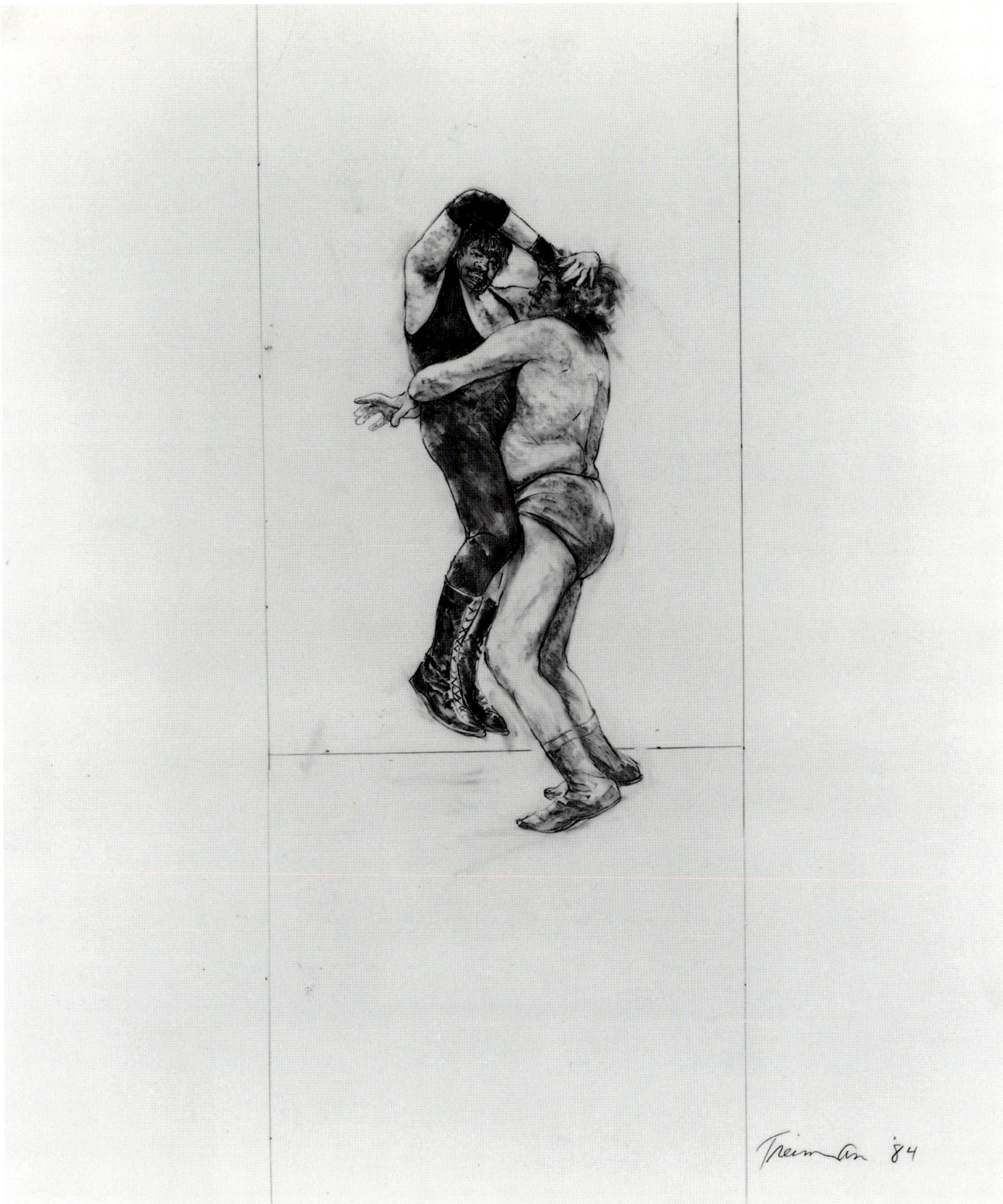

Untitled (Wrestlers)
1984
pencil and colored pencil on paper
$23\frac{1}{4} \times 20\frac{1}{4}$ inches
Courtesy Schmidt Bingham Gallery, New York

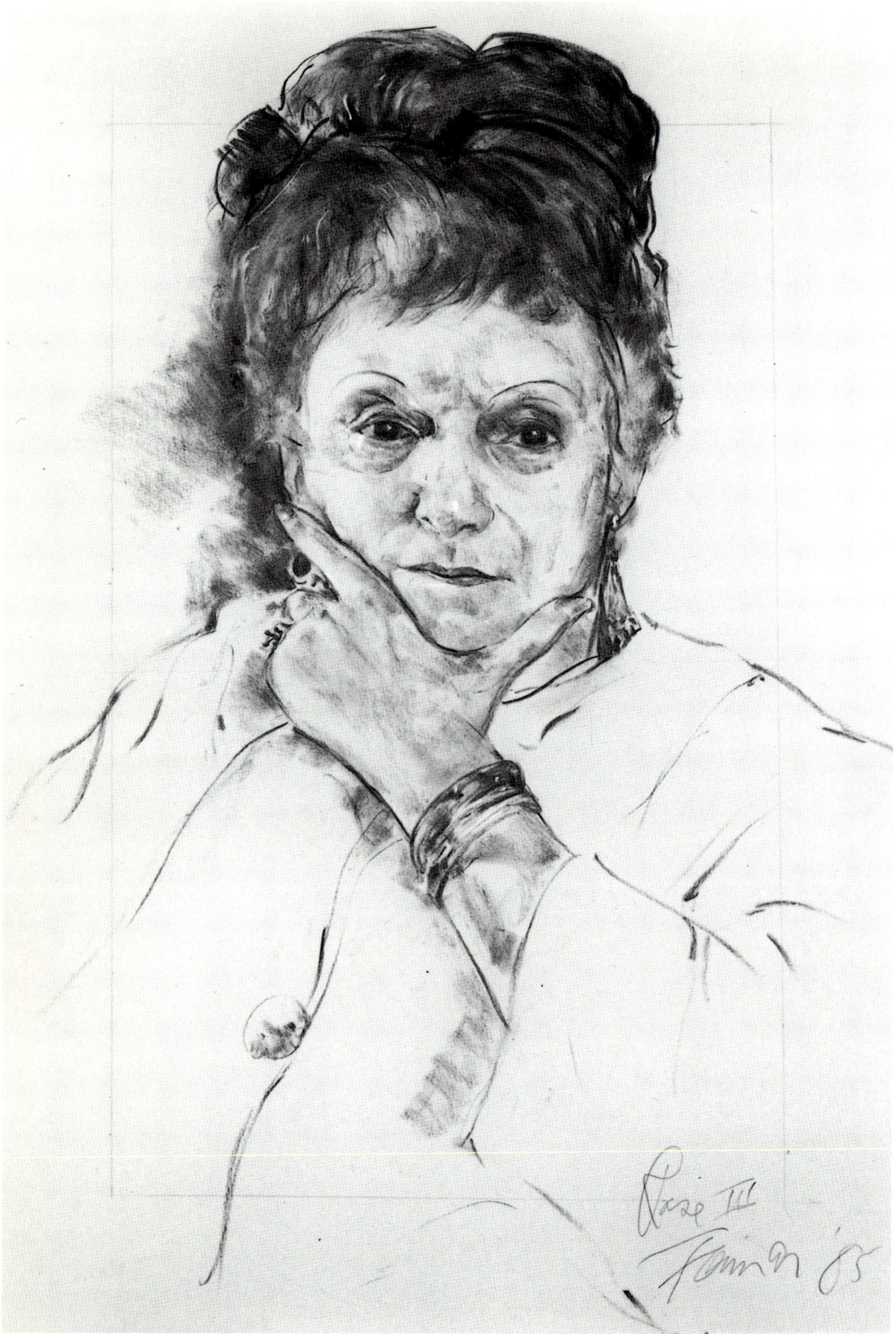

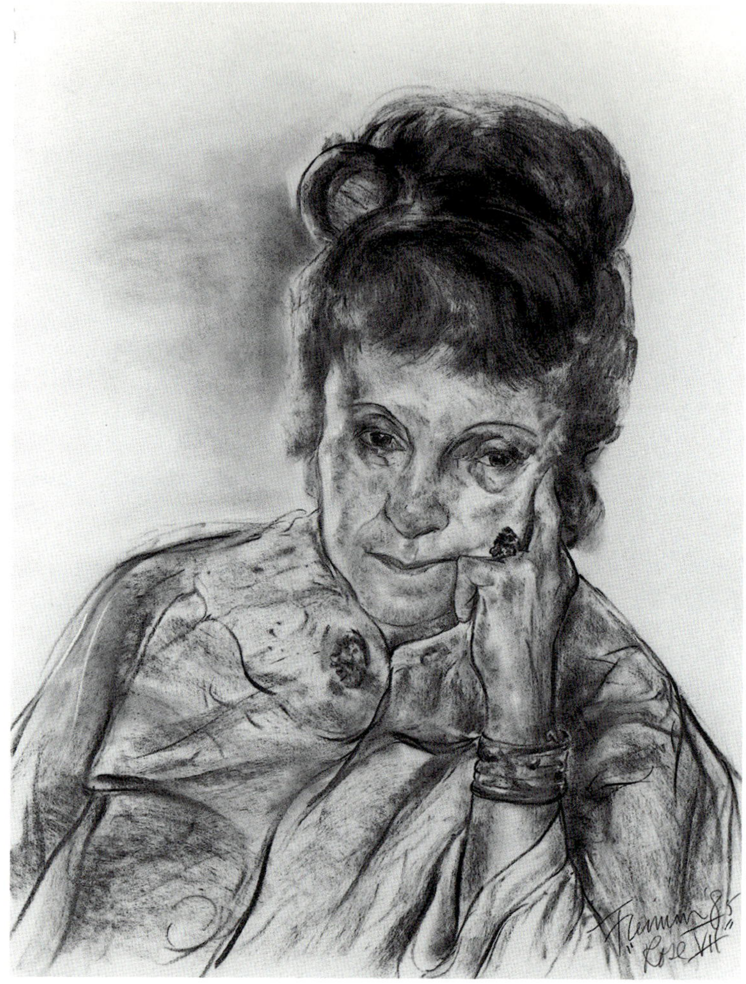

Rose VII
1985
charcoal and pastel on paper
30½ x 22 inches
Collection Donald M. Treiman, Pacific Palisades, California

Rose III
1985
charcoal on paper
30¼ x 20¾ inches
Arkansas Arts Center Foundation Collection, The Tabriz Fund, 1985, 85.57.1

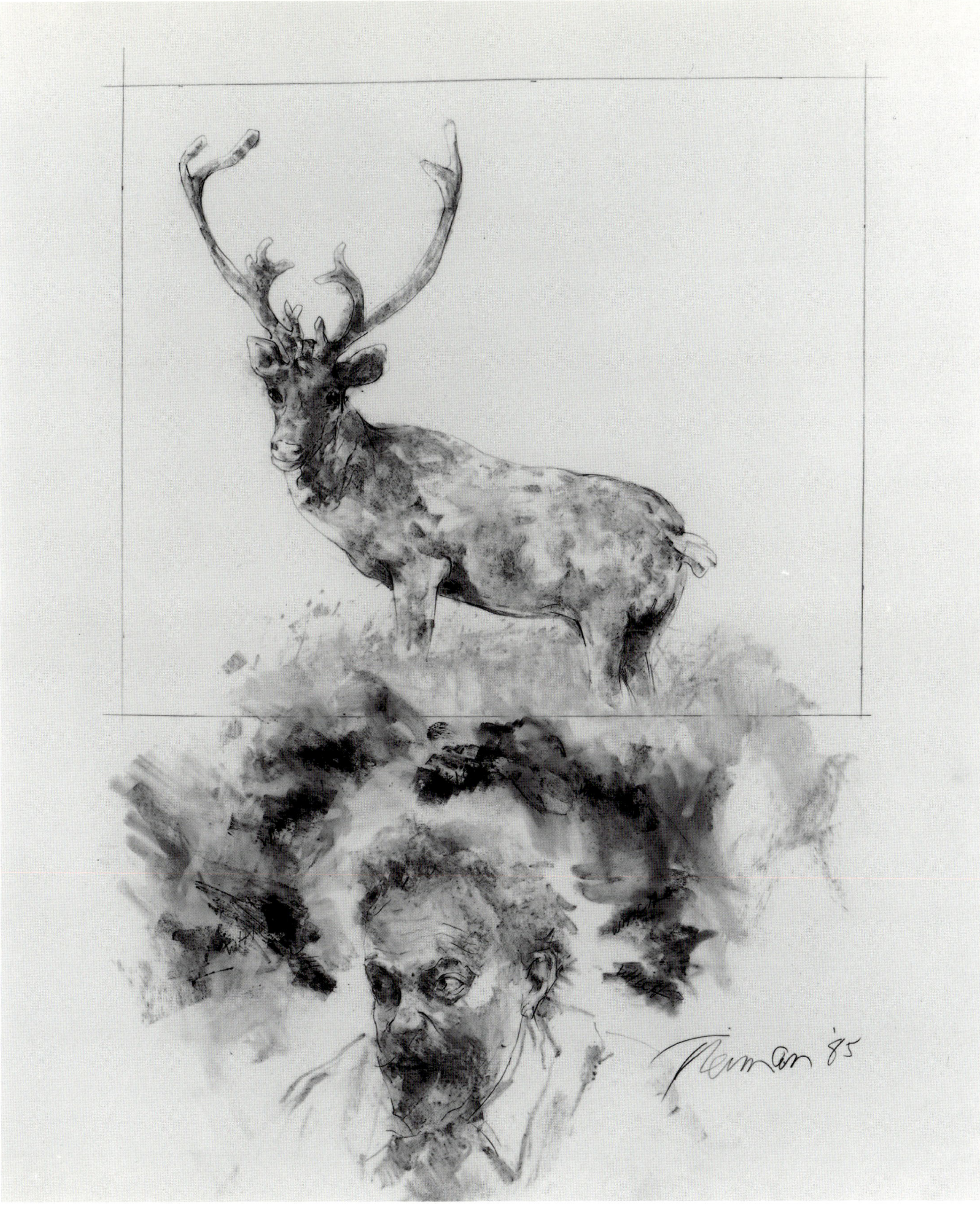

Untitled (Stag and Male Head)
1985
pastel and pencil on paper
17 x 14 inches
Courtesy Schmidt Bingham Gallery, New York

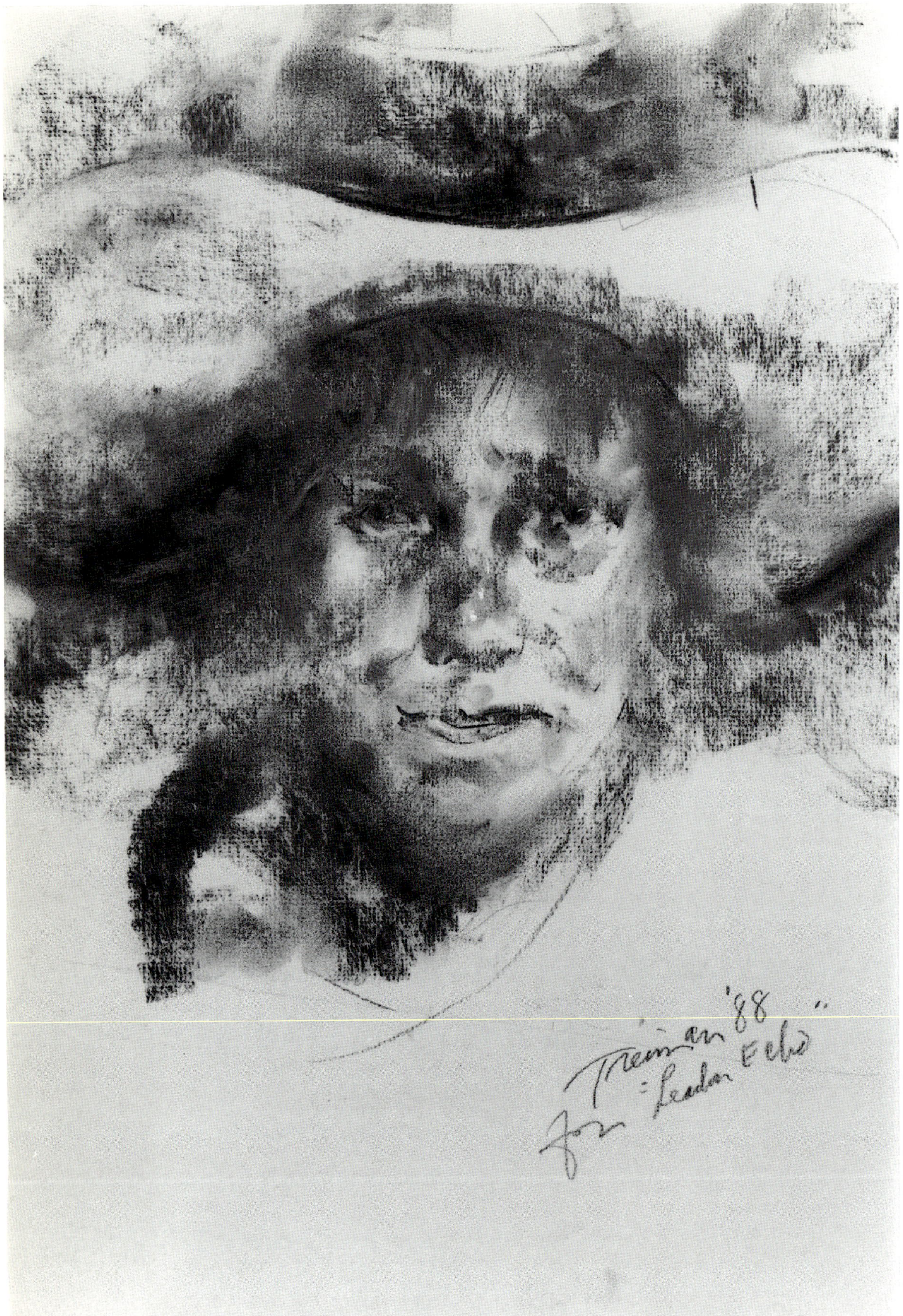

Self-Portrait for "Leaden Echo"
1988
pencil on paper
14 x 11 inches
Collection Donald M. Treiman, Pacific Palisades, California

ME ME ME ME ME: JOYCE TREIMAN AND SELF-PORTRAITURE

MICHAEL DUNCAN

What do we make of Joyce Treiman's odd and haunting post-1970 works? Cropping up in painting after painting, a red-haired, pouty-faced woman eyeballs the viewer. Prominently featured, sometimes holding brushes, this woman signals herself as the pictures' image maker, cast in a variety of unsettled, mysterious dramas. Alternately in a plumed helmet, tiara, cowboy hat, fur coat, Indian headdress, petticoat, and male drag, she strikes moody poses, marking her pictures with mirror images crafted by self-consciousness.

Staring out in a continuing game of "look-away," Treiman challenges the viewer to come to terms with her enterprise. She dares us to dismiss the paintings, confronting us with a dead-pan presence executed with flawless craft. Her gaze reciprocates ours, including us in her elusive, self-reflexive narratives. We, the viewers, become active participants in the narrative process of her enigmatic, challenging works, wrapped up in the drama of the painter's search for meaning.

With her virtuosic draftsmanship and expressive brushwork, Treiman is clearly an artist to contend with. Persisting through the heydays of abstract expressionism, pop, minimalism, and neo-expressionism, she stayed true to the human figure, while keeping pace with—if not exceeding—the dominant artists of those eras in fervor, seriousness, and ambition. Rejecting abstraction after a few experiments—it was "too easy," she said—Treiman developed her own way of extending the narrative concerns of the 1940s figurative painters whom she had admired as a young artist in Chicago.

As a figurative painter, a woman, and—for the crucial part of her career—a Californian, Treiman worked in relative isolation from the art world at large. Her awareness of both art history and the contemporary art scene made that isolation especially painful to bear. Despite the encouragement of her core group of supporters, Treiman knew all too well that her struggle to be acknowledged as an important artist was an "uphill" battle—to quote the title of one of her best late works.

In a remarkable series of paintings begun in 1974, Treiman took matters into her own hands. With a typically American forthrightness, she inserted herself into art history, literally placing herself in the studios of her favorite artists. In the 1980s, in other extraordinary self-portraits and a series of paintings of the Labors of Hercules, she uses her work as an autobiographical forum that is at once classical and postmodern. The complex, ironic self-consciousness of

Untitled (Joker in Black-and-White Shoes)
1984
pencil and colored pencil on paper
14 x 17 inches
Collection Donald M. Treiman,
Pacific Palisades, California

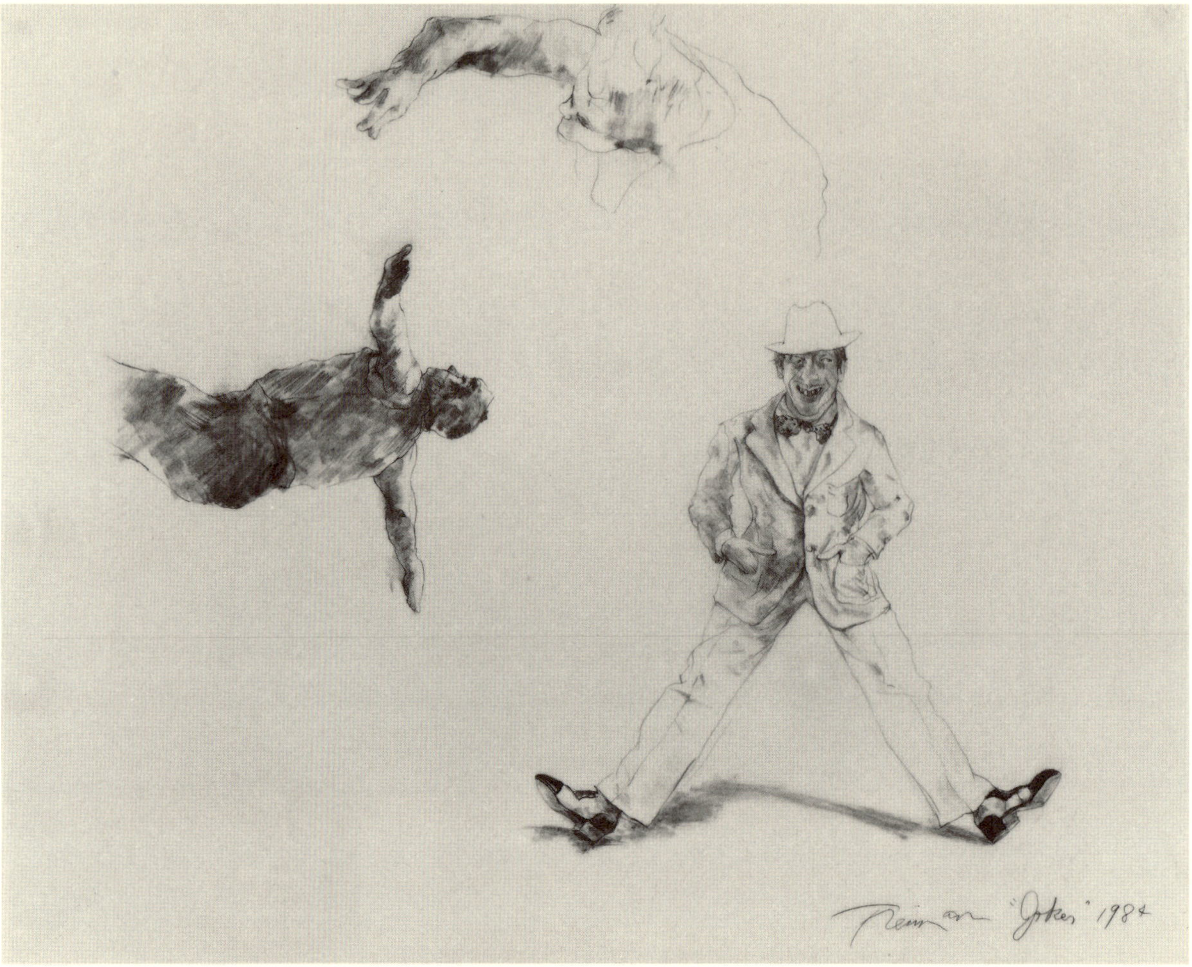

her later work resolves her heroic, lifelong mission to revivify figurative art—both for herself and for a contemporary audience.

Treiman was acutely aware of the problems facing her as a modern representational painter. This century's figurative artists have commonly searched for relevant subject matter to replace the historical, mythological, and genre scenes of traditional painting. For representational artists, the choice of subject matter is particularly crucial because it can so easily invite simplistic critical readings. Figurative artists can quickly be pigeonholed; for artists who do not want to be limited to a particular political issue (such as feminism or ethnic identity) or point of view (such as "modern alienation" or "existentialism"), subject matter must be open-ended. As the critic Lawrence Alloway has cogently pointed out: "Too often Freudian guesses and intimations of alienation . . . have characterized interpretive writings. For example, Edward Hopper has been persistently victimized by 'Modern Man as Lonely Crowd' readings of his work."[1]

Politically charged works face even more obstacles. From the Ashcan school artists to contemporary confabs such as Gran Fury and Group Material, artists whose work deals with social themes have been critically targeted for their mythifying qualities, one-note ideas, and tendencies toward caricature. Even an artist as varied and prolific as Picasso has been considered by the critic John Berger to be an artist who, as a result of his personality cult and political alienation, ultimately lost touch with significant subject matter.[2] Indeed, virtually all of this century's figurative artists have shown an understandable caution in deciding what to paint.

It is particularly fascinating to track Treiman's approach to subject matter. To follow her development is to trace many of the themes and ideas common to the history of midcentury American figurative art as practiced by Treiman's immediate mentors (such as Ivan Albright, Jack Levine, and Raphael Soyer), by her contemporaries (such as Leon Golub, Larry Rivers, and Alfred Leslie), and by more internationally recognized painters (such as R.B. Kitaj, Lucian Freud, Balthus, and David Hockney). For the most part, these artists have been united in their struggle to find a plausible continuity with classical tradition and the great works of the nineteenth century. Not surprisingly, many of these figurative artists—including Treiman—also used the human figure to pursue goals familiar to the dominant art practice of the midcentury: abstract expressionism. A painterly attention to surface and a belief in the psychologically expressive qualities of art are certainly mainstay assumptions of that movement.

A combination of factors determined Joyce Treiman's initial commitment to figurative art. Her interest in painting was solidified at the State University of Iowa, where she obtained a thorough background in art history. Her studio work there was guided by Philip Guston, whose painting at that time dealt with social-realist themes in a style similar to that of Giorgio de Chirico. Under Guston's supervision, the young Joyce Wahl sketched the design for the Civil War section of a 1942 WPA war memorial mural at Camp Dodge in Des Moines, Iowa.[3]

Back in Chicago after art school, Treiman became intrigued with the west-side neighborhoods where her brother was doing his medical internship. Accompanying him on visits to his patients, she became touched by "the very poor, the alcoholics, the separated."[4] Painting at night, she began a series depicting these "lost, isolated people." These works brought her her first success, with a 1947 fellowship from the Louis Comfort Tiffany Foundation and exhibitions in Chicago and New York. In **Street in Motion** (1948) a claptrap sidewalk newsstand—looking ready to collapse—frames a handful of haunted patrons who seem confined by downtrodden self-absorption.

Treiman's allegorical works, dream sequences, and enigmatic narratives of the 1950s and 1960s extend this kind of postwar existential angst into mythological and fantastical realms. In her 1977 autobiographical statement, she looks back on these themes: "This was pretty heavy stuff—but I was young enough to think these things had not been thought of before and that I had to make a statement about the 'condition of man.'" Despite this later jaun-

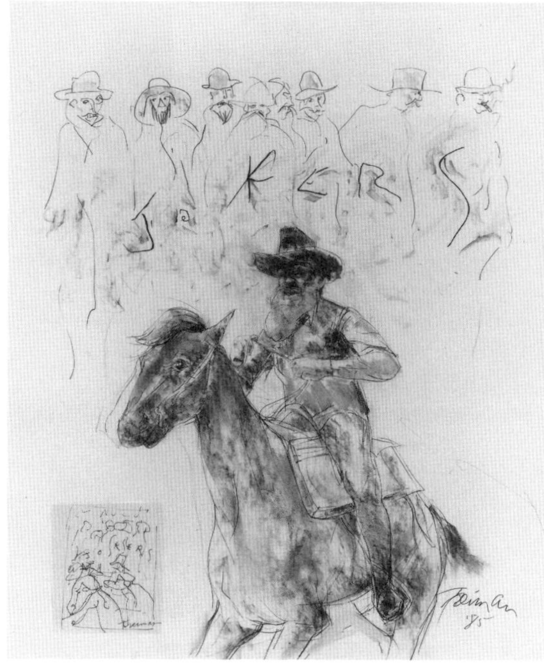

Untitled (Man on Horse with Jokers)
1983
pencil and collage on paper
17 x 14 inches
Collection Donald M. Treiman,
Pacific Palisades, California

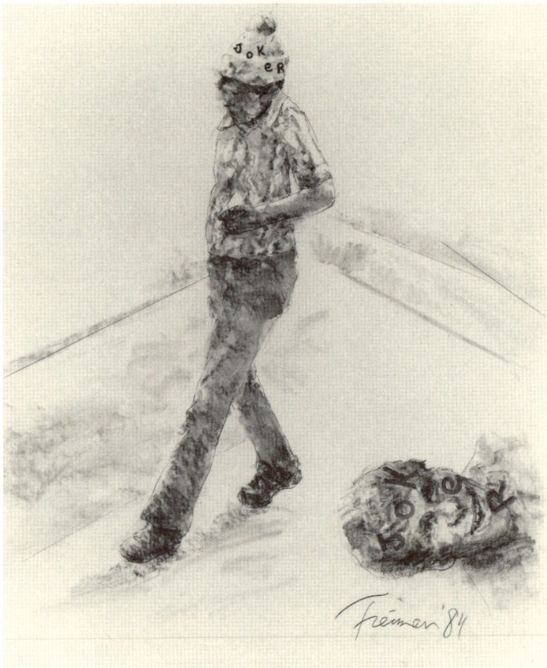

Untitled (Joker Twice)
1984
pastel, charcoal, and pencil on paper
24 x 21 inches
Collection Donald M. Treiman,
Pacific Palisades, California

diced assessment, her subject matter echoed that of much of the art and literature of the period. Through her depictions of grim myths **(Jacob, Man, Angel** [1956] and **Nisus and Scylla** [1951]), troubled fantasies (the 1960s **Dream Sequences)**, and disturbing encounters **(The Birthday Party** [1966–67] and **Rabbit and Pills** [1967–68]), one can trace the development of the skewed American psyche, from the submerged repressions of Eisenhower suburbia to the explosive social upheavals of the late-1960s youth cult.

Treiman attended the School of the Art Institute of Chicago (as did most of the well-known local figures, such as Leon Golub, Seymour Rosofsky, and June Leaf) and shared with other postwar Chicago painters a commitment to the darker, more expressionistic aspects of figuration. Inheriting their tone from Ivan Albright—the city's premier eccentric genius—this Chicago style was later characterized by Golub as one that explored the "notion of how reality is seen, not so much on the surface of things but in terms of instinct, urges, action, violence, myth."[5]

Also crucial in Treiman's commitment to figuration was her first trip in 1955 to Italy and Paris, where she had her first encounters in the flesh with many of her favorite Renaissance, baroque, and impressionist paintings. This experience seemed to tighten her work, focusing her interest on a more precise depiction of the human form. Close study of paintings by Tiepolo, Ribera, Rembrandt, Caravaggio, Velázquez, Goya, and Monet led to the direct appropriations seen in her later drawings.

The Poet (1961–62) is a key work that marks the new formal complexity and classical specificity of her symbolic characters. In a statement she wrote in 1961 about her group of **Poet** paintings, Treiman proclaimed her desire "to put an end to the pussyfooting around about the image."[6] Set in a dramatic moment, the painting presents a contemplative hero sitting off-balance in front of a sleeping muse and encircled by a prowling dog and genielike satyr. The composition has a sense of formal enclosure familiar from Renaissance groupings of saints around the Madonna.

With a typically acerbic verve, Treiman wrote that this sumptuously painted exploration of the "perilous position" of the Poet was intended "to contribute to his health and keep him . . . from dying from a multitude of twentieth-century maladies: creeping Little League, group degeneration of the nervous system, the paralysis of togetherness, and a chronic shut-off of the feeling valve."[7] Treiman has herself acknowledged the influences in her pre-1970 paintings of Raphael Soyer and Jack Levine, clearly evident in her humanistic approach to the human figure and the expressionistic architectural settings for her allegorical dramas.

Treiman's move to Los Angeles from Chicago in 1960 should have been a traumatic one, uprooting her from a city where figuration—while still marginalized in the art world at large—

was a regional tradition. But she was typically undaunted, determined to keep to her own path. Along with a heightened sense of drama, Treiman's 1960s works begin to show evidence of her new West Coast environment. In a letter written soon after her arrival, she stated, "The sharp quality of the light makes a certain clarity inevitable.... This landscape I claim for my own.... The strong lights and the deep rich shadows offer such a contrast and range of values to play with."[8] Soon a specifically Californian light enters her paintings. In **The Birthday Party** (1966–67) two open casement windows flood a suburban living room with a harsh light that enhances the hallucinogenic quality of the bizarre bacchanalia in progress.

In the late 1960s Treiman collected nineteenth-century American drawings that she at first stumbled across in swap meets and junk stores. In studying these works, she became interested in the period's great painters. The off-kilter poses and mysterious psychological nuances of Thomas Eakins's portraits especially struck a deep chord, as did the tinselly glitter and lavish exoticism of John Singer Sargent's works. The raw, unsettling, "masculine" quality of Eakins's work seemed to appeal to Treiman as a way to toughen and sharpen her portrait subjects. Sargent's love of detail is reflected in Treiman's repeated use of fanciful costumes and fabric patterns.

Particularly inspired by these works, as well as by the self-portaits of Rembrandt, Treiman began to focus on a more refined form of portraiture in the 1970s. The array of alienated characters in **Anomie** (1970) gave Treiman a chance to experiment with painting styles, subtly melding the fussily baroque with the psychologically expressionistic. This breakthrough painting is the first major work to include the artist in its cast of isolate, neurotic characters. Its eight figures are dressed in various period costumes and range from a Caravaggiesque man in a flowing dressing gown to a pensive, shifty-eyed businessman out of Eakins who stands lumpy and awkward in his three-piece suit with watch chain. By including herself in this group of sequestered souls, Treiman annuls her position as an objective narrator; the teller has become part of the tale. But the point is that there is no single tale; each character is trapped in a stilted pose, cut off from outside contact. **Anomie** ironically finds subject matter in its own frigid paralysis. Treiman was once quoted as saying, "The painting is about society and its nonrelationships."[9] Demonstrating the impossibility of making narrative art amid social fragmentation, it is the cool painterly equivalent to grim, self-enclosed, modernist literature such as T. S. Eliot's "Waste Land" or Jean Paul Sartre's **No Exit.**

For the next decade, Treiman experimented with similarly disparate groups of characters, ever increasing the psychological complexity of their unlikely encounters. **The Adventure** (1970) is the first in a series of paintings to depict various characters' reactions to disturbing, unresolved incidents that occur outside the frame. Theatrically lit, the figures' surprised responses accent their lonely, yet fully formed individualities. In the **Adventures** and **Incidents** series, Treiman continues to keep the action off-canvas; depicting reactions after

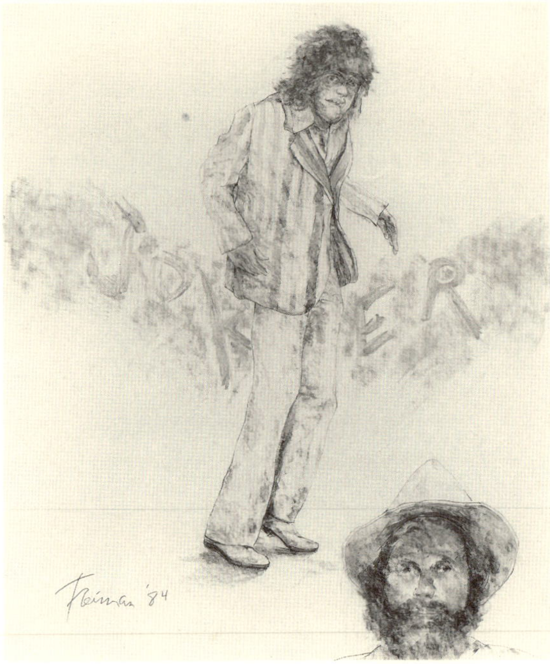

Untitled (Joker in Blue Striped Jacket)
1984
pastel and pencil on paper
24 x 21 inches
Collection Donald M. Treiman,
Pacific Palisades, California

the fact, the paintings themselves are evidence of the impossibility of rendering crucial modern events with the straightforward, symbolic assurance of a David or a Poussin. Treiman includes herself in these casts of confused and concerned onlookers, adding herself to the ranks of the dissociated voyeurs. Like the viewer, she, too, is responding to the inscrutable.

As her work gets more autobiographical, this self-reflexiveness begins to have less to do with generalized statements about contemporary experience. Lured by the variety and lushness of the California landscape—which fed into her ongoing fascination with nineteenth-century American themes—Treiman began to play with the idea of the western frontier. In the wide-open mountainscape of **Self-Portrait with Cowboy Ken** (1970–71), she inserts herself and her husband on horseback—in real life a highly unlikely couple of equestrians. With its pair of riders halted in midfield, this odd, deadpan fantasy becomes a kind of allegory of a relationship bound by separateness. The somewhat awkward placement of the figures in the foreground also wryly reflects the traditional fate of newcomers to California who find themselves suddenly plopped down in the middle of what is still the American frontier.

Treiman's use of western locations and themes particularizes the 1970s enigmatic narratives. In **Americana III and Me** (1972) a disparate group including Wild West gunslingers, prospectors, an Indian chief, and Treiman are arrayed like isolated cliff dwellers on a sheer mountainside. In **Dear Friends** (1972) she meticulously details the costumes of a similar group of eight western characters with a virtuosity worthy of Sargent. With his hands-on-hips stance, the bearded cowboy in furry chaps has a particularly American buoyance. By including a self-portrait in the guise of a dour little Indian girl, Treiman hints at her fantastical relationship to this larger-than-life western world. **Dear Friends** is in the 70-by-70-inch-square format that Treiman began to prefer for her major narratives, writing that it provided her with open-ended "possibilities and ambiguousness."[10]

Treiman's paintings using favorite artists as subjects are even odder fantasy-dramas, additionally cast with friends, models, and well-known artworks, and with herself as the unlikely star. The idea of making art about art was not new to her; in 1953 her feeling for art was the springbroad for perhaps her best-known abstract painting, **Homage to Rodin.** Her 1969 correspondence with the realist critic and painter Sidney Tillim discusses their mutual search for appropriate subject matter for what she called "major figurative narrative art." Fascinatingly, Tillim, after dismissing any interest in portraiture, tosses off the idea that modern figuration "must show a new sense of the history of art. That is, we must understand art history in such a way as to make representation plausible now."[11] Treiman did not respond directly to this idea, but clearly it struck a deep chord.

The first of these paintings, **Thomas Eakins Modeling in California** (1974), is loosely inspired by Eakins's painting **William Rush Carving His Allegorical Figure of the Schuylkill**

River (1876–77, fig. 1). That work focuses on Rush's nude female model, depicting her from the rear, dramatically lit in his darkened studio. Asserting the power of realism over allegory, Eakins's painting leaves in the shadows the idealized sculpture that the sculptor Rush carves, instead focusing attention on the fleshy model herself—and her disarrayed jumble of ruffled undergarments.

Reversing the sexes of the William Rush painting in her homage, Treiman depicts Eakins himself as a nude model. The fey blond woman who beckons him down from his pedestal refers to another work by Eakins.[12] Following Eakins's penchant for using friends and family as subjects, Treiman surrounds this action with two groupings of disinterested observers—including her son, Raphael Soyer, and the art historian Maurice Bloch. A hunched-over Treiman presides center stage, in a shawl and Indian headdress that comically mark her as what she called "the outsider," eyeballing the viewer with a scrutinizing glare.[13]

The chiaroscuro of Eakins's works has disappeared; Treiman floods the studio with California light, depicting all ten of the painting's subjects with the heightened luminosity that the earlier painter typically reserved for his central figures. Her notes describe this change: "The color in this painting was also different from the darkness I had been working with during my stay in the 19th century. Somehow I was bringing my 'heroes' up to the light with me." Setting her own self-deprecating portrait in the foreground, she has dragged the artist figure of Eakins's painting out of the shadows and into the spotlight. In so doing, she one-ups Eakins, further demythifying and analyzing the nature of art making. This and the other works of the series, **The Big Sargent** (1975), **Big Lautrec and Double Self-Portrait** (1975–76), and **Rose, Bonnard, and the Artist Twice** (1977), are theatrically conceived, self-referential paintings in the tradition of Velázquez's **Meninas.** But unlike the figures in the Spanish studio, the characters in Treiman's fantasies have shifting art-historical references and a contemporary sense of social unease.

On its tilted, perspectival plane, **Degas, Cassatt, and Me** (1979) presents the two nineteenth-century artists and contemporary versions of their models. In this modern reworking of these painters' trademark subjects, Cassatt's little girls and Degas's ballerina are set free from center-stage scrutiny. Treiman makes an odd kind of revisionist history painting, pointing a self-reflexive mirror at traditional art-historical subject matter.

Filtering events through a unique sensibility is a common trope of modernism, most familiar through the use of "stream of consciousness" in novels such as James Joyce's **Ulysses** and Virginia Woolf's **Waves.** The appropriation of history through an individual consciousness reached its modernist apotheosis in Ezra Pound's **Cantos,** whose sprawling structure was built from an eccentric and cantankerous assimiliation of literary history, autobiography, and the histories of China, Renaissance Italy, and Jeffersonian America.

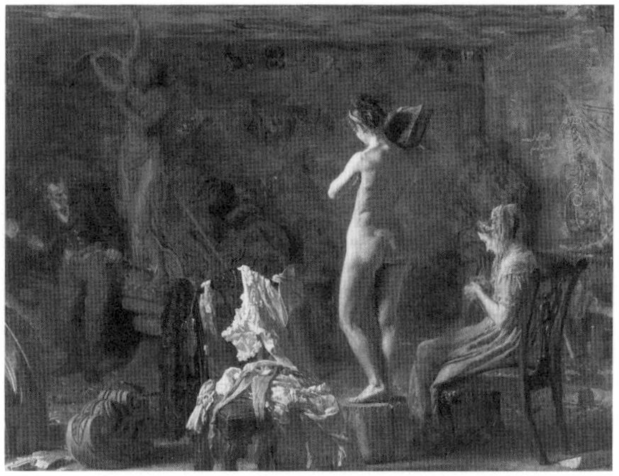

Thomas Eakins
William Rush Carving His Allegorical Figure of the Schuylkill River
1876–77
oil on canvas on Masonite
20 1/8 x 26 1/8 inches
Philadelphia Museum of Art:
Gift of Mrs. Thomas Eakins and
Miss Mary Adeline Williams

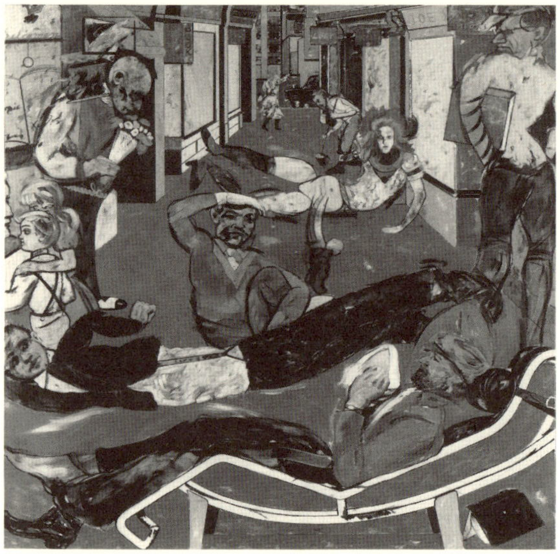

R. B. Kitaj
Cecil Court, London WC4 (The Refugees)
1983–84
oil on canvas
73¼ x 73¼ inches
The Tate Gallery, London

With its fixation on abstraction and constant formal experimentation, modern art has avoided this kind of historical assemblage. Treiman is one of only a handful of midcentury figurative artists (including Larry Rivers, Alfred Leslie, May Stevens, and Sylvia Sleigh) who have attempted to construct modernist, historical, narrative paintings. Perhaps the best-known and most complex of these documenters of the fragmented twentieth-century consciousness is R. B. Kitaj. Using borrowings from art history, Kitaj's allegorical paintings reference Jewish history, political theory, modern literature, and autobiography (fig. 2). Like Treiman's, his interests have stood outside the concerns of the art world at large.

In the 1980s Treiman's more explicit and direct use of autobiography enabled her to simplify her historical narratives. **Déjeuner** (1981), for example, one of Treiman's most buoyant pictures, both commemorates a French vacation with some close friends and lushly alludes to impressionism and the wild colors of the Fauves. The painting keeps its art-historical references light and open-ended, claiming the French landscape for its female revelers as it jokingly reverses the sex of Manet's nude picnicker.

Treiman was extremely close to her mother, Rose, whose death in 1976 is the subject matter for the extraordinary painting **The Parting** (1983), intended "as an hommage to my favorite painter, Rembrandt, and my favorite person, my mother, Rose Wahl."[14] Brightly lit, in a nightgown and earrings, Rose rises up behind sleeping sentinels like a risen Christ; she is parting from Joyce who stands awkwardly, hands in the pockets of her painter's pants, crowned in a plumed helmet from Rembrandt.[15] The virtuosic loose brushwork, dramatic composition, and masterful control of light suitably reflect the stylistic mastery of the Dutch painter. But rather than depicting an enigmatic event or disjunctive grouping, Treiman here has rendered a crucial event in her own life. She finds an expressive intermediary for her own grief through stylistic references to Rembrandt, an artist whose work she deeply cherishes. The sly ironies of the art-historical borrowings only increase her work's emotional content. Treiman's "heroic" appropriation of the mantle of the Dutch master becomes the means for the expression of her own personal history.

In the full-length **Self-Portrait in Titus's Hat** (1983) Treiman portrays herself in the feathery hat worn in Rembrandt's portrait of his son, Titus.[16] Wearing a flouncy dress and posing with a dolled-up terrier, Treiman seems as exotic and unlikely a model as Rembrandt himself in his own **Self-Portrait in an Oriental Costume with a Dog** (1631, fig. 3). As her many sketches and drawings attest, Treiman relates to Rembrandt's penchant for self-portraits featuring exotic costumes, gestures, and comic poses. Furthermore, his virtuosic, somber, late self-portraits are important sources for the best works of Treiman's last decade.

Like Treiman, postmodern artists of the 1980s, such as Cindy Sherman, Sherrie Levine, Mike Bidlo, and the theater ensemble the Wooster Group, used fragments from art and literary histories to remake new aesthetic objects that both comment on the past and take on new meanings. Perhaps closest in concept to Treiman's works are Cindy Sherman's **History Portraits** (1989–90), the photographer's staged self-portraits that allude to paintings from the Renaissance and the nineteenth century. **Untitled #204** (1989, fig. 4), for example, loosely borrows its pose, lighting, and setting from Ingres's **Madame Moitessier** (1856, National Gallery, London). In other photographs, Sherman poses as subjects from paintings reminiscent of those by artists such as Caravaggio, Raphael, François Boucher, Jean Fouquet, and Georges de La Tour. The illusion of Sherman's re-creations is undercut by her use of obviously false wigs, extravagantly applied makeup, and body prostheses.

Although beautifully lit and elegantly staged, Sherman's series seems intent on demystifying the sanctified paintings of the past, emphasizing the grotesquerie of her own assumption of these bodies and costumes. The critic Arthur Danto praises Sherman for "draining the old masters and their subjects at once of a certain power by showing the artifice, the convention, the transparent fakeness of the worlds [that] they believed were solid and unshakable and real—reducing them to conventions one can slip in and out of without believing them the final truth of being."[17] Sherman's works—whose profound ambiguities have made them key texts for postmodern and feminist theory—share a slippery attitude toward the art of the past, one that is both satirical and probing.

Less deconstructive, Treiman's maverick stance seems more assimilative and ultimately more ambitious. A lifetime of painting—and of trying to invigorate figurative traditions—enables Treiman to adapt art history to her own expressive purposes. **Self-Portrait in Titus's Hat** uses Rembrandt's profound and playful self-portraiture as a model for a psychologically compelling portrait of Treiman's own innocence, delusion, and spunk. The four self-portrait panels—sometimes collectively referred to as **Mortality** (1982–83)—extend the Rembrandt-like self-analysis in a loose and extravagant neo-expressionistic style. In the most intense of these panels, **The Smoker No. 21** (1983), Treiman in a housecoat and jeweled tiara evokes her own demon in the upper reaches of her cigarette smoke. Her grimly ironic self-portrait stamps the work with painterly authenticity.

In perhaps Treiman's most haunting painting, **Thanatopsis** (1983), she literally embraces death, in the figure of a chummy, squatting skeleton. A pastel-stroked sunset presides over the two figures who directly face the viewer over a pile of long-stemmed red roses. The expressionistic horror of these works does not seem gratuitous or sentimental; in fact, it amazingly presages the lung cancer with which Treiman was diagnosed late in the year.

Treiman's **Hercules** series can be seen as an extension of her self-portraiture, with the underlying analogy drawn between the epic hero's labors and the artist's own struggle to recharge figurative painting. By using self-portrait observers in **Hercules and the Nemean Lion**

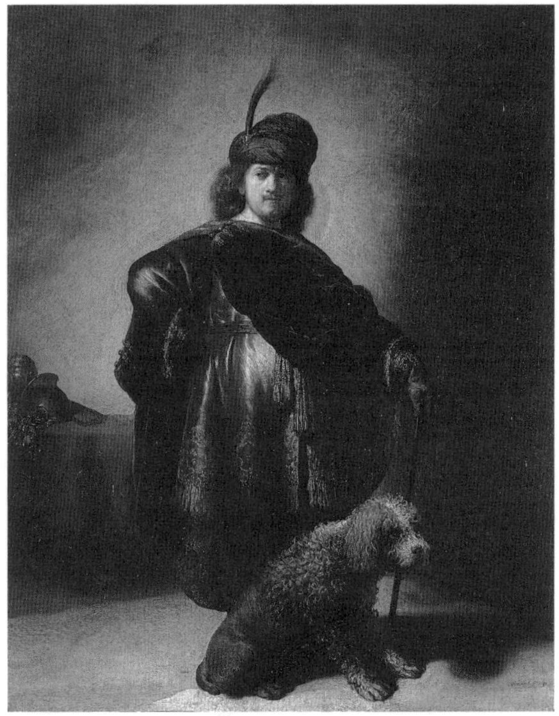

Rembrandt van Rijn
Self-Portrait in Oriental Costume
1631
oil on panel
63 x 56 inches
Ville de Paris, Musée du Petit Palais

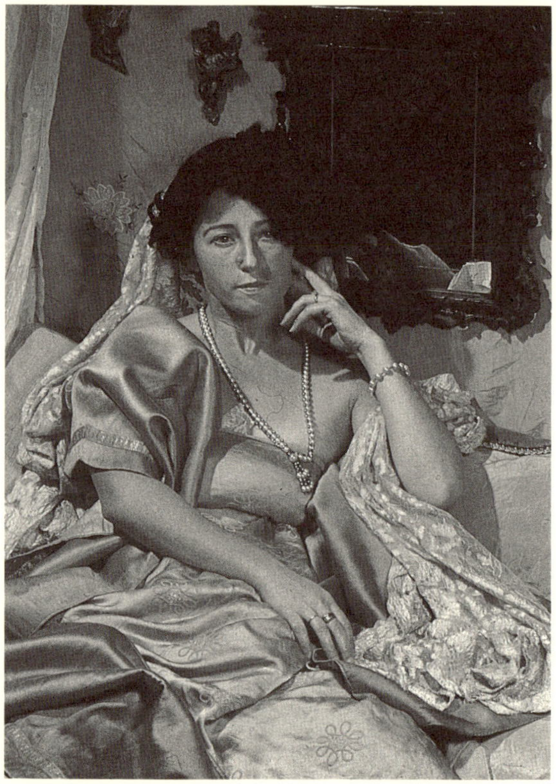

Cindy Sherman
Untitled #204
1989
color photograph
59¾ x 53¼ inches
Courtesy of the artist and Metro Pictures

(1983), **Hercules and the Arcadian Stag** (1983), and **Hercules and Cercopes** (1983) as analogues for the hero, Treiman implies that the creation of each painting is as heroic as the act it depicts. The fervor and extravagance of her paint handling define the works as genuinely heroic labors. Yet, as in all her work, the reality of the representation triumphs over its idealization. The critic Betty Brown observed how in the Cercopes painting Treiman insistently left exposed the underpainting on Hercules' head, "revealing the process of execution and, at the same time, addressing the ambiguity of man/hero/sculpture that the Hercules image cannot help but evoke."[18]

The **Joker** series, begun during Treiman's recovery from cancer, similarly uses self-portraiture to endow allegories with expressionistic feeling and meaning. These paintings and drawings trace Treiman's flirtatious battle with a mostly malevolent male figure who variously represents death, sexual manipulation, oblivion, vanity, and corruption. The works become a forum for death-haunted fantasy and autobiographical reverie. In **Sailing Away** (1985) an off-balance Treiman is ushered by a less sardonic version of the Joker toward an ominously departing ocean liner. In **Joker Looking Down and Me** (1986) Treiman's self-portrait assumes the hairstyle and earrings of her departed mother, Rose.

In her last major paintings, Treiman returned to the western imagery of earlier works such as **Dear Friends** and **Americana III.** In **Friends and Strangers** (1987) a duplicitous Joker and an ominous Indian on horseback sandwich two full-length, off-kilter versions of Joyce. The text uttered by the Treiman-in-a-headdress—"Moi?"—suggests by its self-doubt that each of the characters is both a "friend" and a "stranger." On the similarly barren western landscape of **The Last Parade** (1987), a tuba-playing Joker ominously guides into oblivion a reeling, ceremonially dressed Joyce. Treiman's heroic/antiheroic stance charges these late paintings with meaning. **Uphill** (1988) perfectly describes the artist's genuinely Sisyphean efforts; undaunted, the aging cowgirl spurs her horse on, seemingly against his will. Her ride represents a melodramatic western that is both comic and heroic, continuing regardless.

Enhanced by extraordinary painterly qualities and draftsmanship, the autobiographical nature of Treiman's quest for meaning in figuration has a literary quality unique among her peers. Her use of art history as source material has firm roots in modernism and intersects with postmodern appropriation in a fascinating way. Treiman's conceptual complexity can be said to match that of contemporary figurative artists such as Mark Tansey, David Salle, or Eric Fischl—whose works pale before hers in terms of craft. The expressive power of her late autobiographical works transcends the ambiguity and simplistic irony of most postmodern figuration.

Treiman must also be considered as a breakthrough female artist, one who inserted herself without special pleading into the top ranks of male artists. Although rarely espoused by feminists, her work bears fascinating comparison with that of other iconoclastic women artists from the 1970s who toyed with autobiography and art history: May Stevens, Eleanor Antin, Faith Ringgold, Sylvia Sleigh, and Lil Picard. Her works as well bear comparison with those of contemporary male artists obsessed with self-image, such as Robert Arneson, Lucas Samaras, and Jonathan Borofsky.

Working intuitively, Joyce Treiman managed to find forms to combine her interests in the world around her with her enthusiasms for the great art of the past. Through the filter of her consciousness, she was able to reconceive the traditions of the past using self-portraiture as a vehicle. In the largely unwritten history of twentieth-century figurative painting, Treiman's vigorous and ambitious voice should not be ignored. In a letter from the 1960s to her friend and dealer, Sally Fairweather, she defined her goals for a kind of allegorically specific, figurative art: "When it all boils down, I am trying to say hallelujah to the particular, slightly frightened, existing being.... I want my work to make us see again the importance of the individual, the singular one.... The singular momentous event is what I am prowling for, and to me these events are a summing up and a viva."[19]

NOTES

1. Lawrence Alloway, "The Renewal of Realist Criticism," **Art in America** 69, no. 7 (September 1981): 111 n. 9.
2. John Berger, **Success and Failure of Picasso** (Harmondsworth, Middlesex: Penguin Books, 1965).
3. "War Art Shop Has New Order," **Iowa Press-Citizen** (Iowa City), November 27, 1942, p. 2.
4. Joyce Treiman, unpublished manuscript, June 1977, notes for Barnsdall retrospective, Los Angeles, under the auspices of the Los Angeles Municipal Art Gallery, in the Treiman estate.
5. Barbara Tannenbaum, "Painting in Chicago, 1945–1965," in **Chicago: The City and Its Artists, 1945–1978** (Ann Arbor: The University of Michigan Museum of Art, 1978), p. 18. From an interview with the artist, October 8, 1977.
6. Joyce Treiman, "**The Poet**... Series of Paintings: A Proclamation for 'Man,'" document in unfilmed 1960s scrapbook, Treiman Archive, Archives of American Art, Smithsonian Institution, Washington, D.C.
7. Ibid.
8. Joyce Treiman, unfilmed letter to Marian [?], July 27, 1960, Treiman Archive, Archives of American Art.
9. Michael Kurcfeld, "Making Faces," **California Magazine** 8, no. 4 (April 1983): 101.
10. Treiman, "Notes on Paintings, 1968–74, 1985, 1986, 1989," unfilmed journal, Treiman Archive, Archives of American Art.
11. Tillim, unfilmed letter to Treiman, August 13, 1969; Treiman, unfilmed rough draft of response to Tillim, August 16, 1969, Treiman Archive, Archives of American Art.
12. In Eakins's later painting **William Rush and His Model** (1907–8, Honolulu Academy of Arts), Rush helps the brightly lit female nude down from her modeling pedestal. According to her journal, Treiman based her nude depiction of Eakins on a period photograph.
13. Treiman, "Notes on Painting."
14. Treiman, "Notes on Paintings," unfilmed journal dated 1985, Treiman Archive, Archives of American Art.
15. Rembrandt, **Man with a Gilt Helmet,** Staatliche Museen, Berlin. As with many works long attributed to Rembrandt, the authorship is now in question.
16. Although Rembrandt's portrait is commonly referred to as **Portrait of the Artist's Son,** the identity of the sitter is actually in dispute.
17. Cindy Sherman, **History Portraits,** with a text by Arthur Danto (New York: Rizzoli, 1991), p. 13.
18. Betty Brown, "Believing in the Human Spirit," **Artweek** 14, no. 43 (December 17, 1983): 6.
19. Treiman, unfilmed draft of letter to Sally Fairweather, ca. 1960–64, Treiman Archive, Archives of American Art.

The Party
1945
oil on canvas
$25\frac{3}{4}$ x 20 inches
Collection Donald M. Treiman,
Pacific Palisades, California

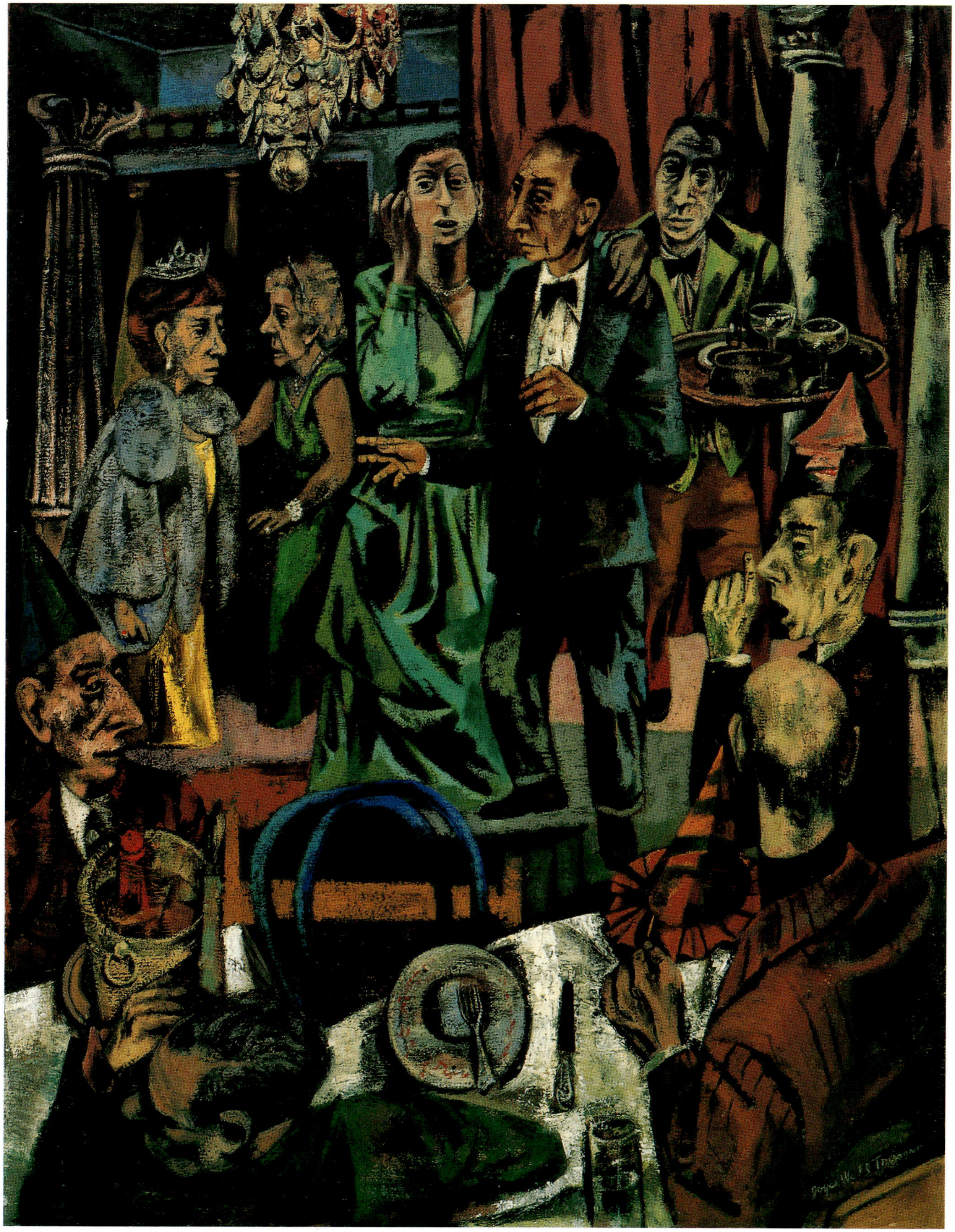

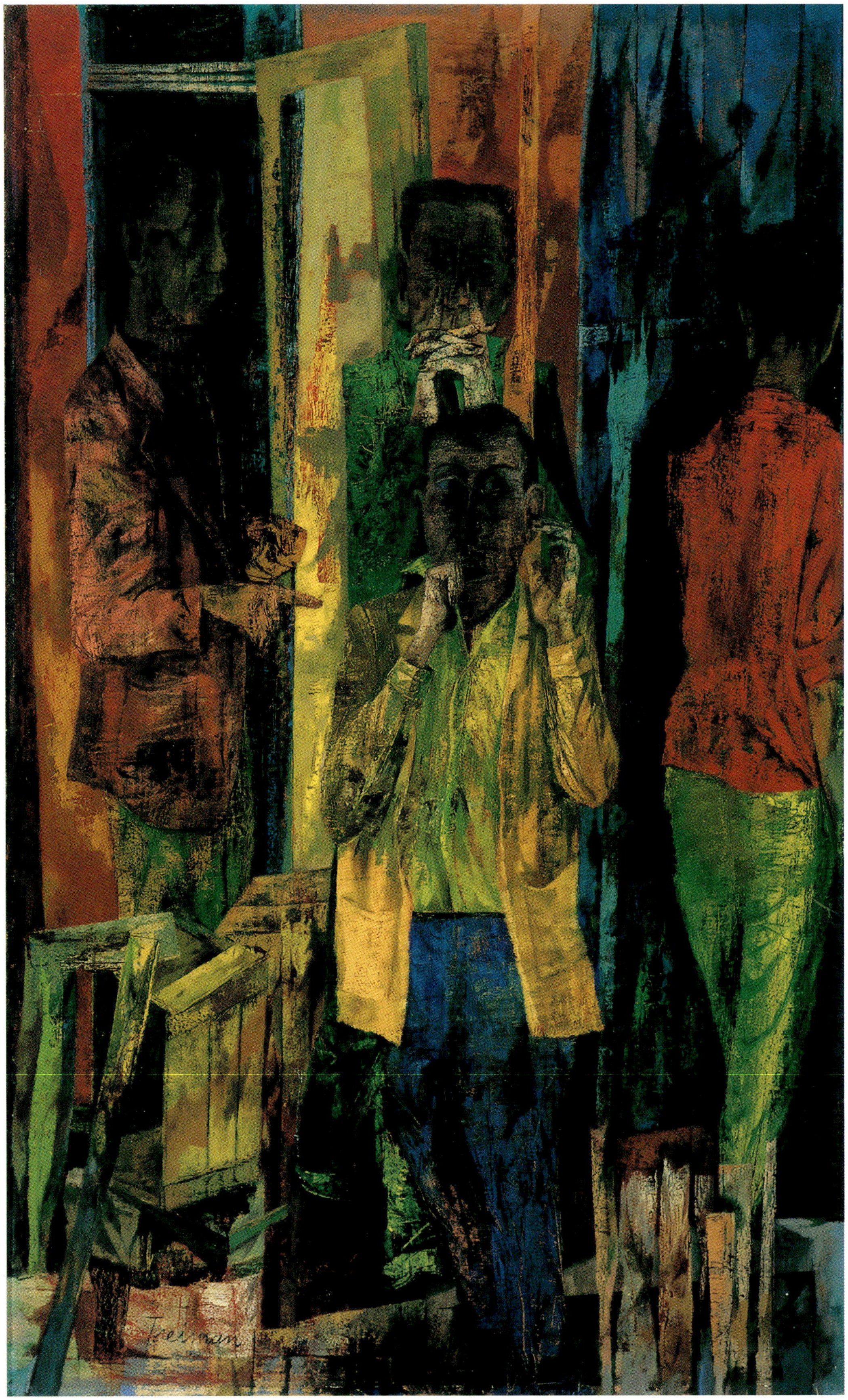

The Wanderers
1946
oil on canvas
50 x 38 inches
Lisa and John Pritzker

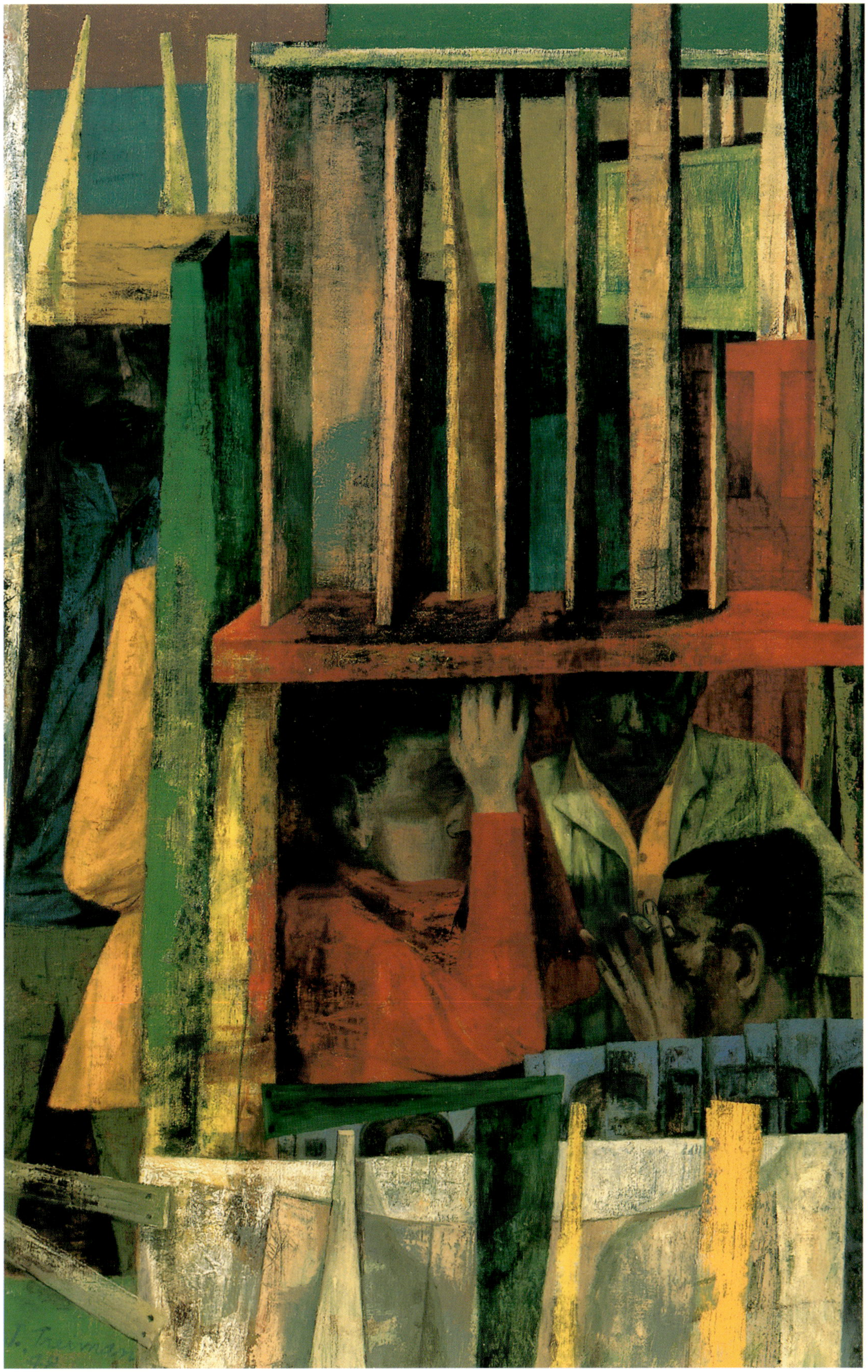

Conversation
1948
oil on canvas
44 x 28 inches
Denver Art Museum, Helen Dill Collection, 1948.20

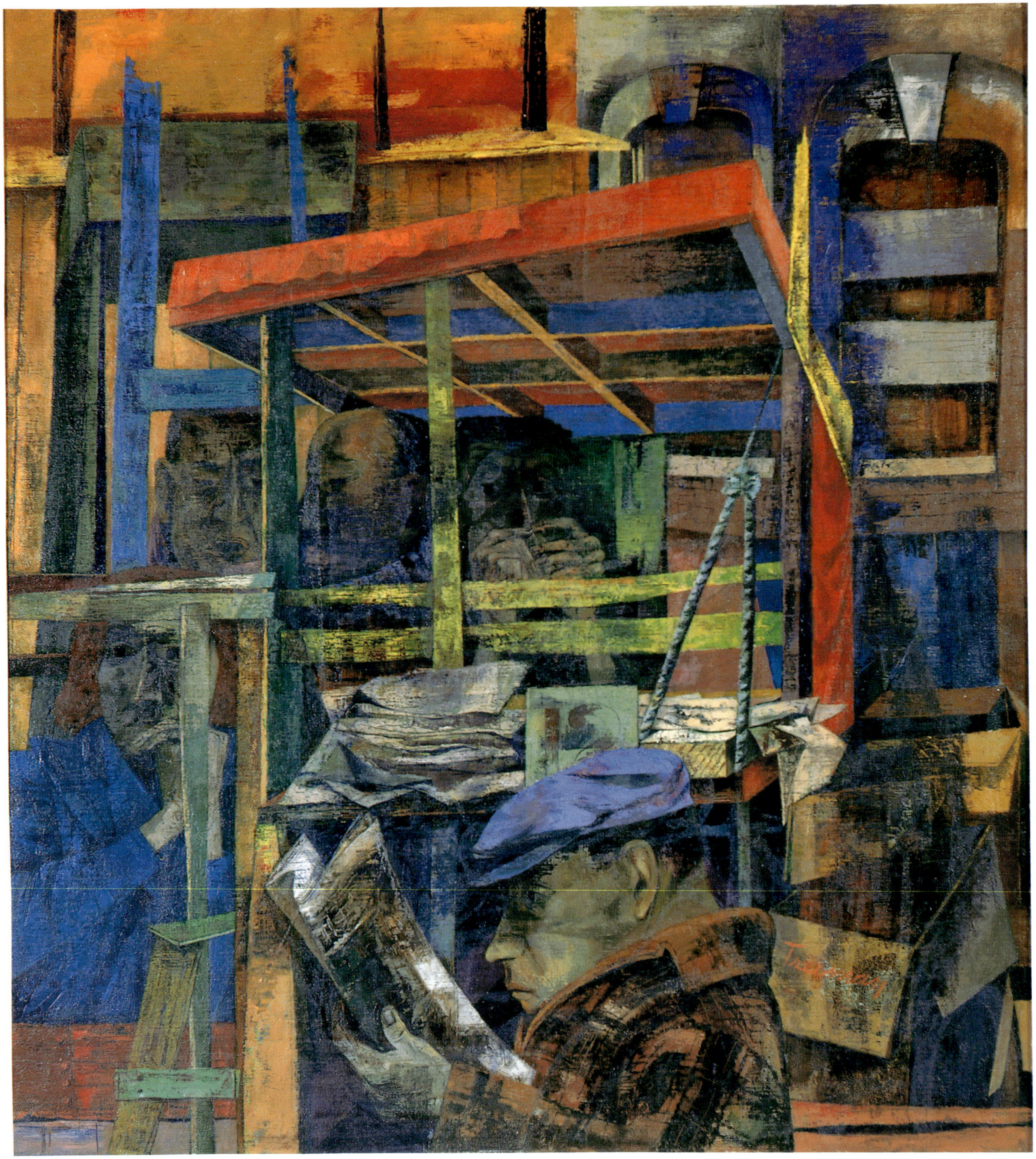

Street in Motion
1948
oil on canvas
37 x 34 inches
Collection of the Illinois State Museum, Springfield

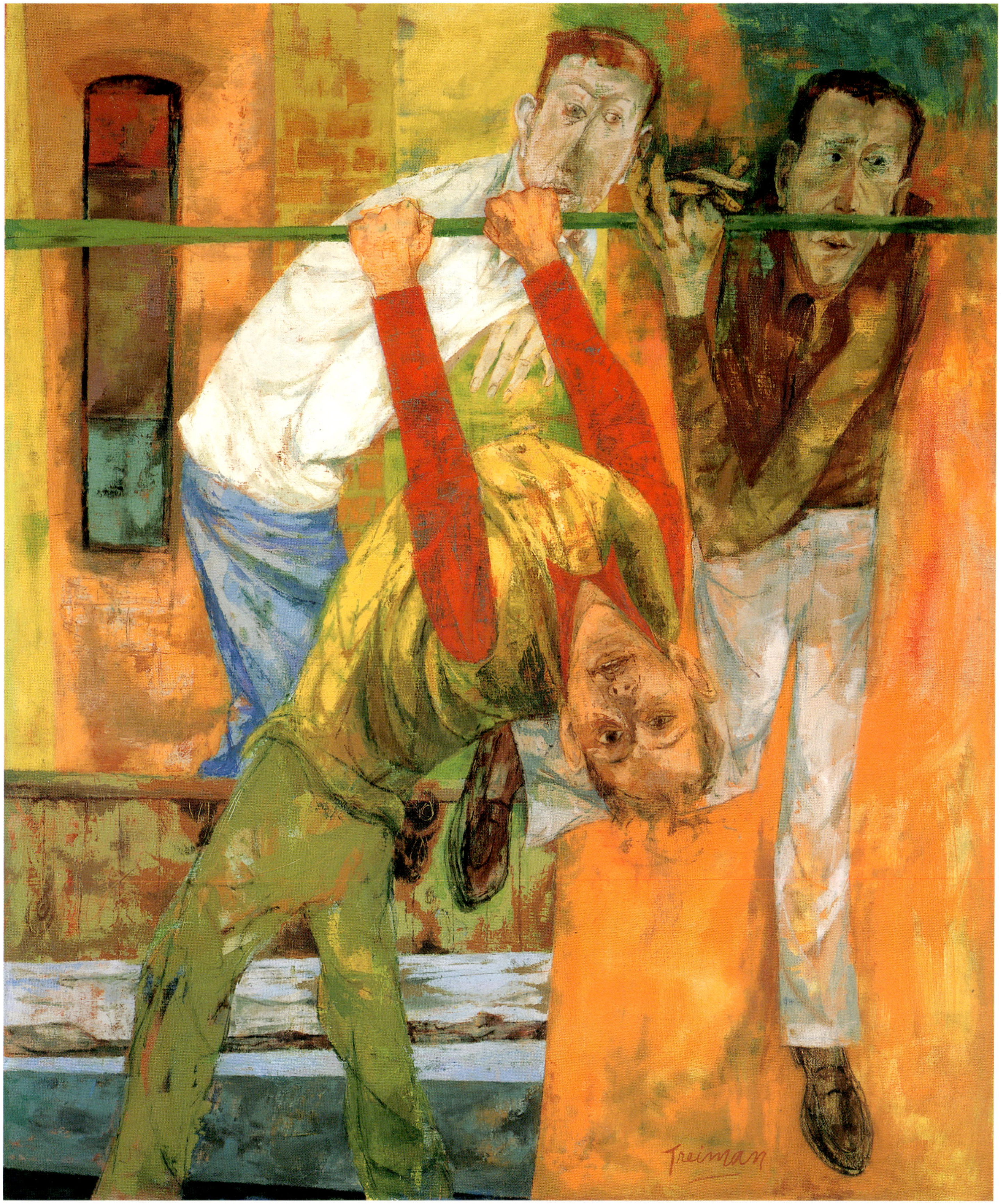

Escape
1950
oil on canvas
44 x 36 inches
The Art Institute of Chicago,
Mr. and Mrs. Frank G. Logan
Purchase Prize, 1951.130

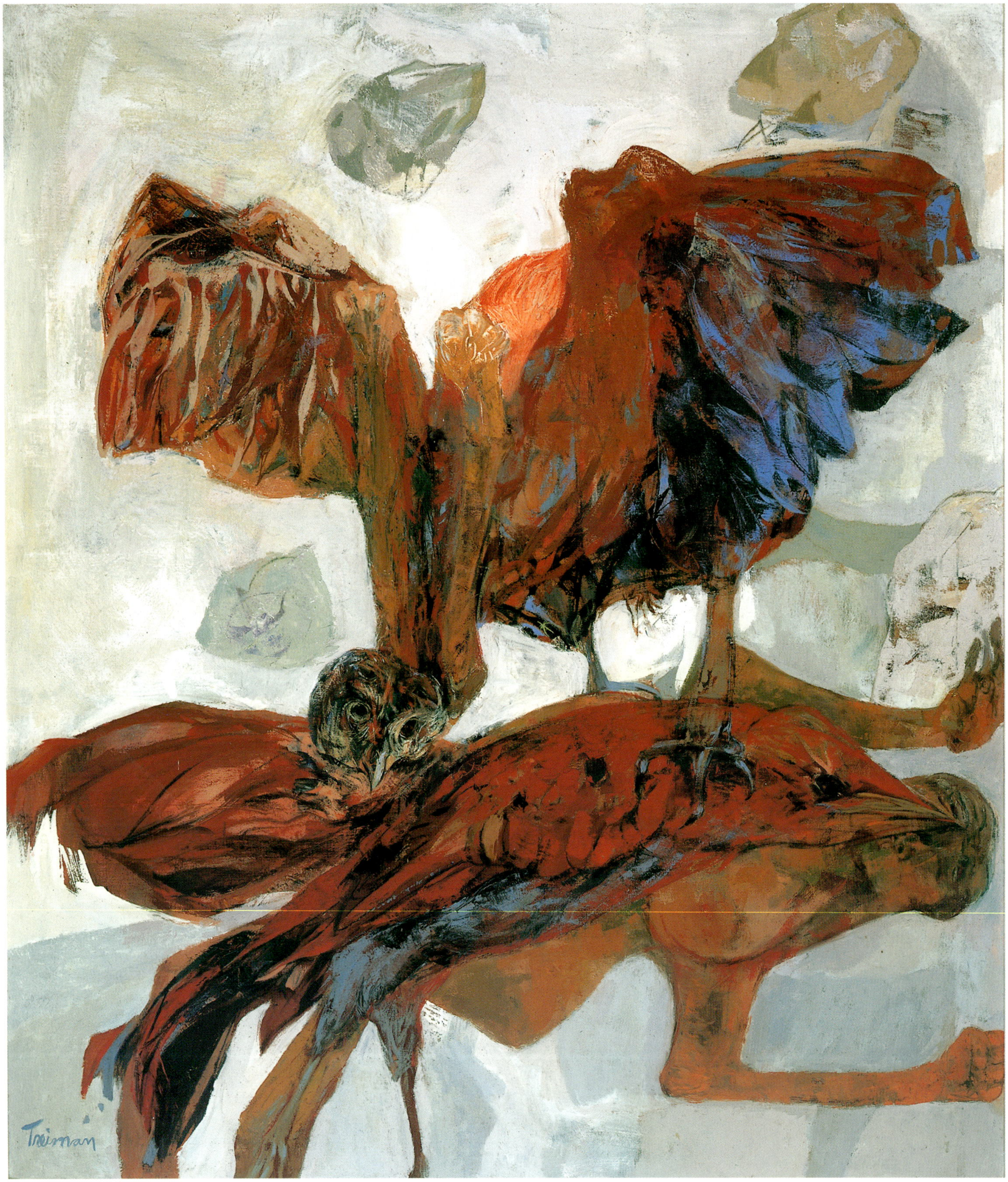

Nisus and Scylla
1951
oil on canvas
41 × 34¾ inches
Santa Barbara Museum of Art, Gift of Ann and Aaron Nisenson, 1991.65.2

The Poet
1961–62
oil on canvas
70 × 70 inches
Collection of Alex and Corrine Koper

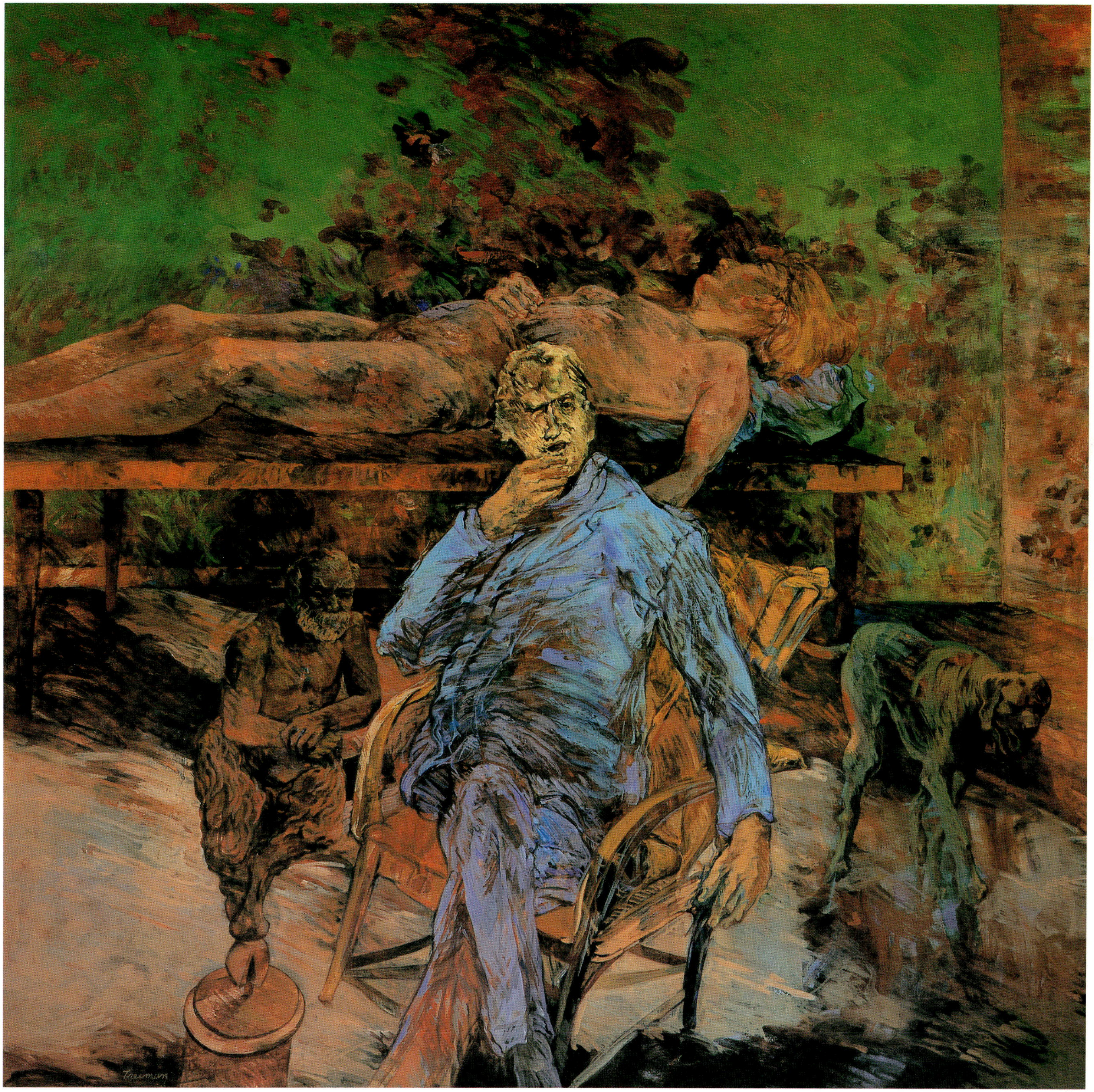

Angel for Abraham
ca. 1952
acrylic on canvas
$51\frac{5}{8} \times 38\frac{3}{4}$ inches
Collection Museum of Contemporary Art, Chicago,
Gift of Joseph and Jory Shapiro, 92.47

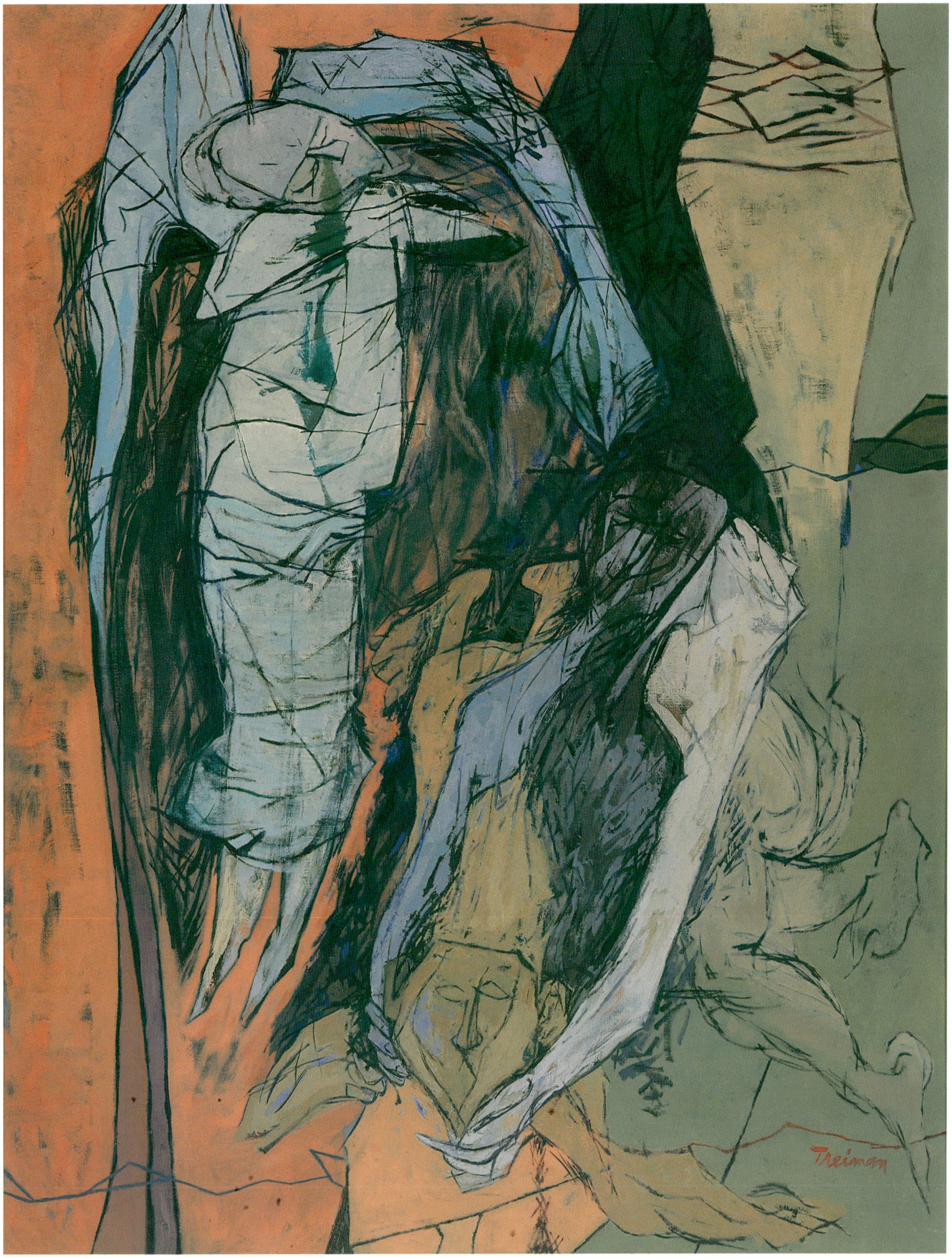
Treiman

Jacob, Man, Angel
1956
oil on canvas
48 x 40 inches
Courtesy Schmidt Bingham Gallery, New York

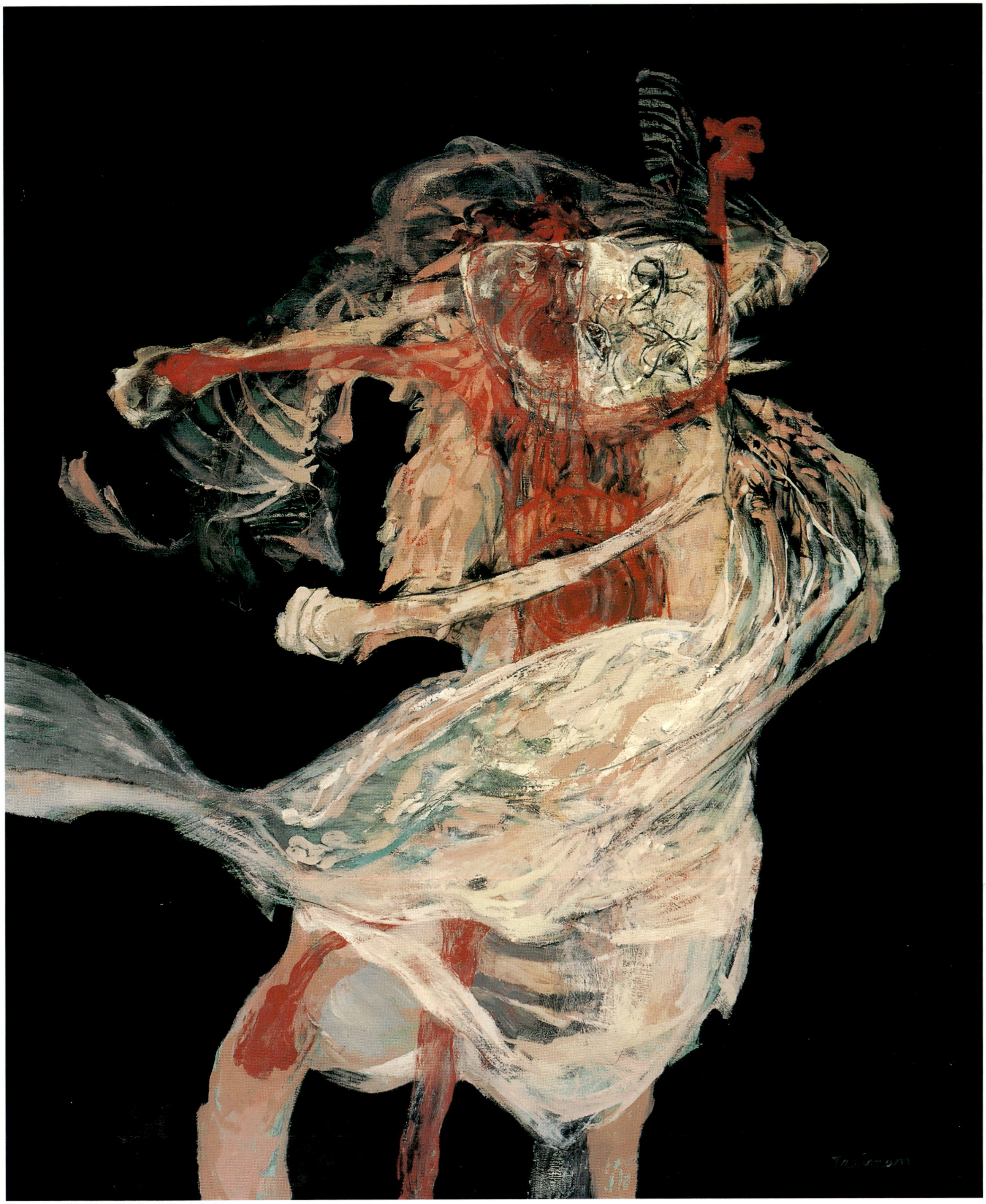

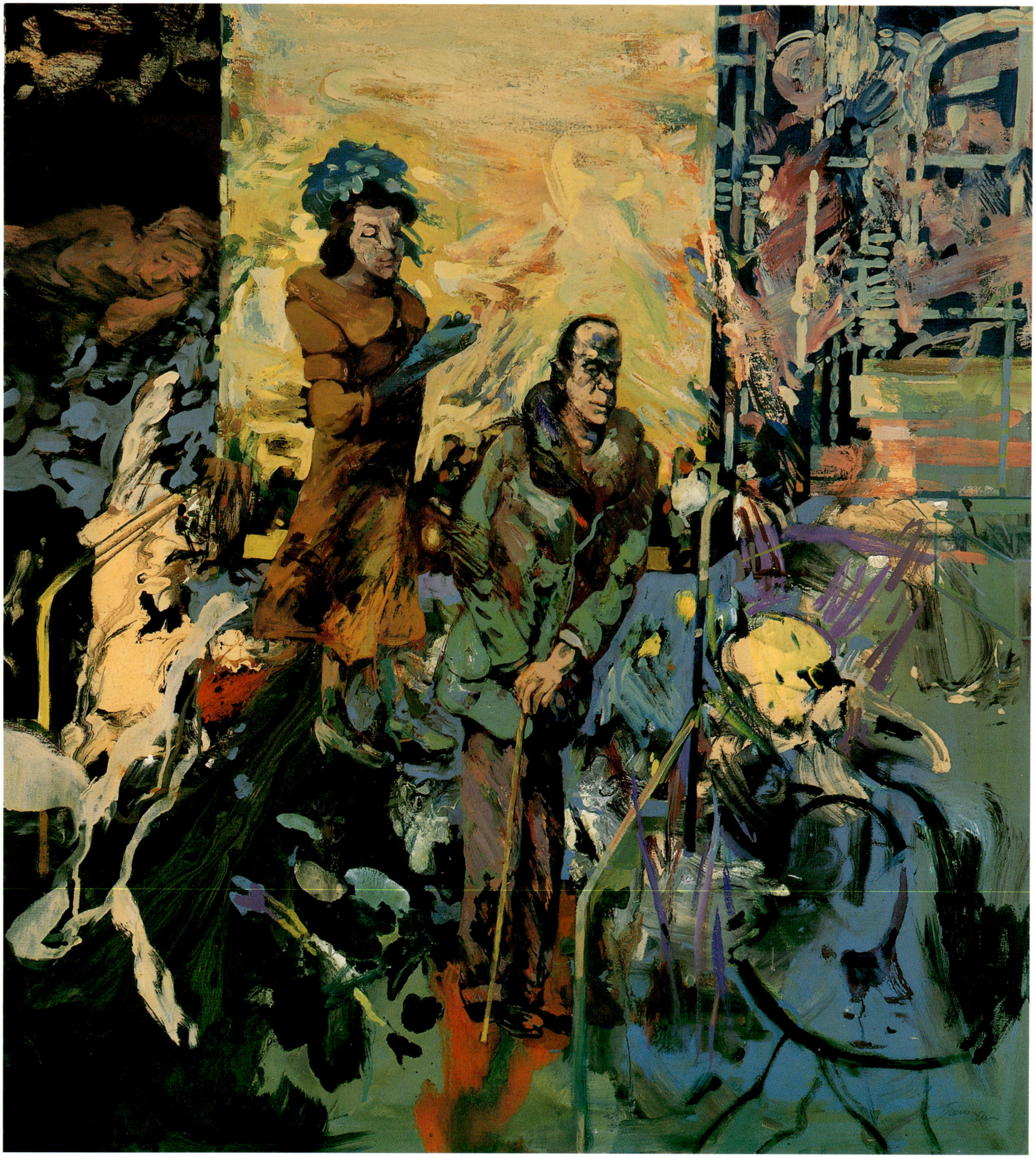

Dream Sequence (The Couple)
1962
oil on canvas
36 x 32 inches
Courtesy Schmidt Bingham Gallery, New York

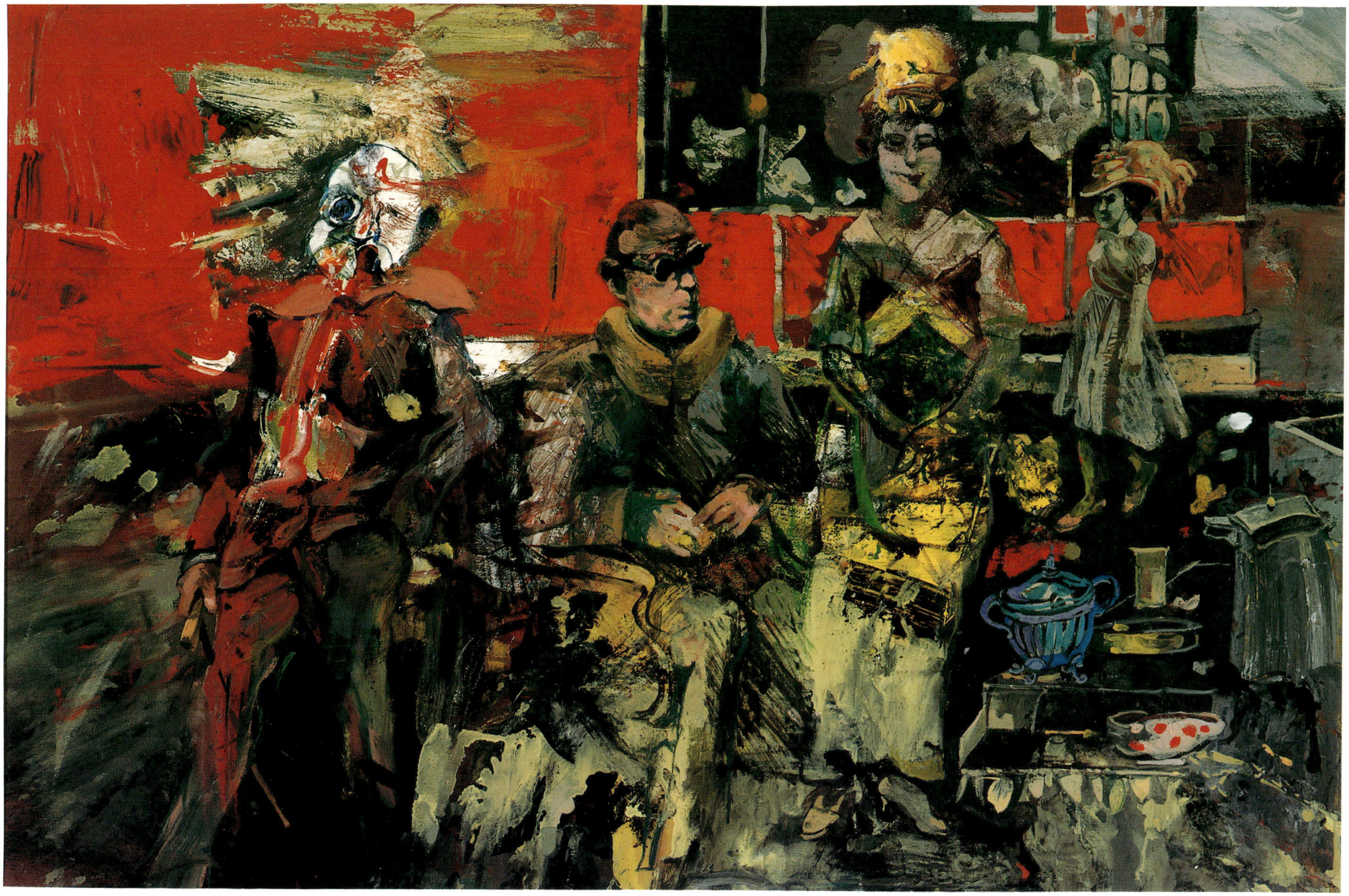

Man with Monocle No. 1
1962
oil on canvas
24 x 36 inches
Collection of J. B. and M. K. Pritzker

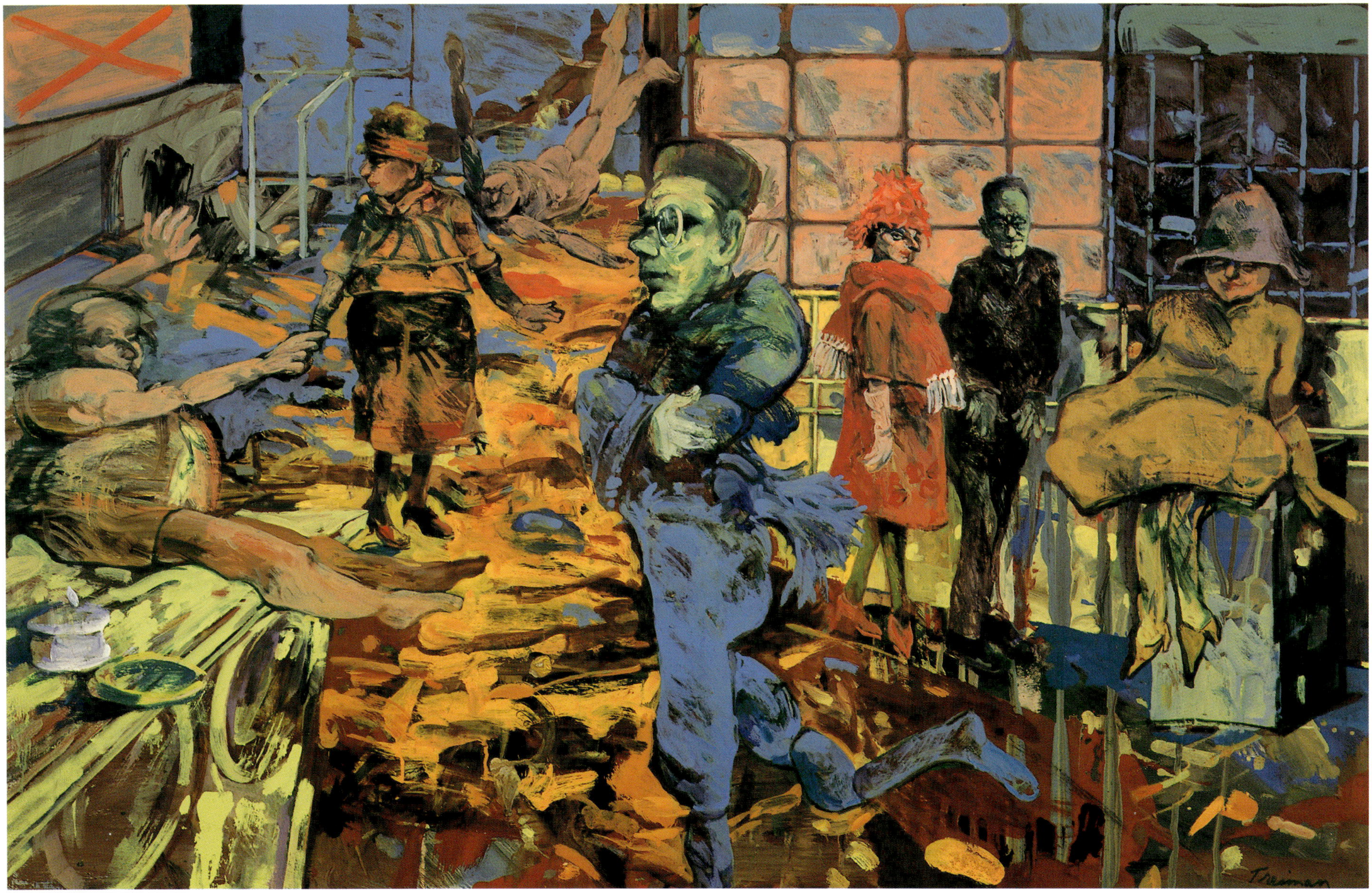

Dream Sequence
1964
oil on canvas
$30\frac{1}{4} \times 46\frac{1}{8}$ inches
Collection of Alex and Corrine Koper

The Fish Pond
1964
oil on canvas
60 x 50 inches
Portland Art Museum, Gift of Donald Treiman, 83.50

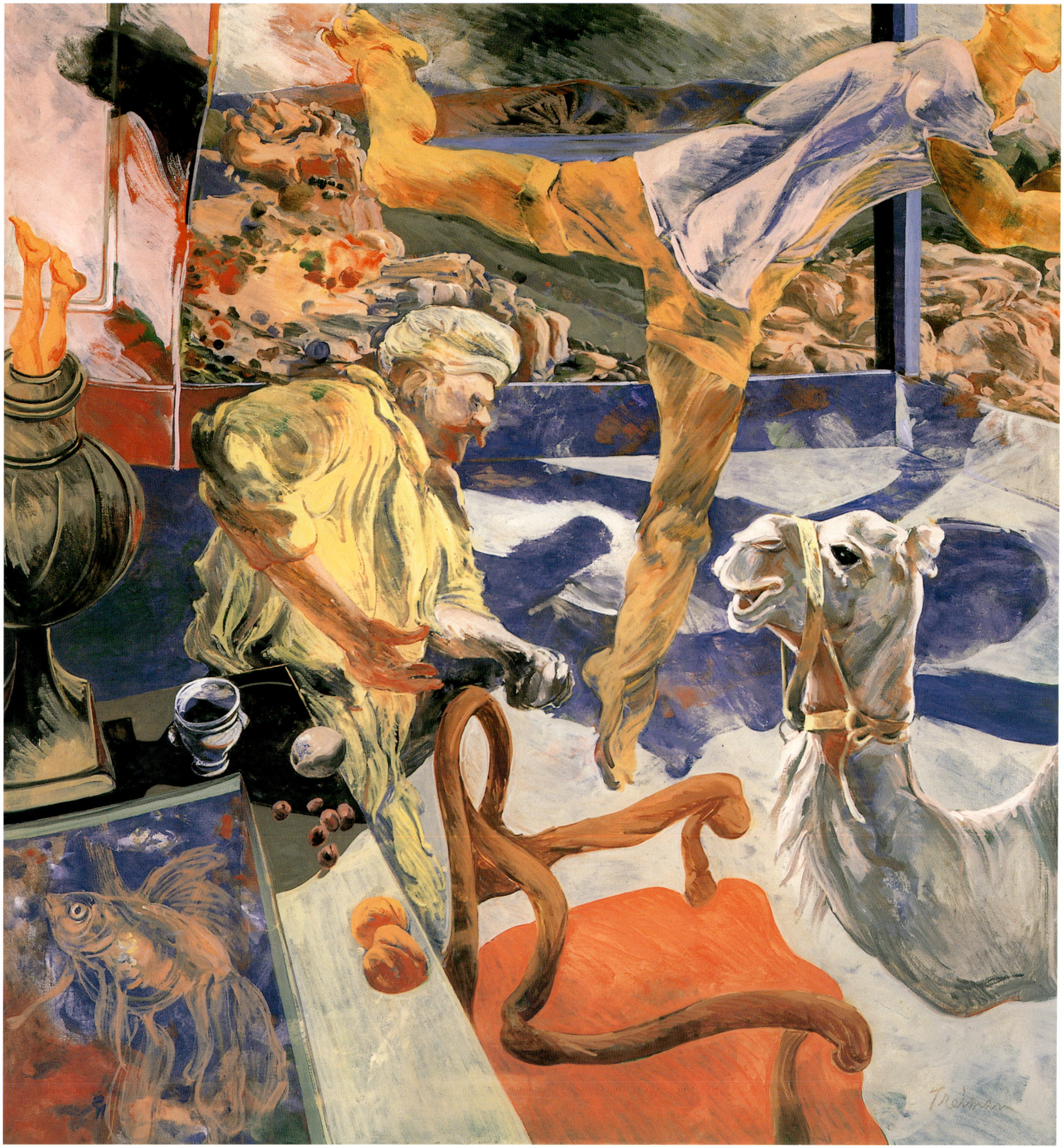

A View of Any Arrival
1964
oil on canvas
40 x 40 inches
Joseph Cecil

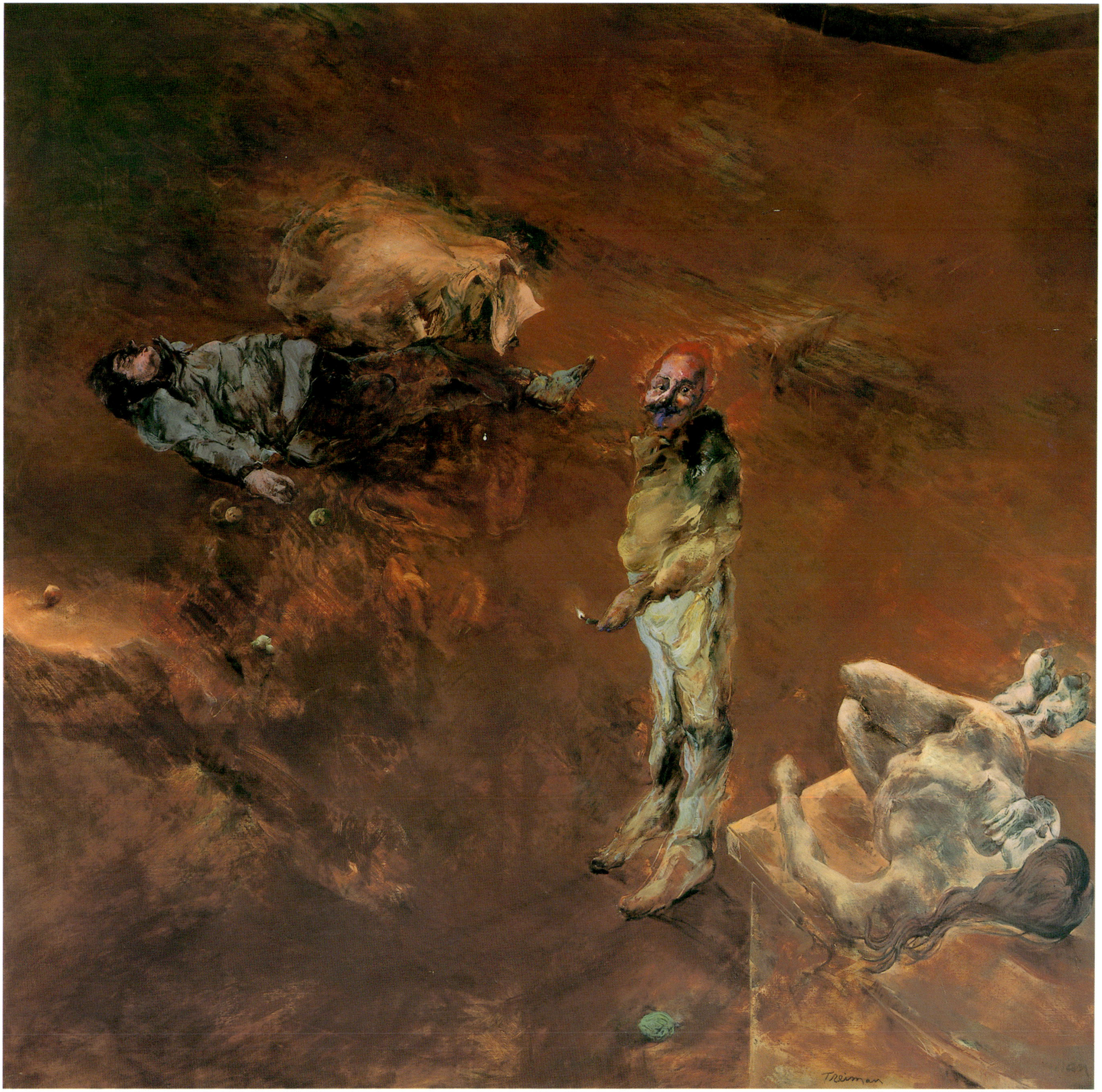
Treiman

The Birthday Party

1966–67

oil on canvas

70 x 70 inches

Partial and promised gift to the Los Angeles County Museum of Art by Ann and Aaron Nisenson

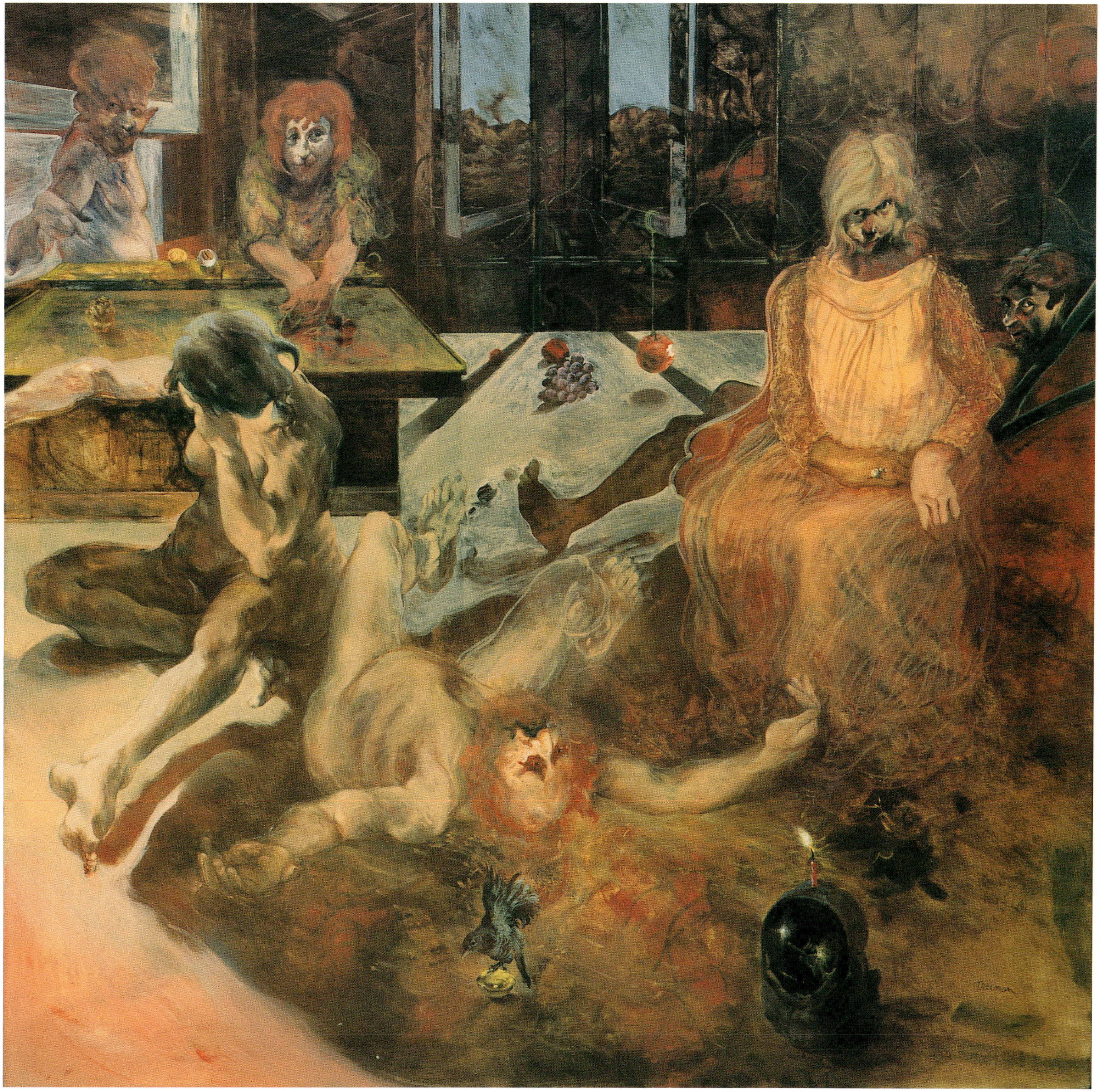

Rabbit and Pills
1967–68
oil on canvas
60 x 50 inches
Collection of Alex and Corrine Koper

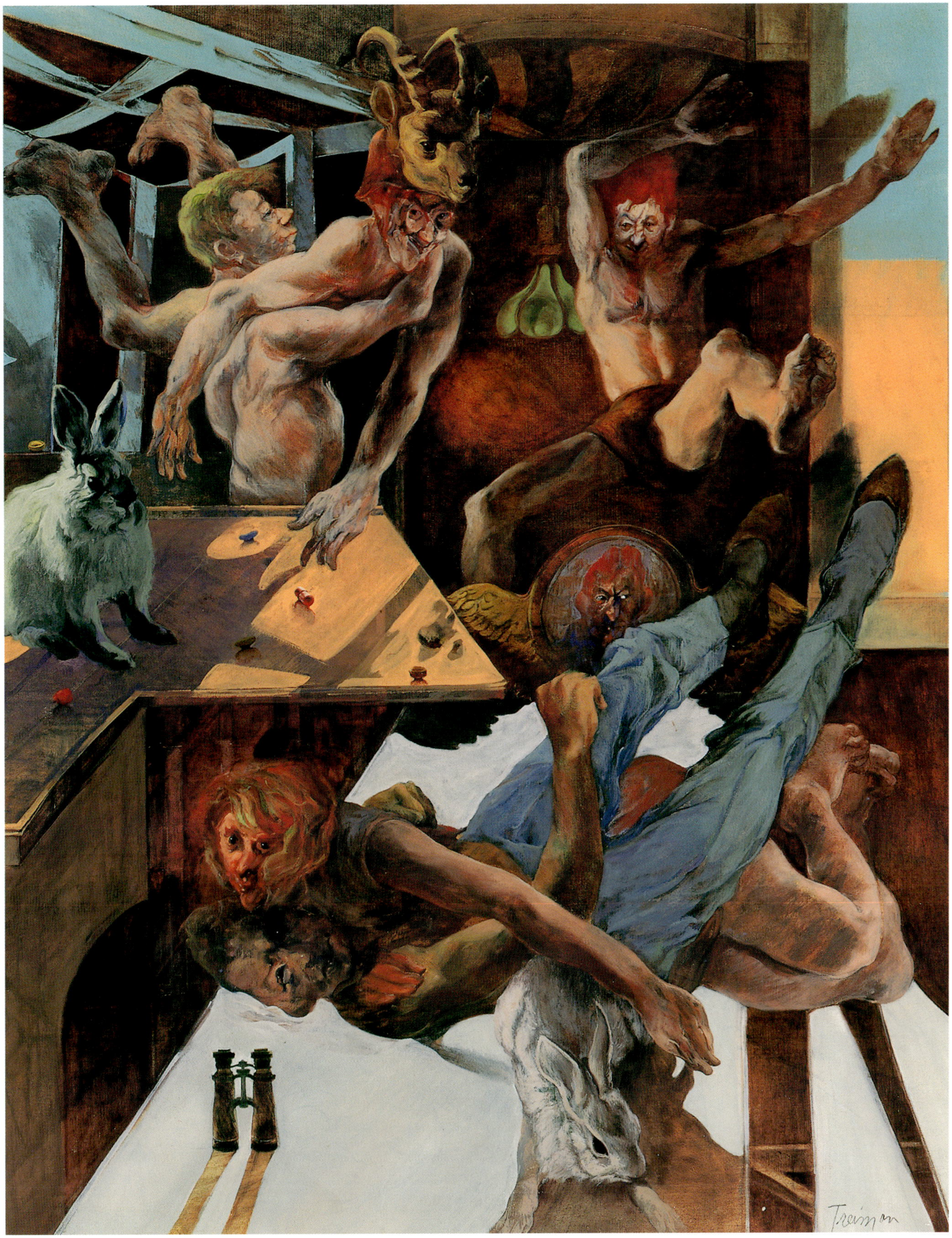

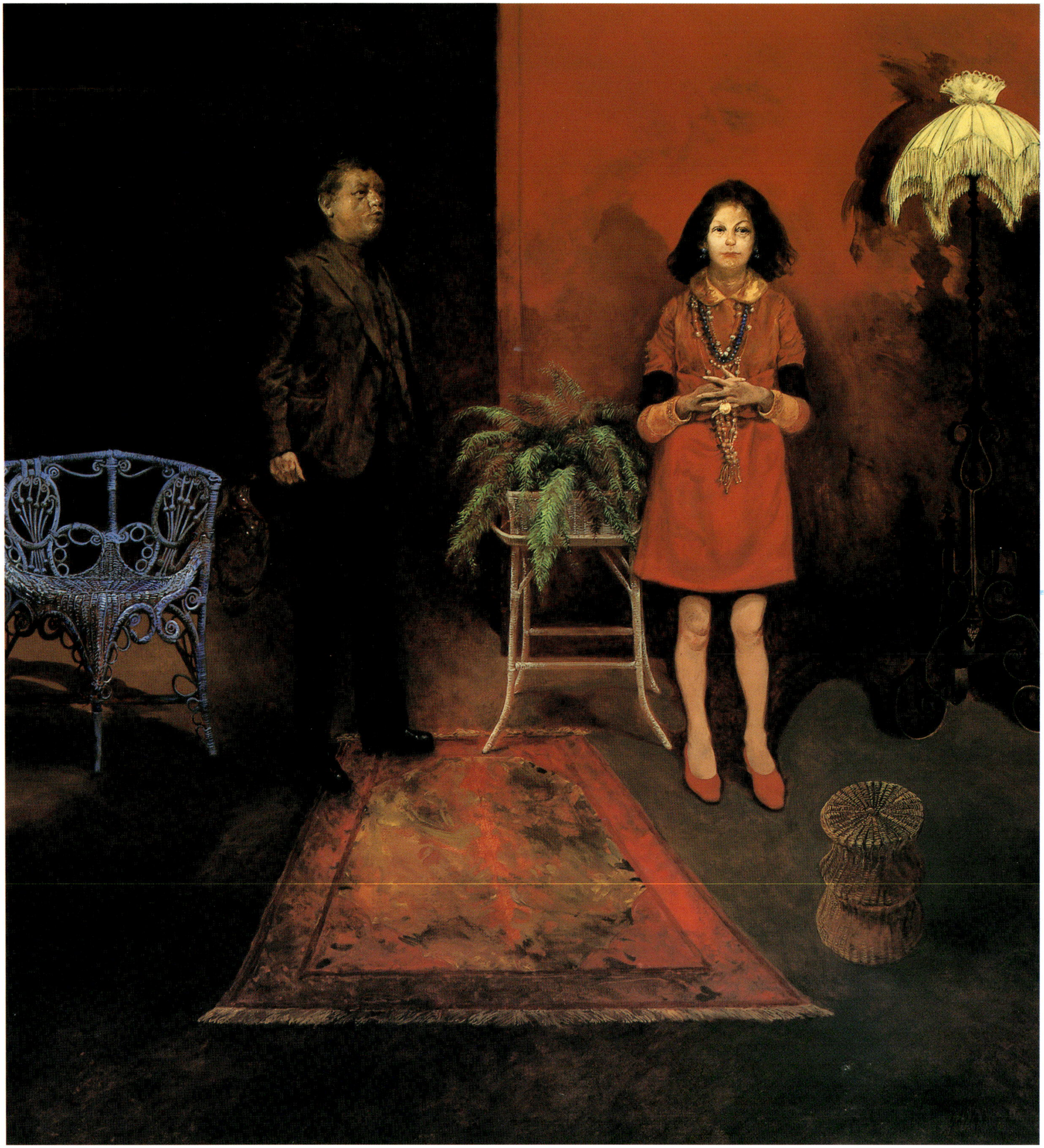

The Yellow Lampshade
1968–69
oil on canvas
40 x 36 inches
Charles and Carol Greenberg

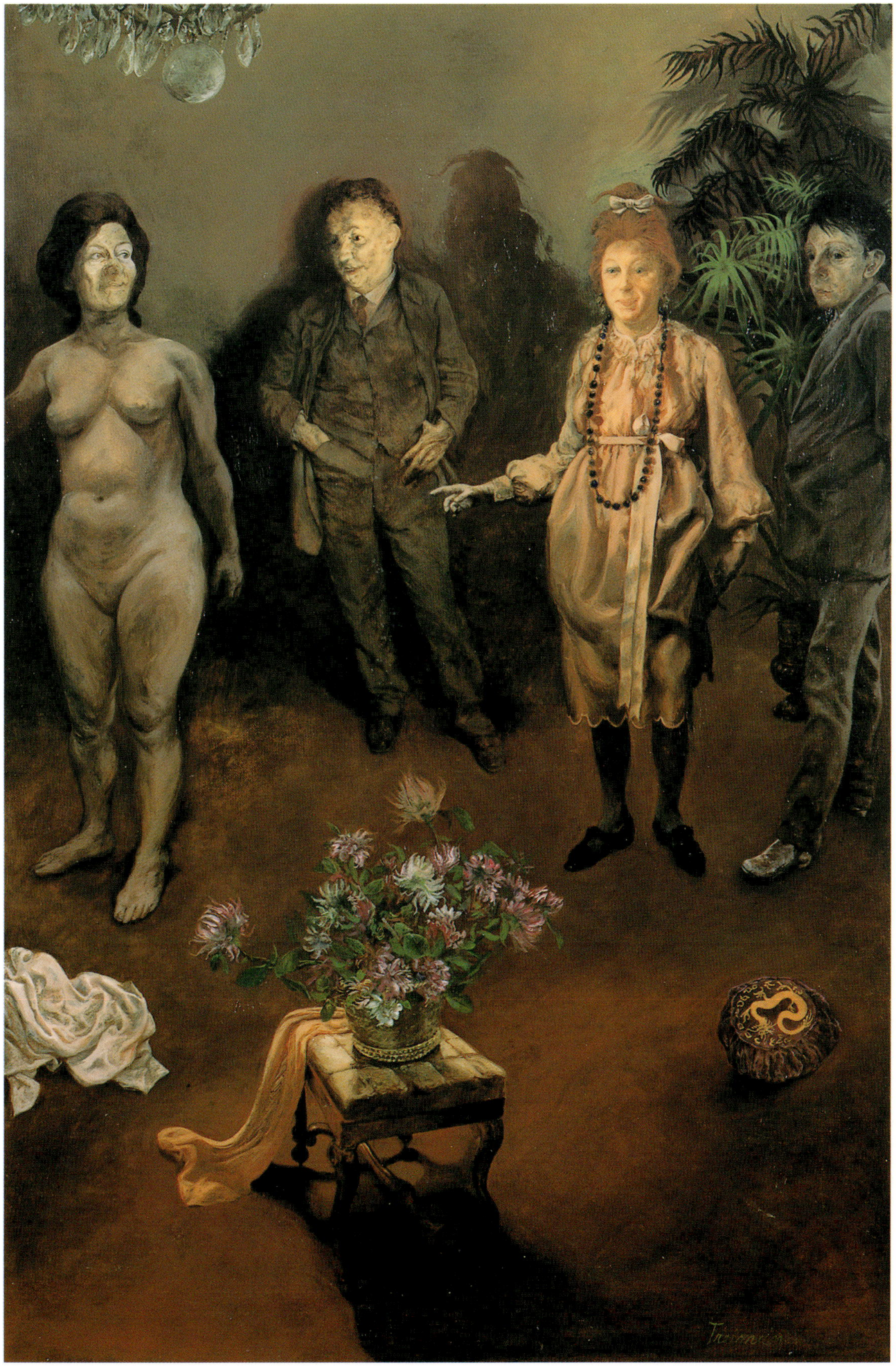

The Bouquet
1969
oil on canvas
36 x 24 inches
Collection of Harry Saunders

The Adventure
1970
oil on canvas
48 x 60 inches
Nancy Cooper Federman
and the late Ronald Harrison Cooper

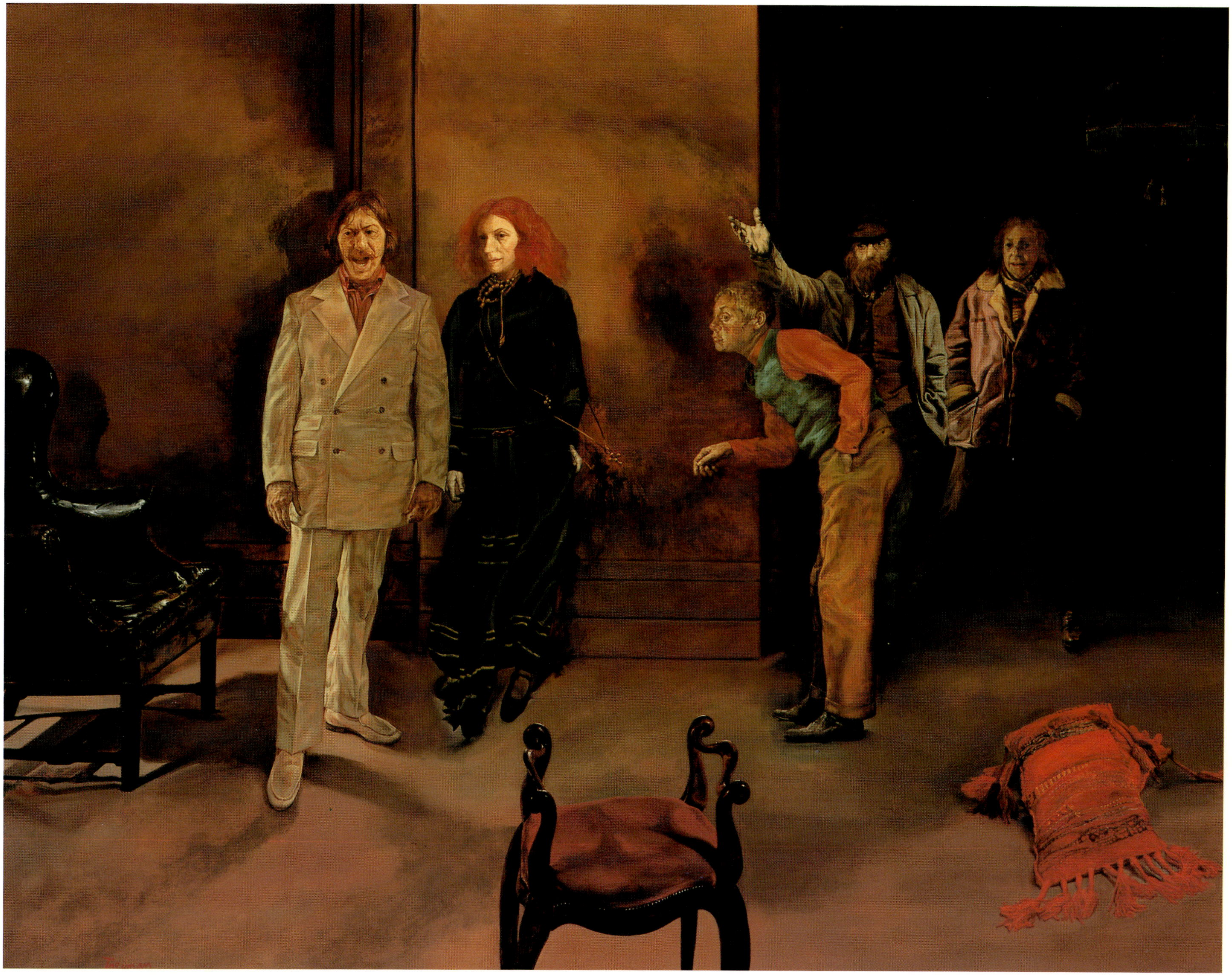

Standing Man
1968–69
oil on canvas
40 x 30 inches
Collection Donald M. Treiman,
Pacific Palisades, California

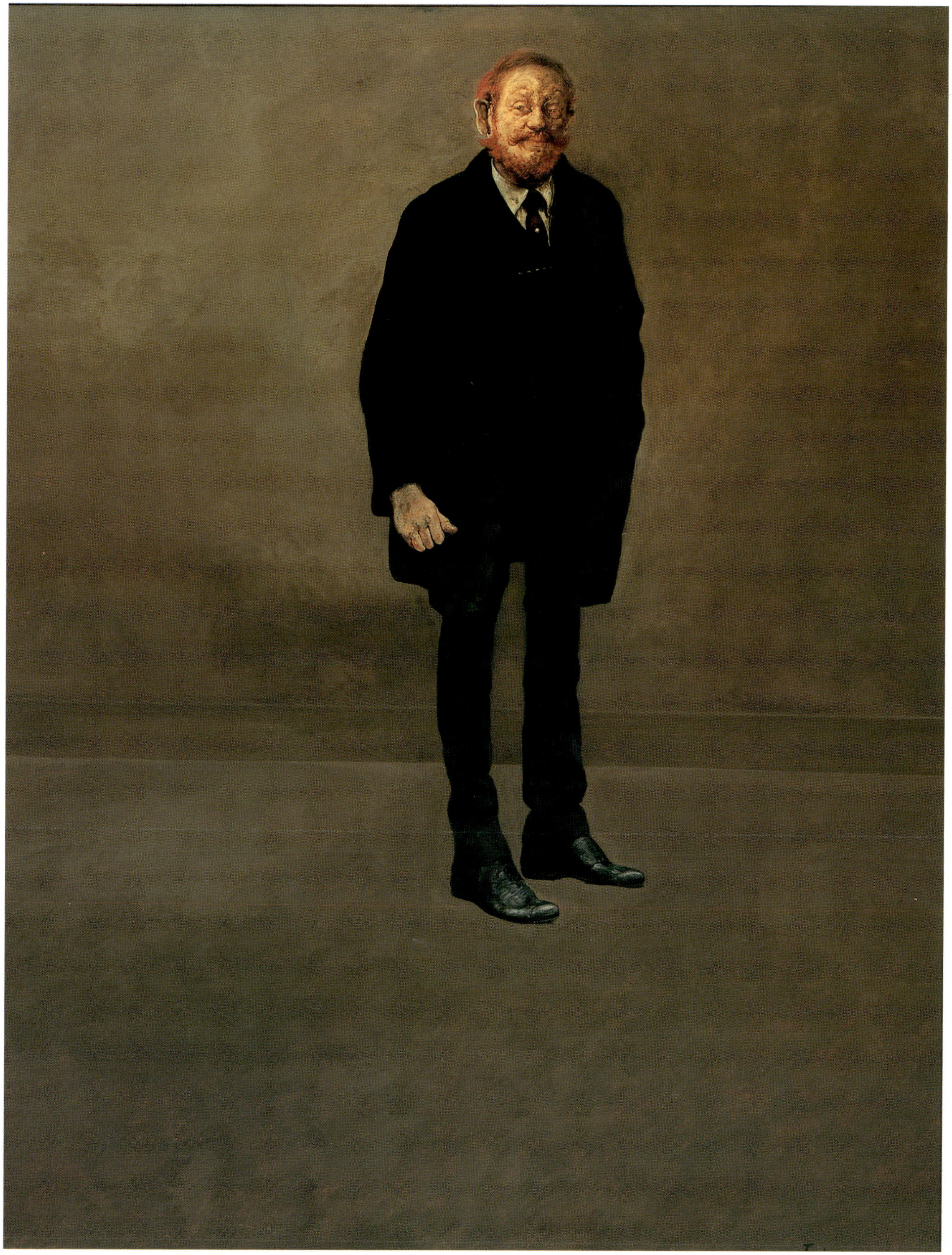

Anomie

1969–70

oil on canvas

70 x 70 inches

Whitney Museum of American Art, New York,
Gift of an anonymous donor, 71.227

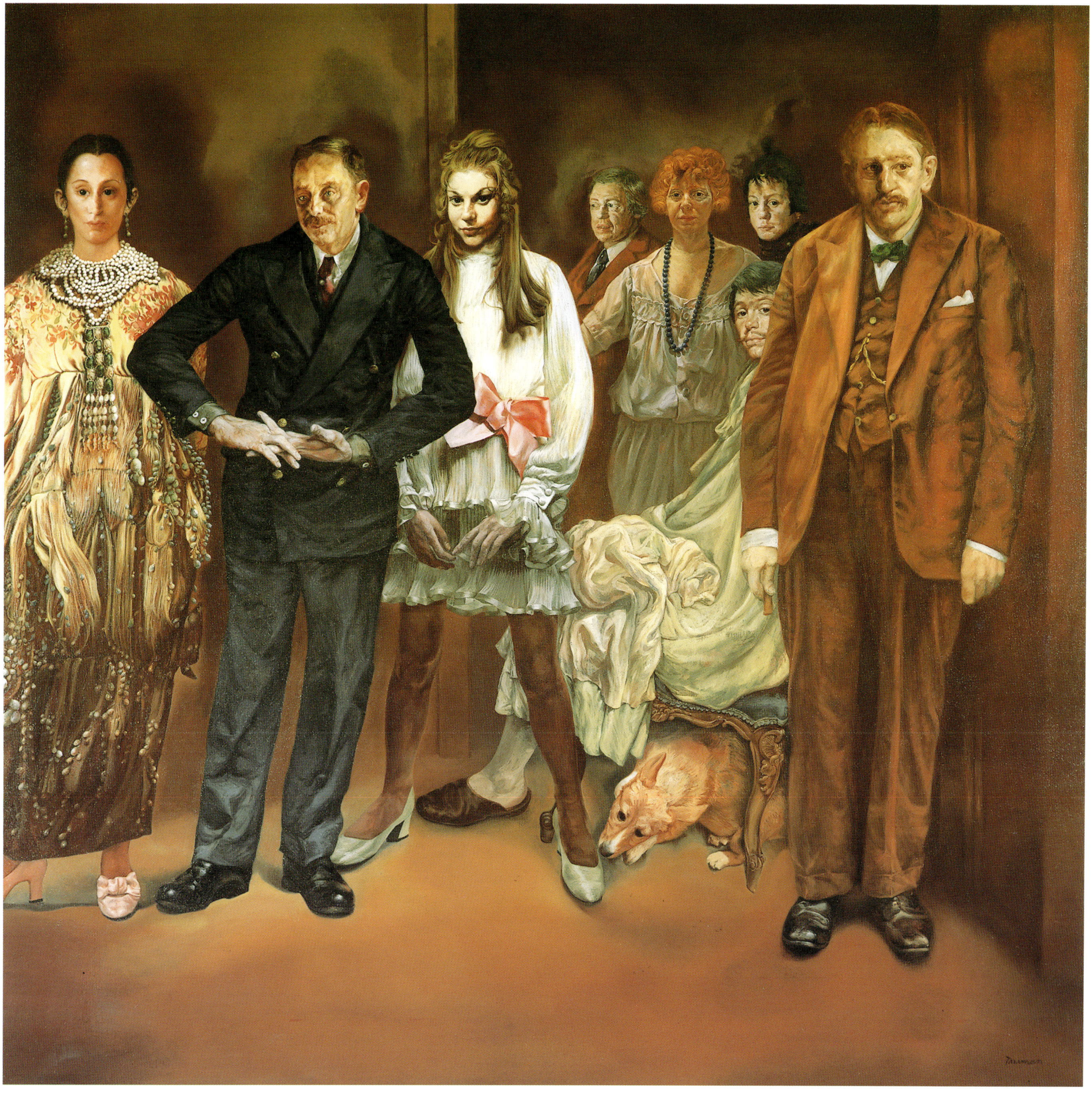

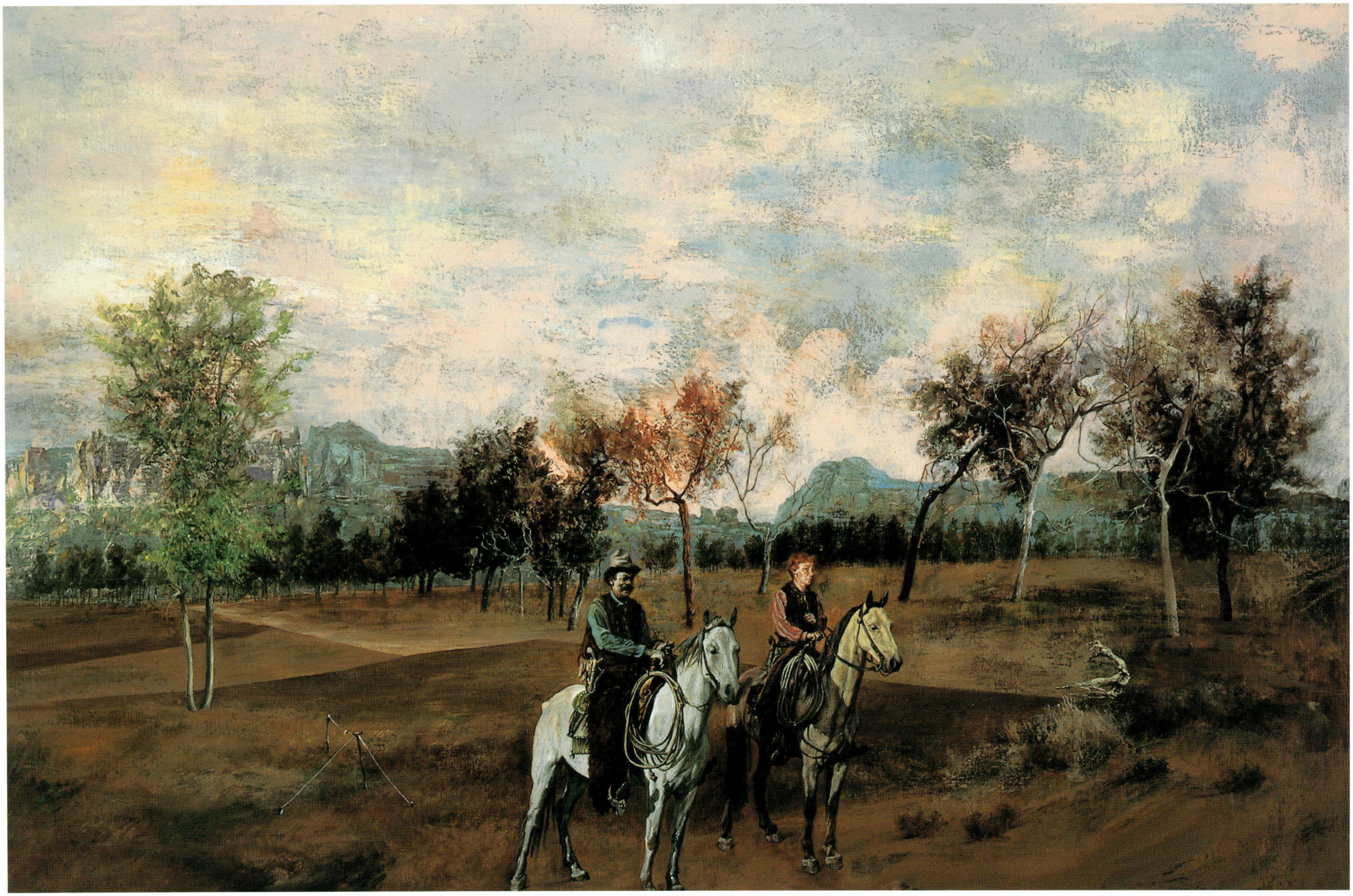

Self-Portrait with Cowboy Ken
1970–71
oil on canvas
24 x 36 inches
Collection of the City of Los Angeles, Gift of Home Savings and Loan

Dear Friends
1972
oil on canvas
70 x 70 inches
Lisa and John Pritzker

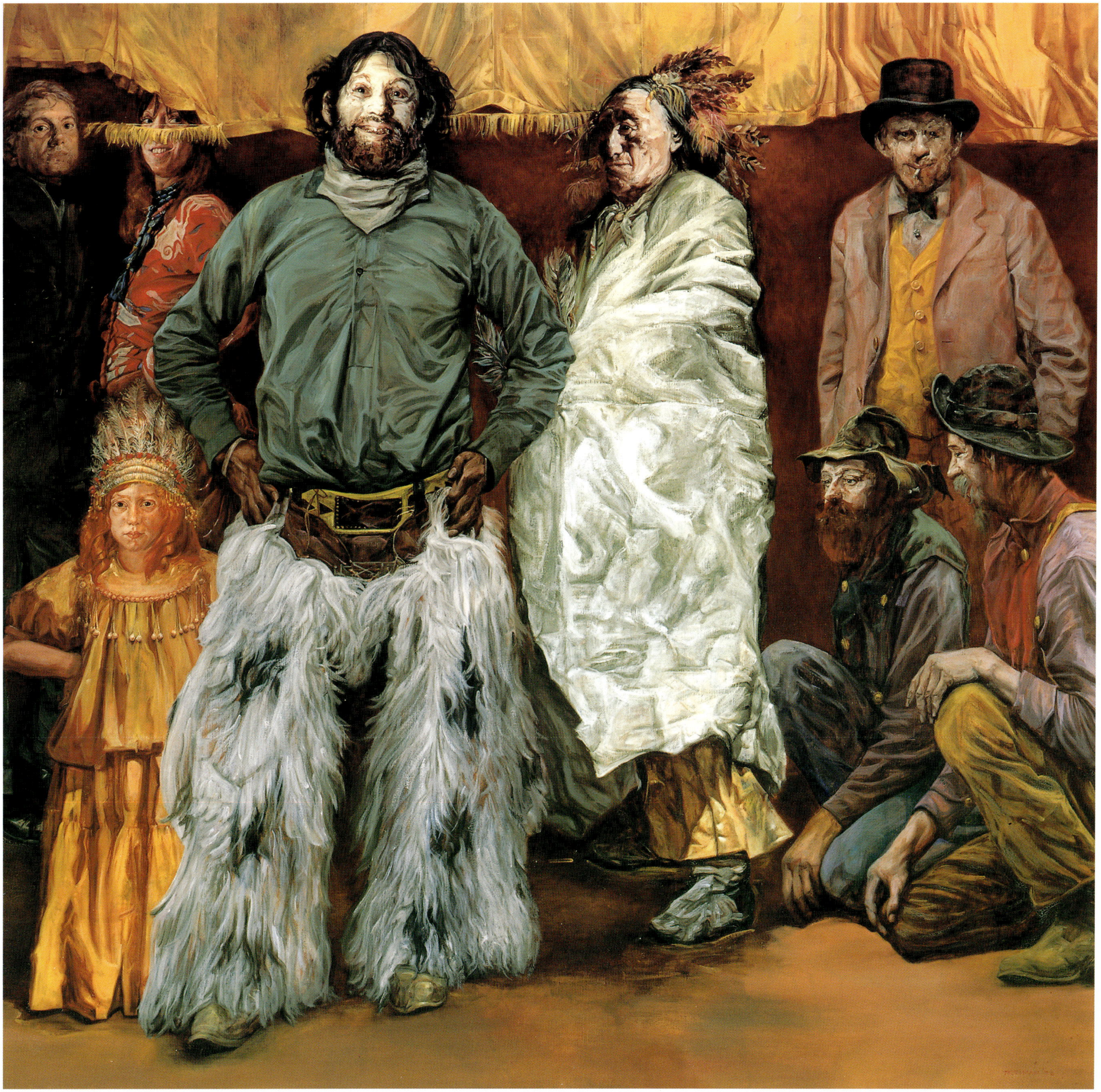

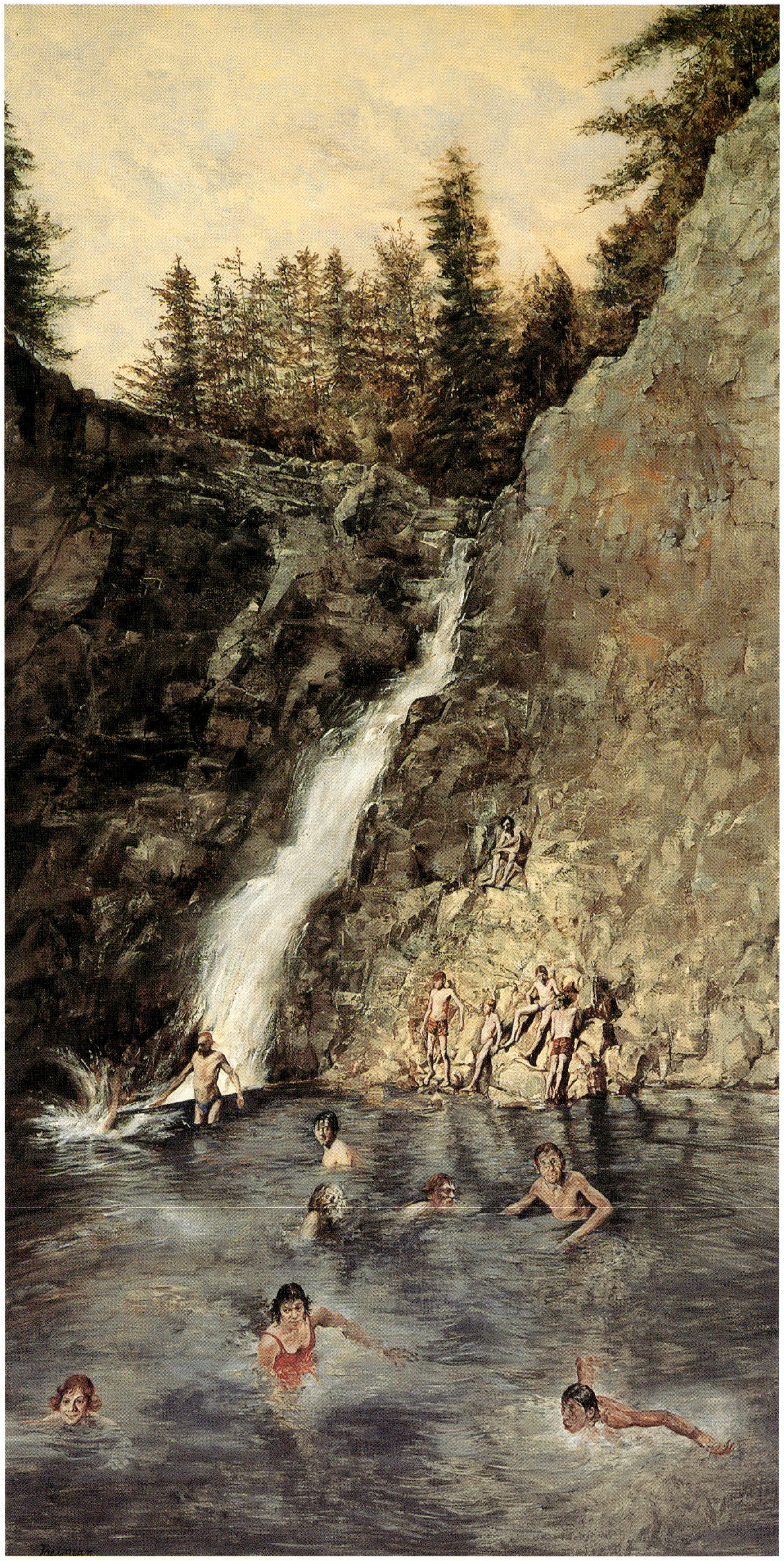

Swimmers: Antibes, Topanga
1971
oil on canvas
$48\frac{1}{2} \times 23\frac{1}{2}$ inches
Collection of the Long Beach Museum of Art,
Gift of the artist

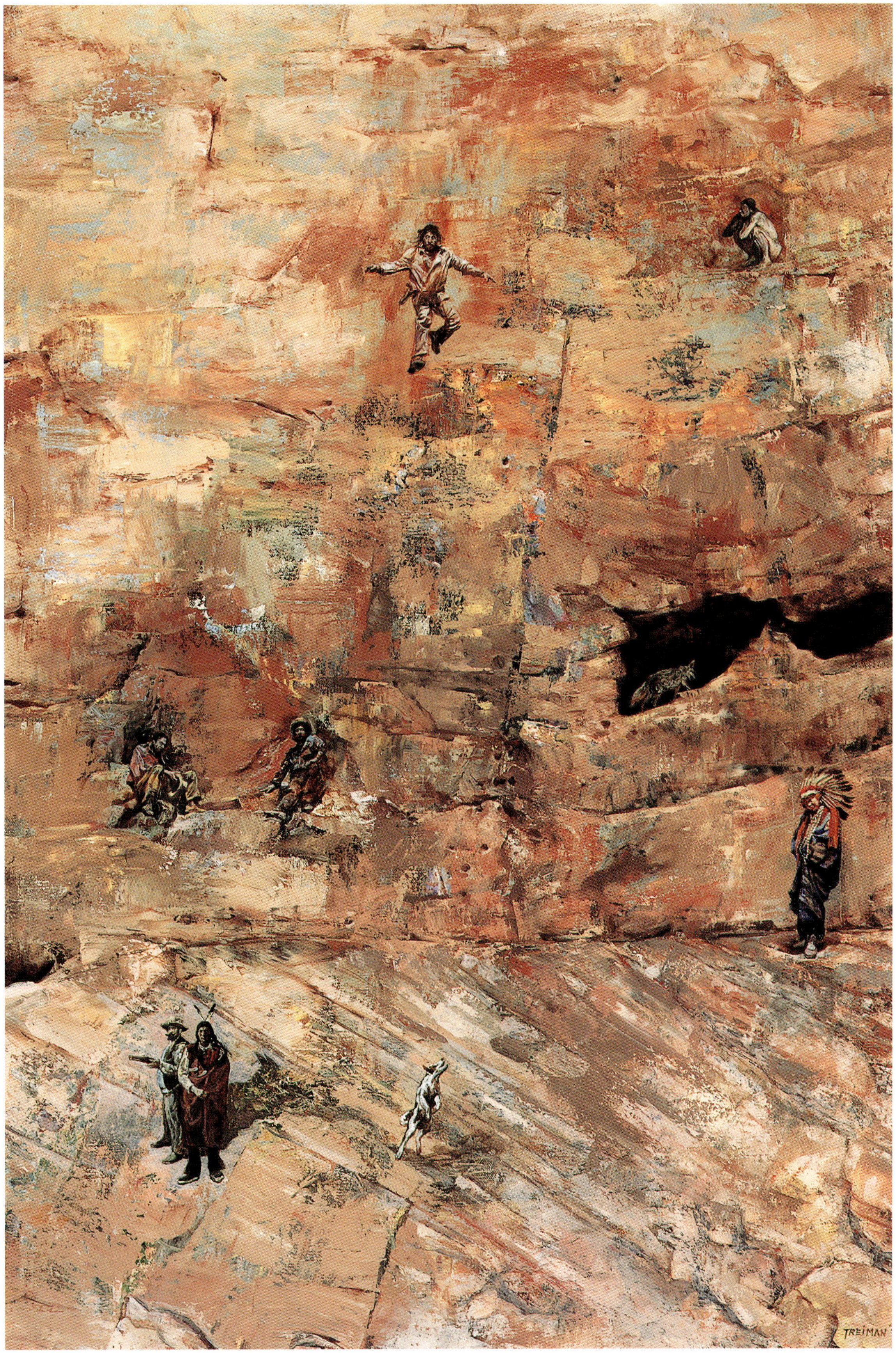

Americana III and Me
1972
oil on canvas
36 x 24 inches
Collection of Mr. and Mrs. Calvin J. Goodman

Thomas Eakins Modeling in California
1974
oil on canvas
70 x 70 inches
Mark E. B. Pinney

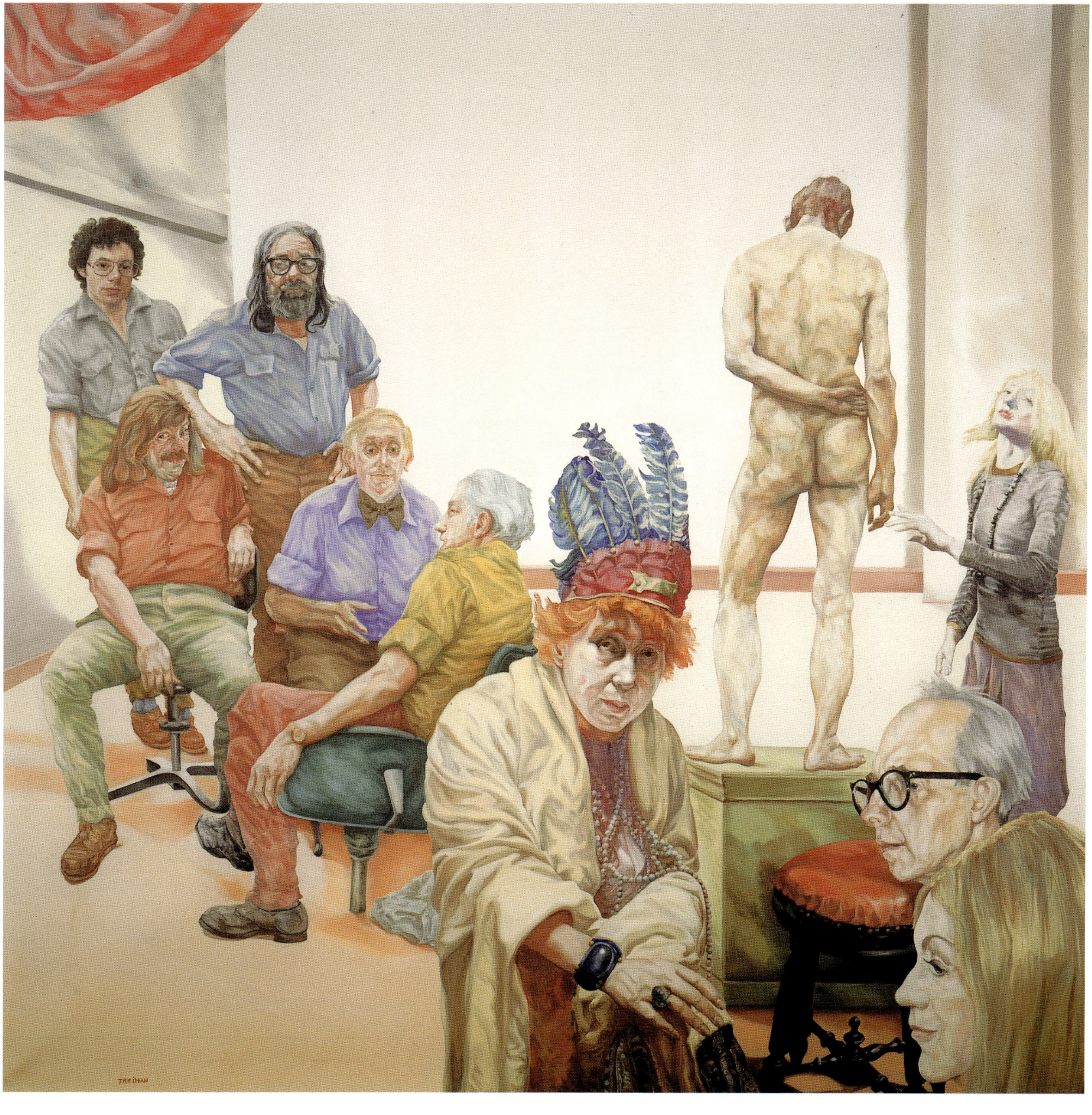
TREIMAN

The Big Sargent
1975
oil on canvas
70 x 70 inches
Mrs. Charlene and Dr. S. Sanford Kornblum

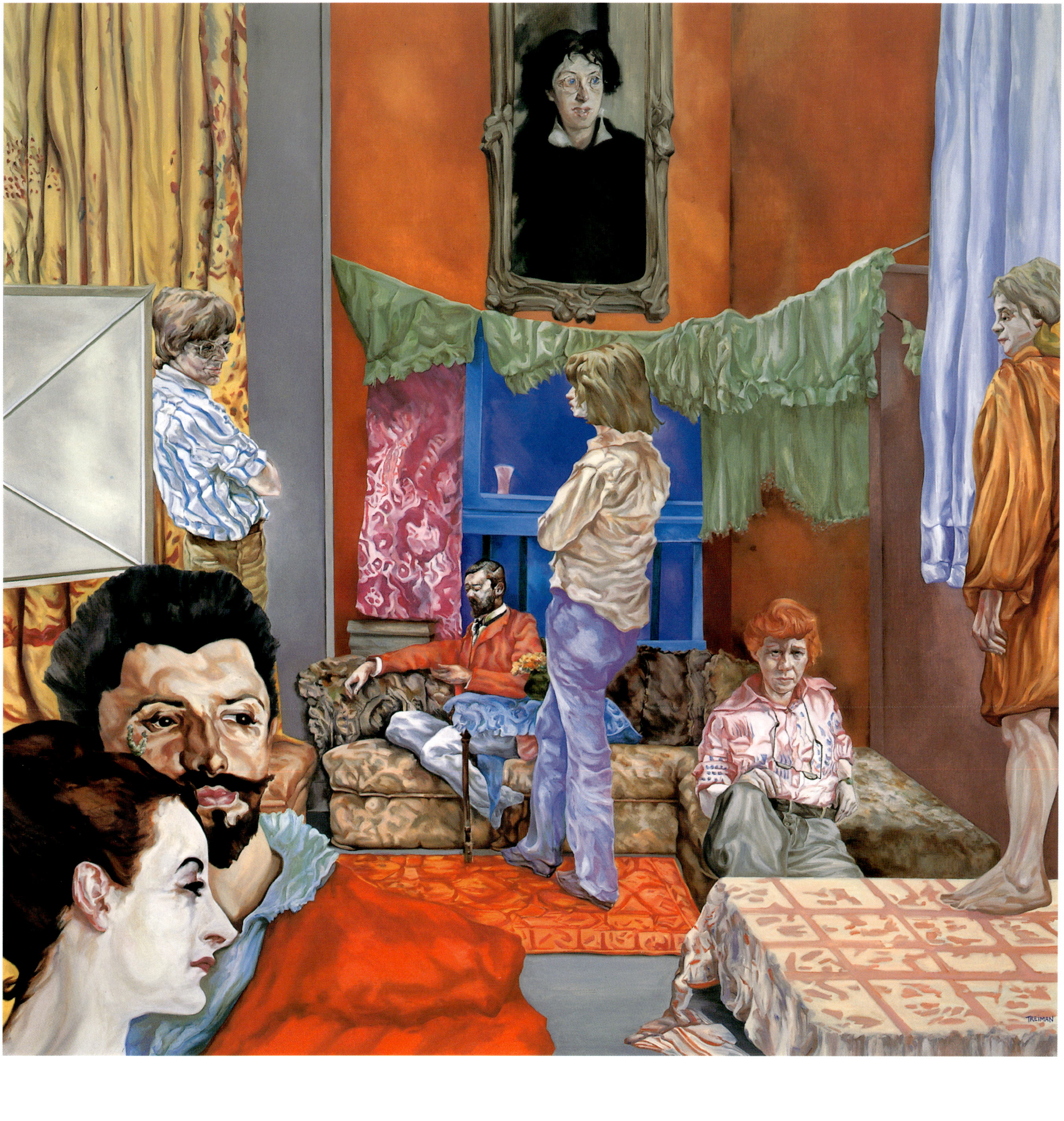
TREIMAN

Big Lautrec and Double Self-Portrait
1975–76
oil on canvas
70 x 70 inches
In the Collection of
Kemper National Insurance Companies

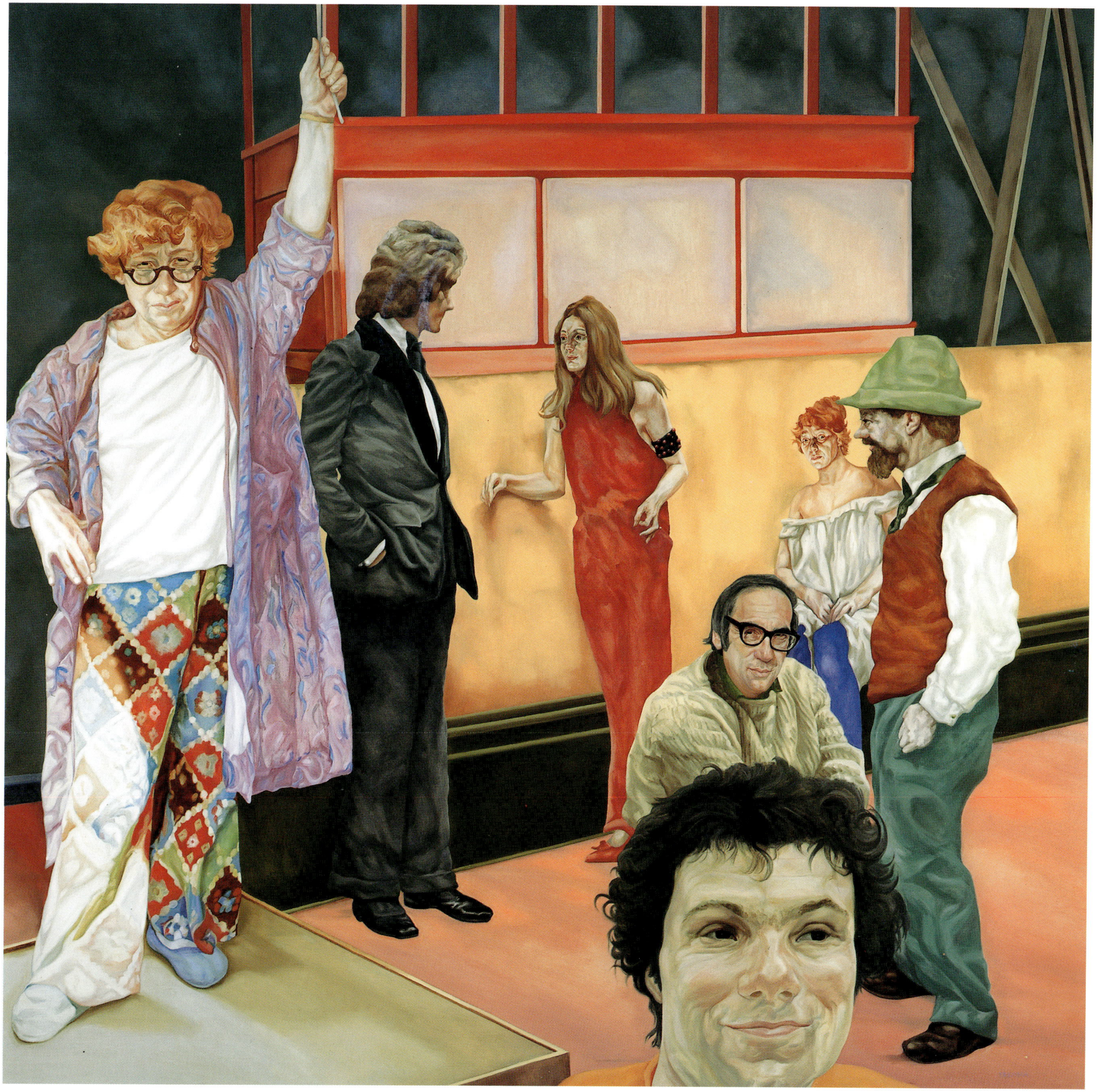

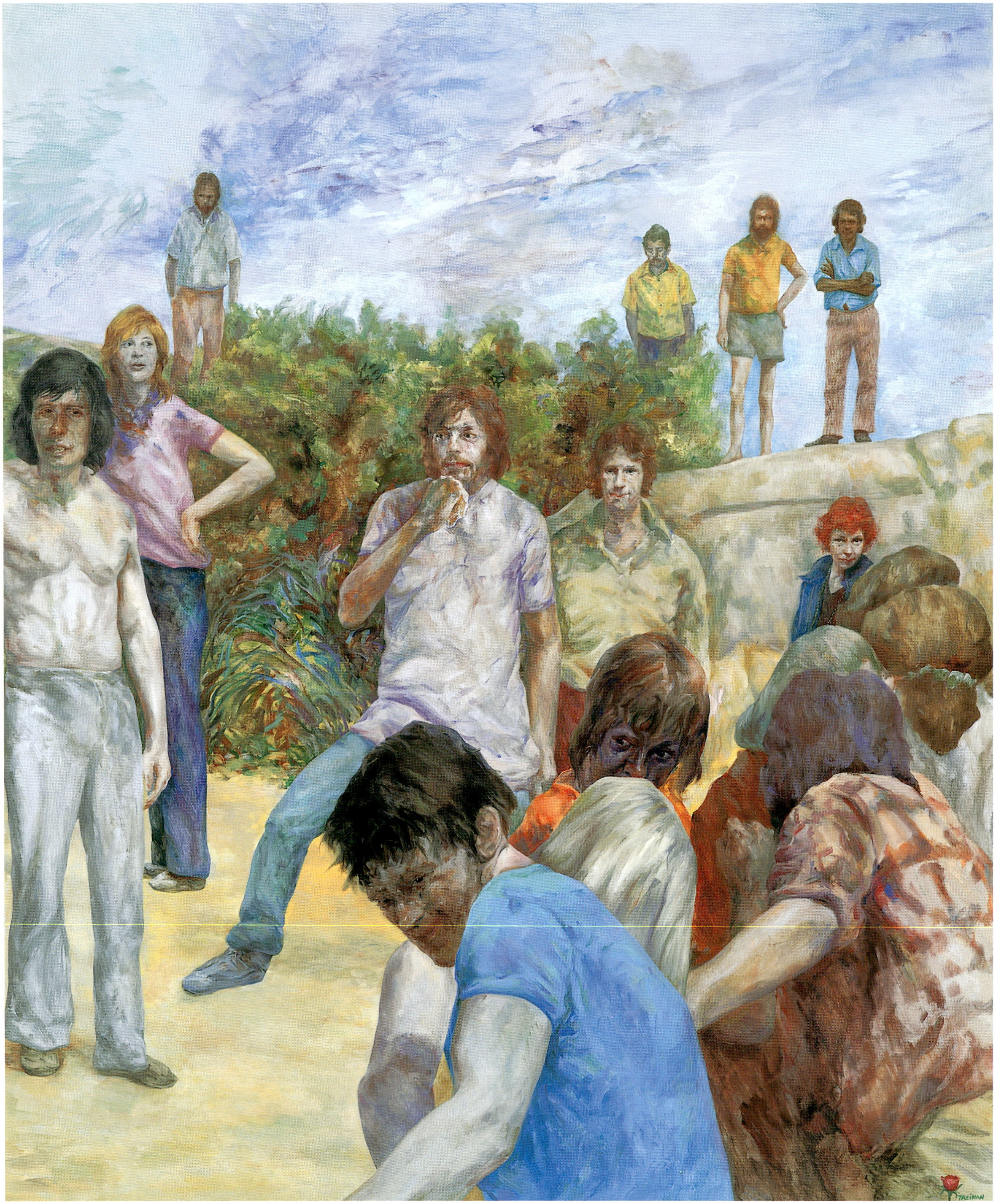

Incident I
1976
oil on canvas
60 x 50 inches
Courtesy Schmidt Bingham Gallery, New York

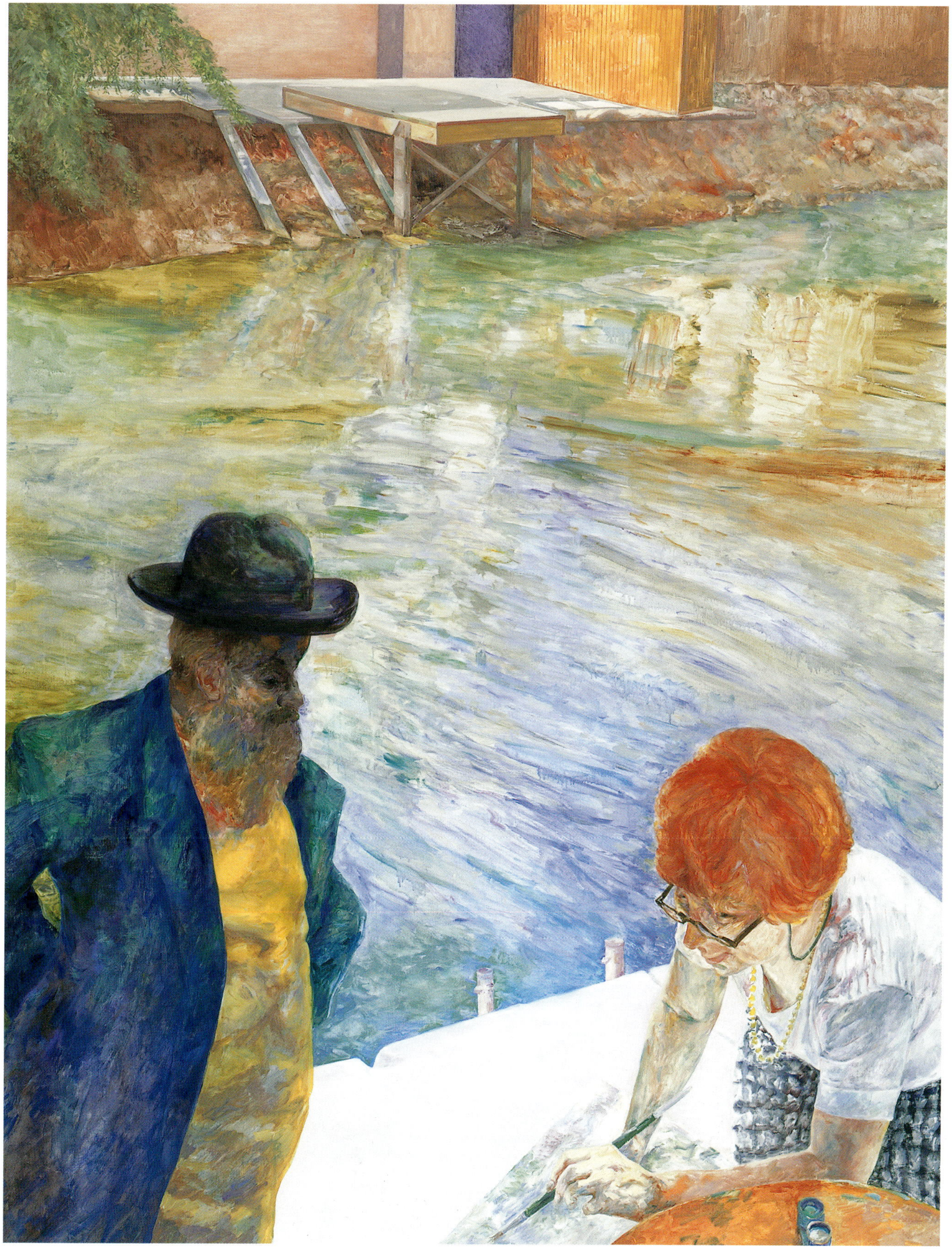

Monet and Me at the Venice Canals
1977
oil on linen
80 x 60 inches
BankAmerica Corporation Art Collection, San Francisco

Rose, Bonnard, and the Artist Twice
1977
oil on canvas
70 x 70 inches
Cindy and Jay Pritzker

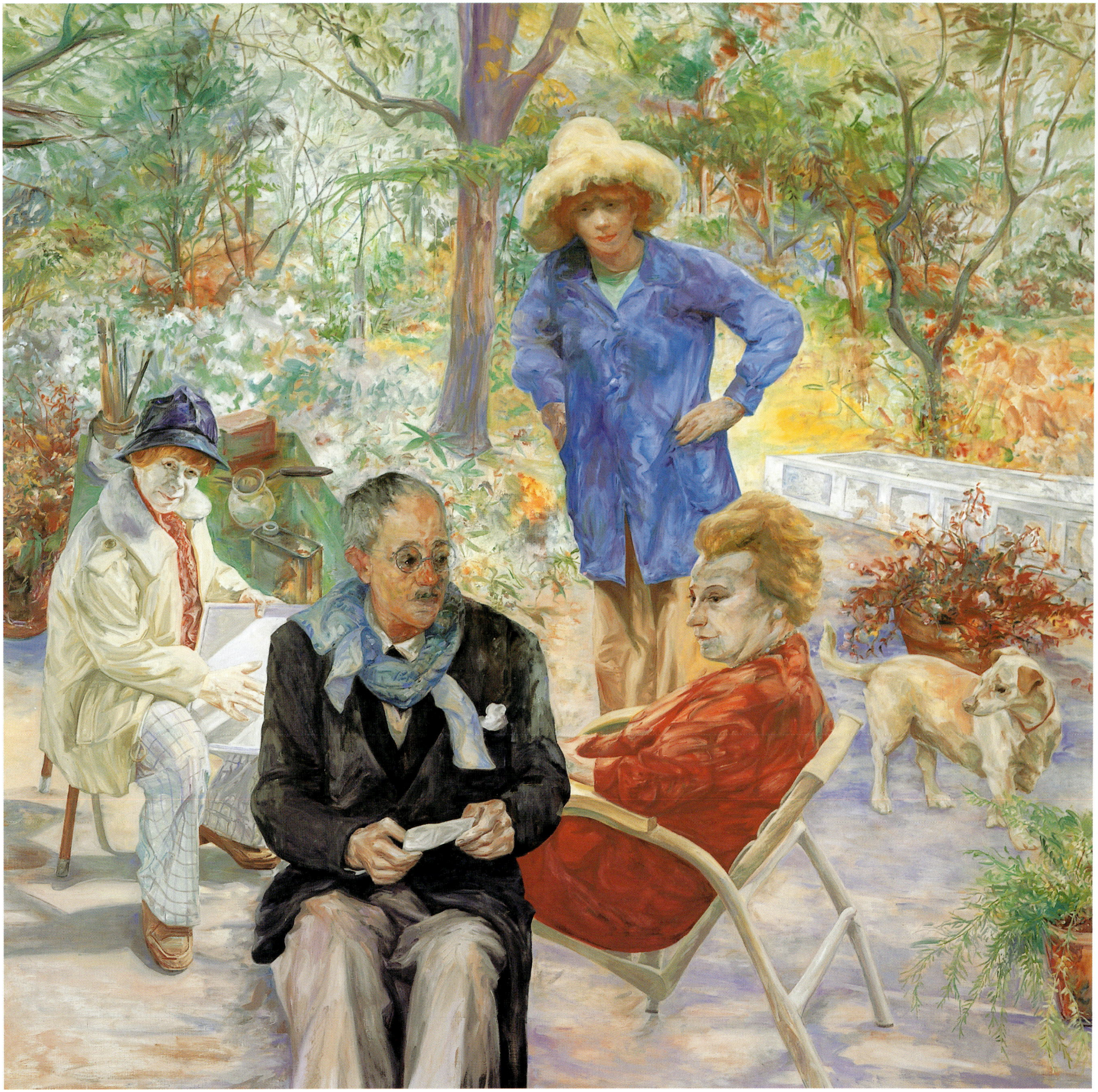

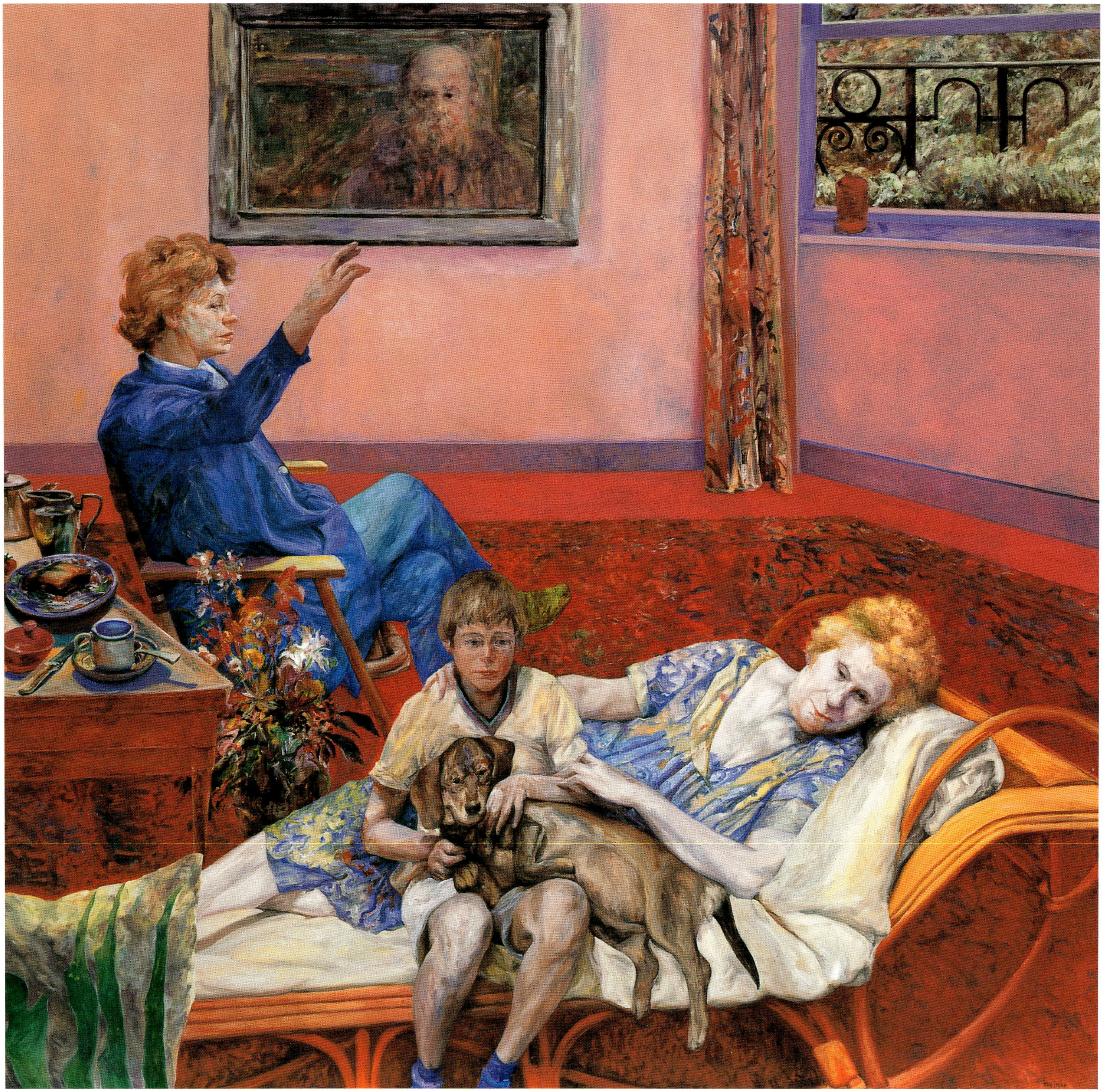

Rose, Vuillard, and Me
1978
oil on canvas
70 x 70 inches
Mrs. Charlene and
Dr. S. Sanford Kornblum

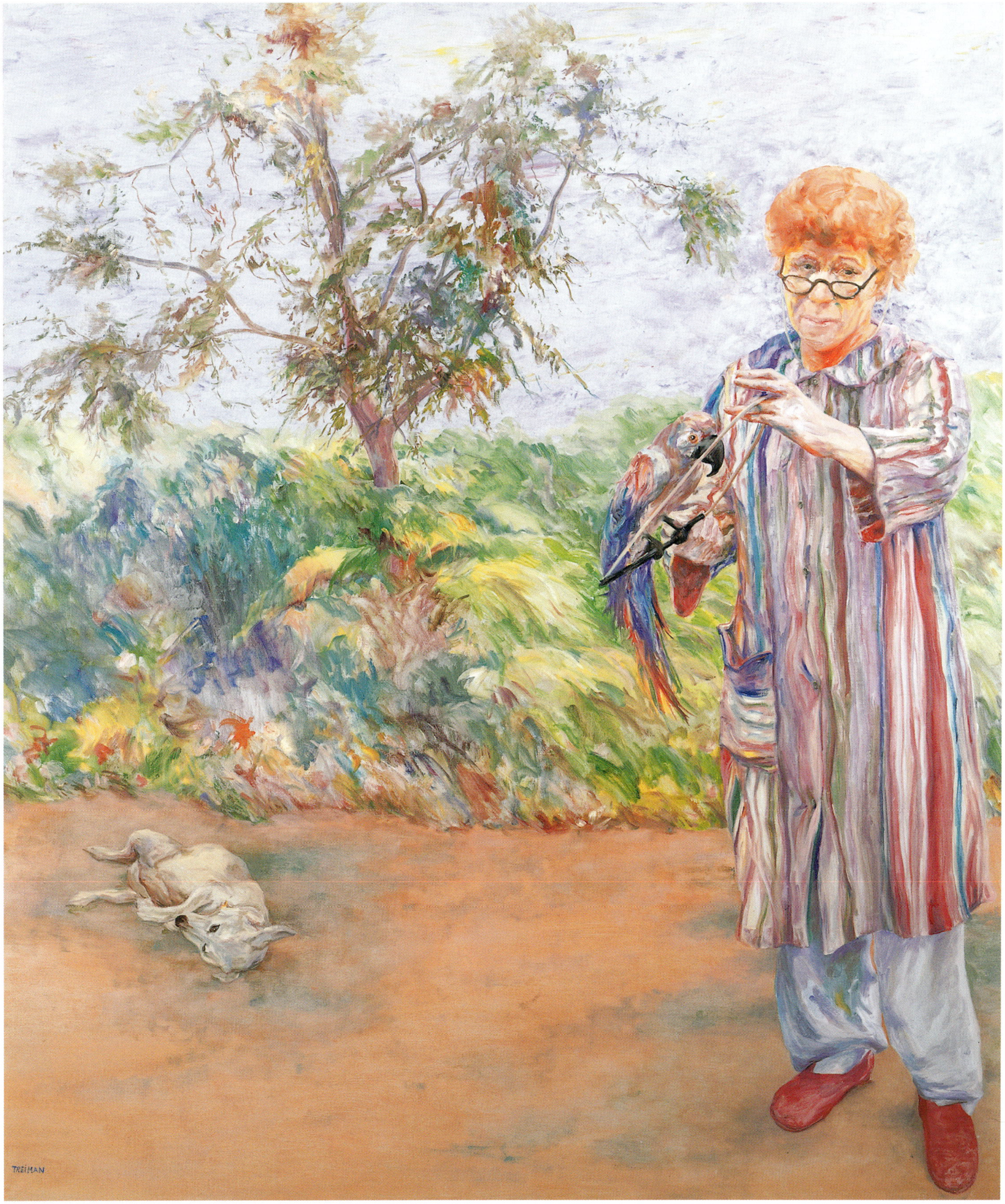

Schatzie and Me with Fake Parrot
1978
oil on canvas
60 x 50 inches
National Academy of Design,
New York City

Adventure III
1979
oil on canvas
50 x 50 inches
Courtesy Schmidt Bingham Gallery, New York

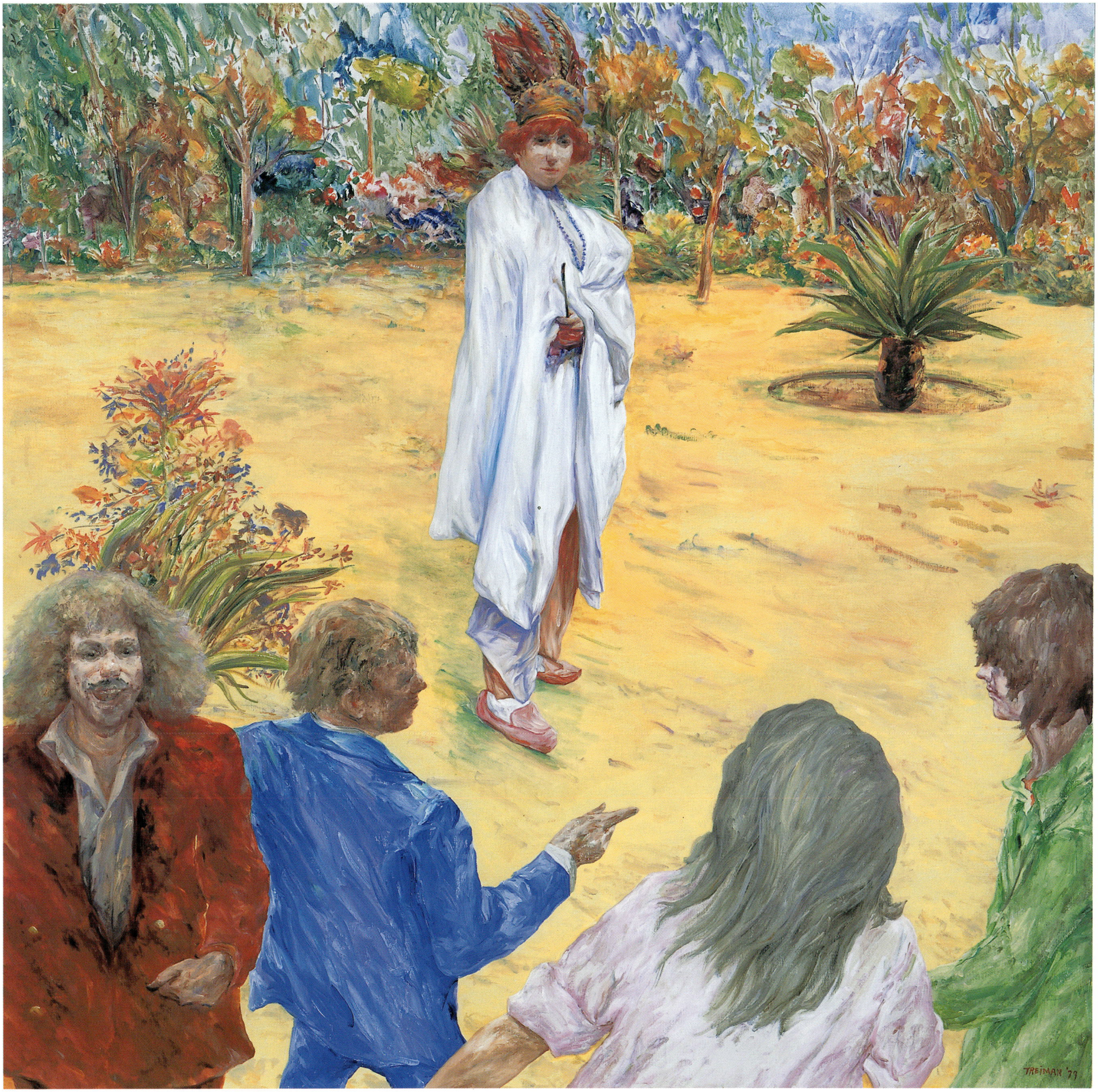

Degas, Cassatt, and Me
1979
oil on canvas
70 × 70 inches
Collection of Harry Saunders

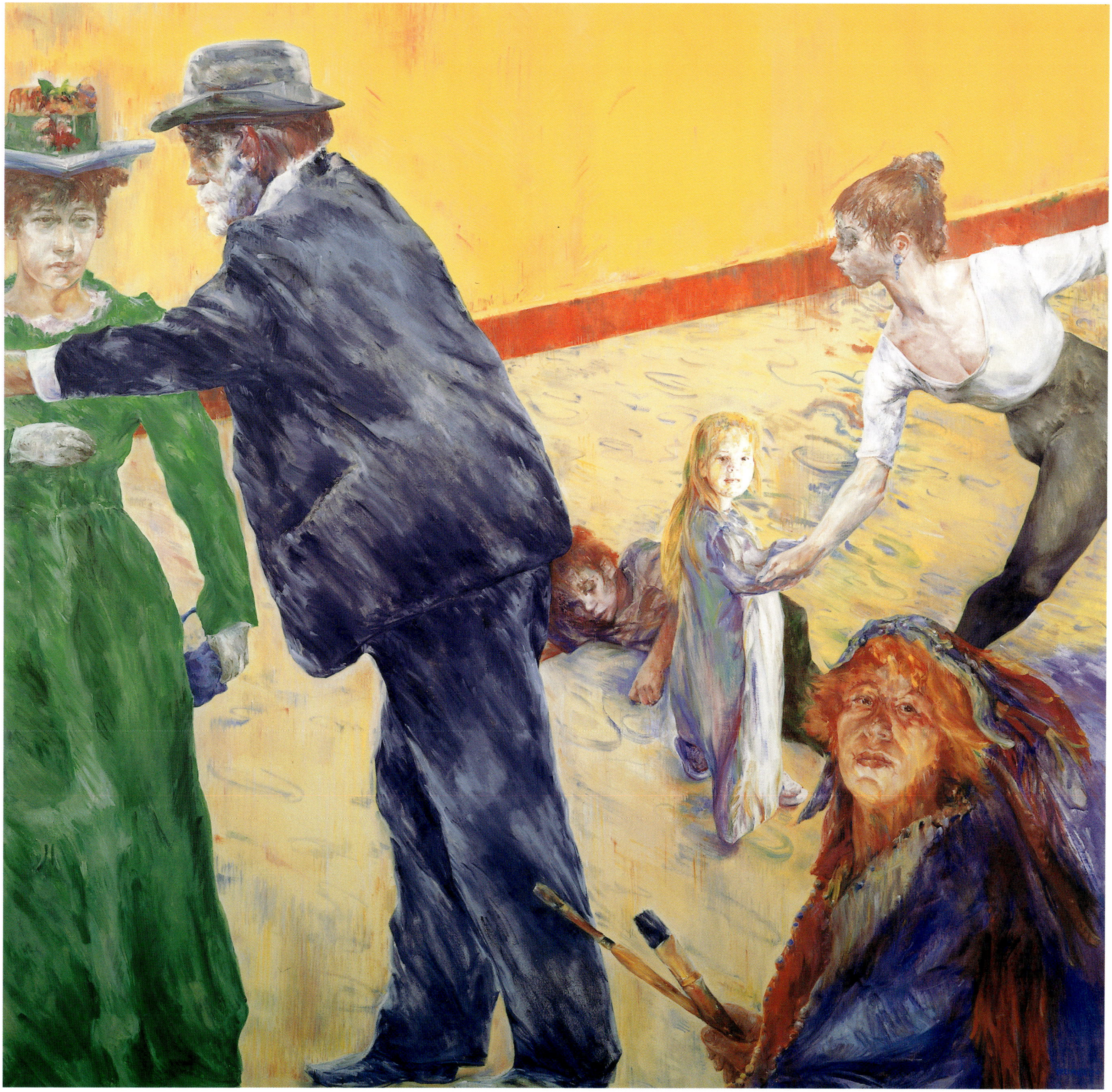

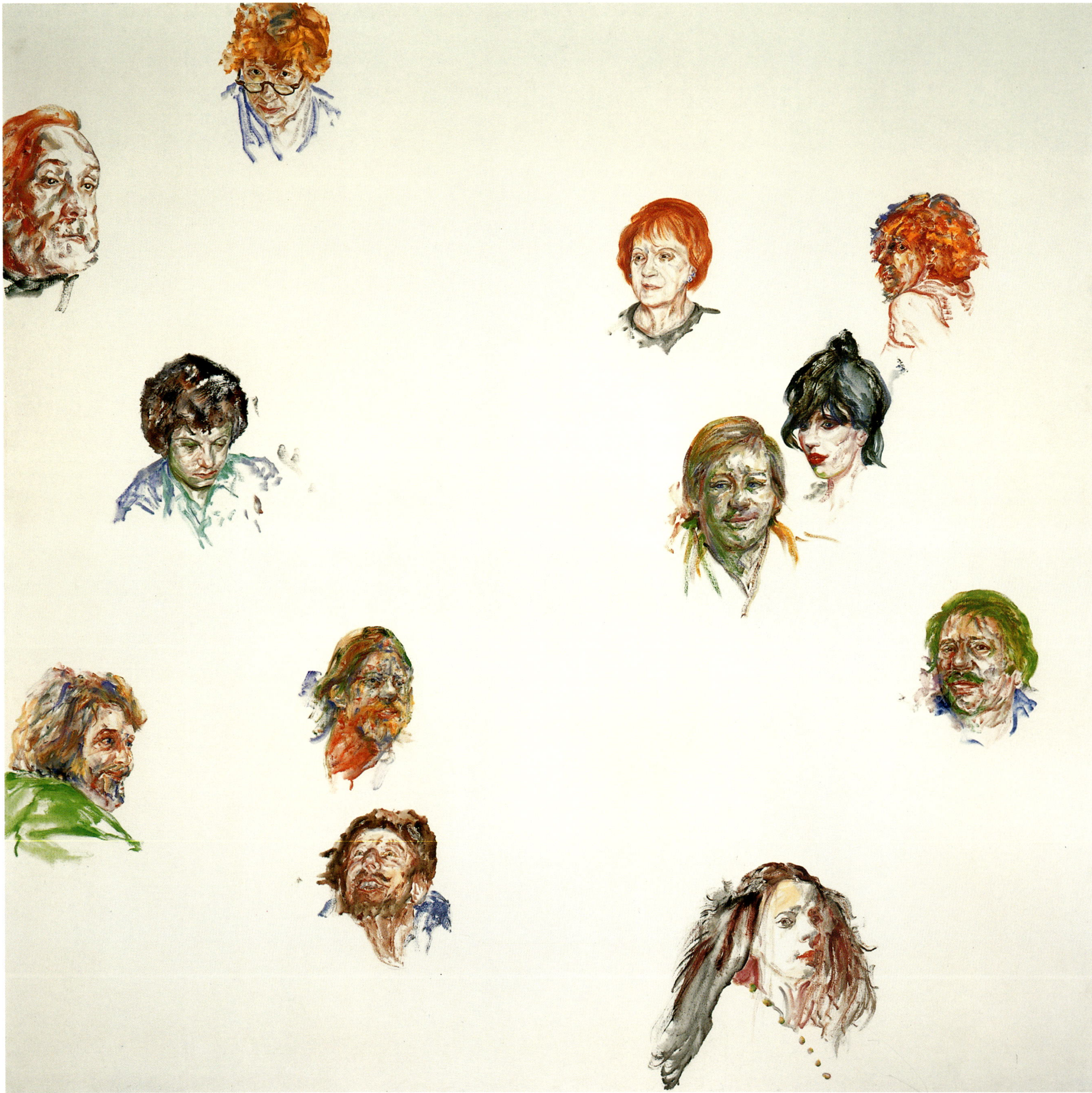

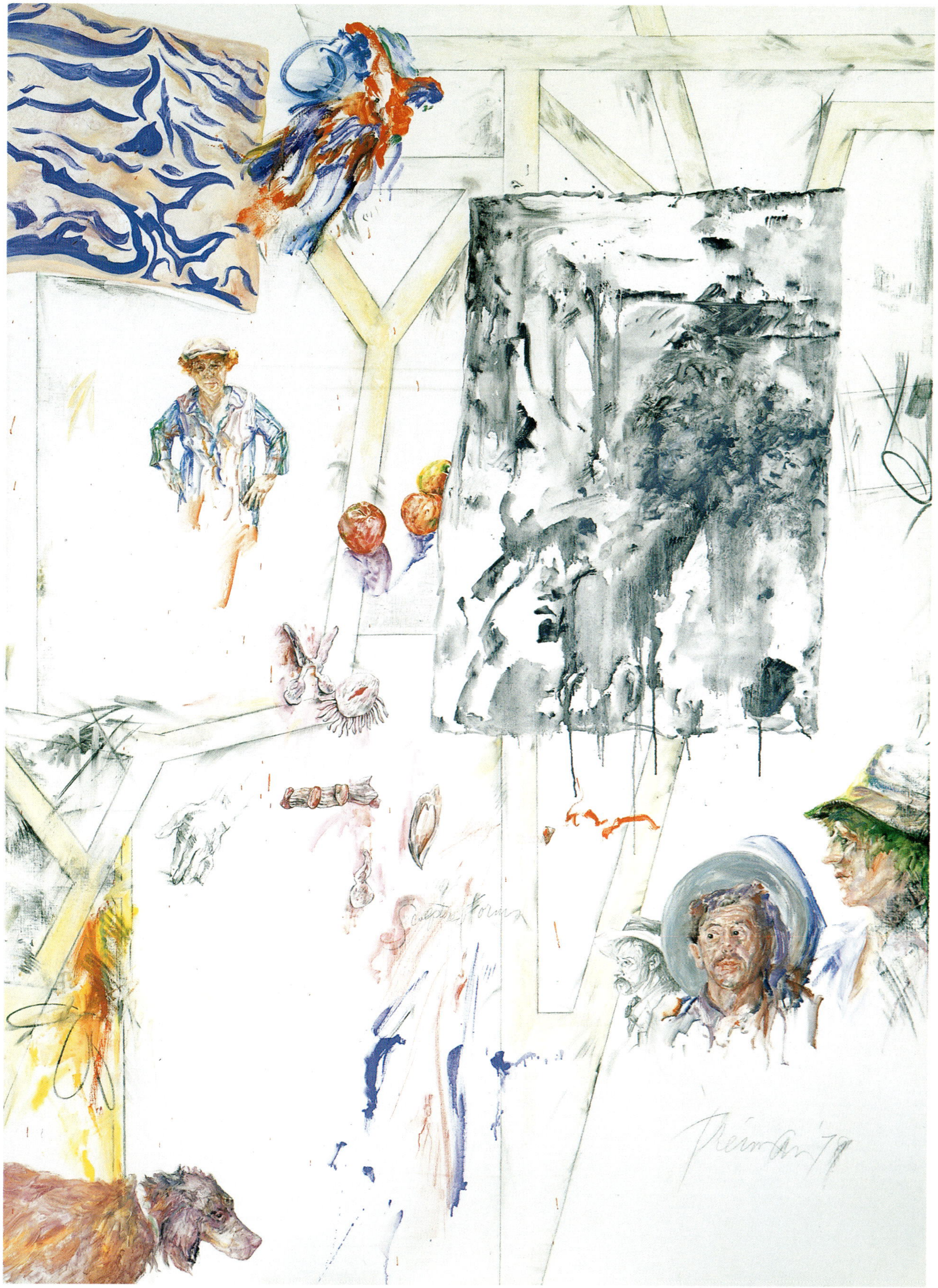

Page One
1979
oil on canvas
70 x 70 inches
Collection Donald M. Treiman,
Pacific Palisades, California

Page Two
1979
oil on canvas
70 x 50 inches
Lisa and John Pritzker

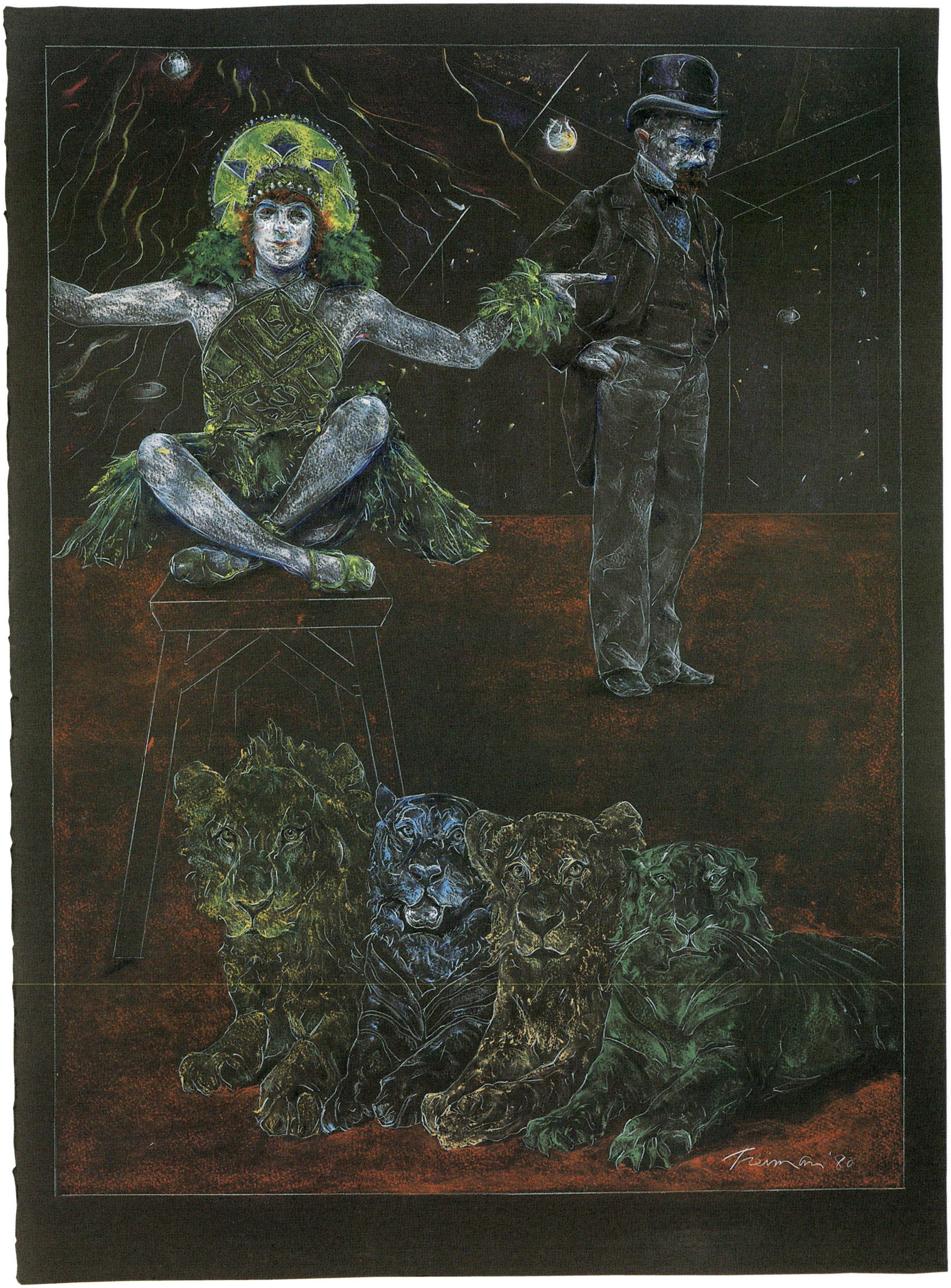

Night Series (Tiger, Tiger, Burning Bright)
1980
pastel on paper
30 x 24 inches
From the collection of Sandra and Robert Jackman

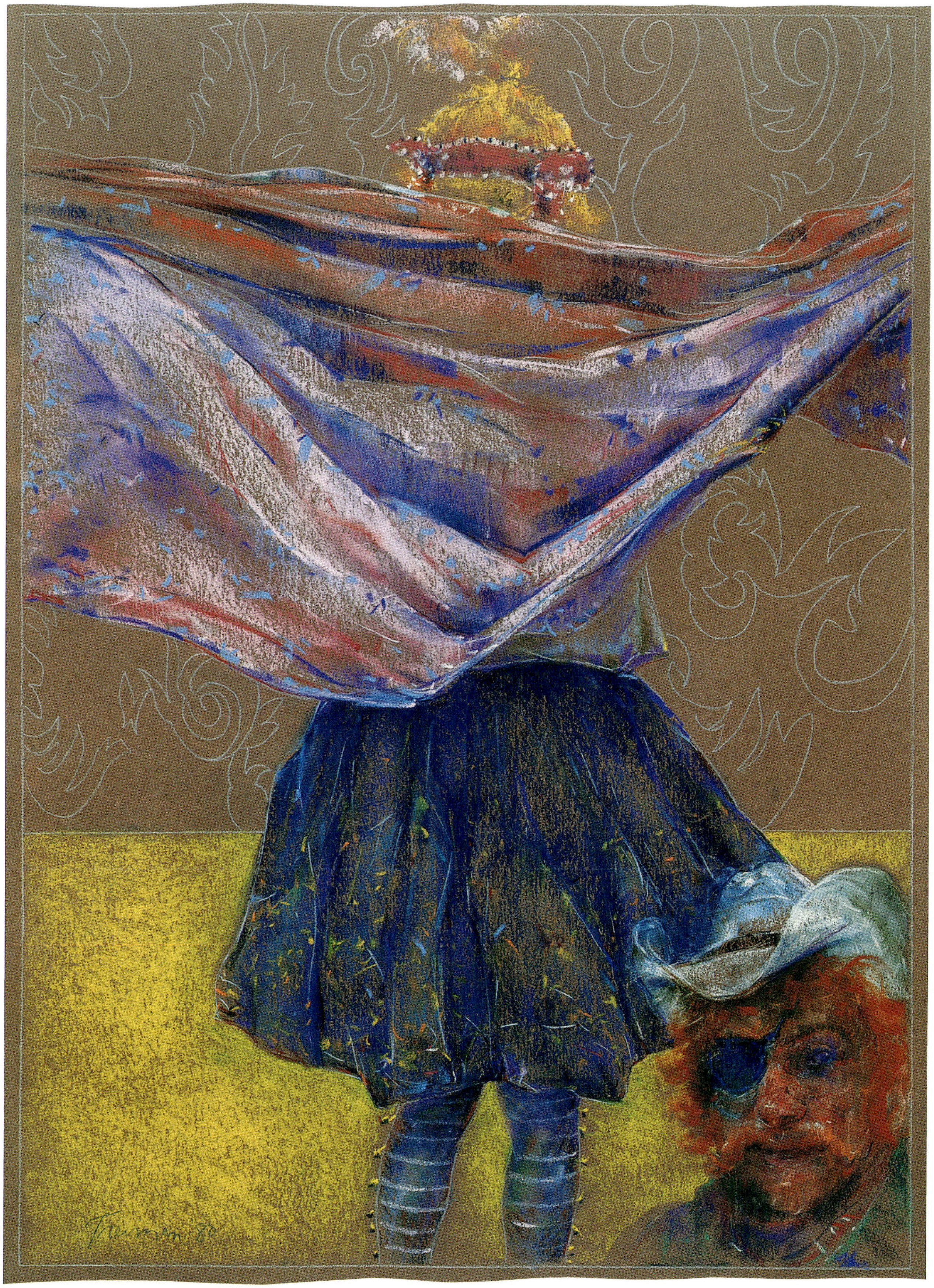

Pink Cloth
1980
pastel on paper
24 × 18 inches
Sally and Conrad Kuzma, Bloomington, Indiana

Déjeuner
1981
oil on canvas
80 x 60 inches
Collection of Harry Saunders

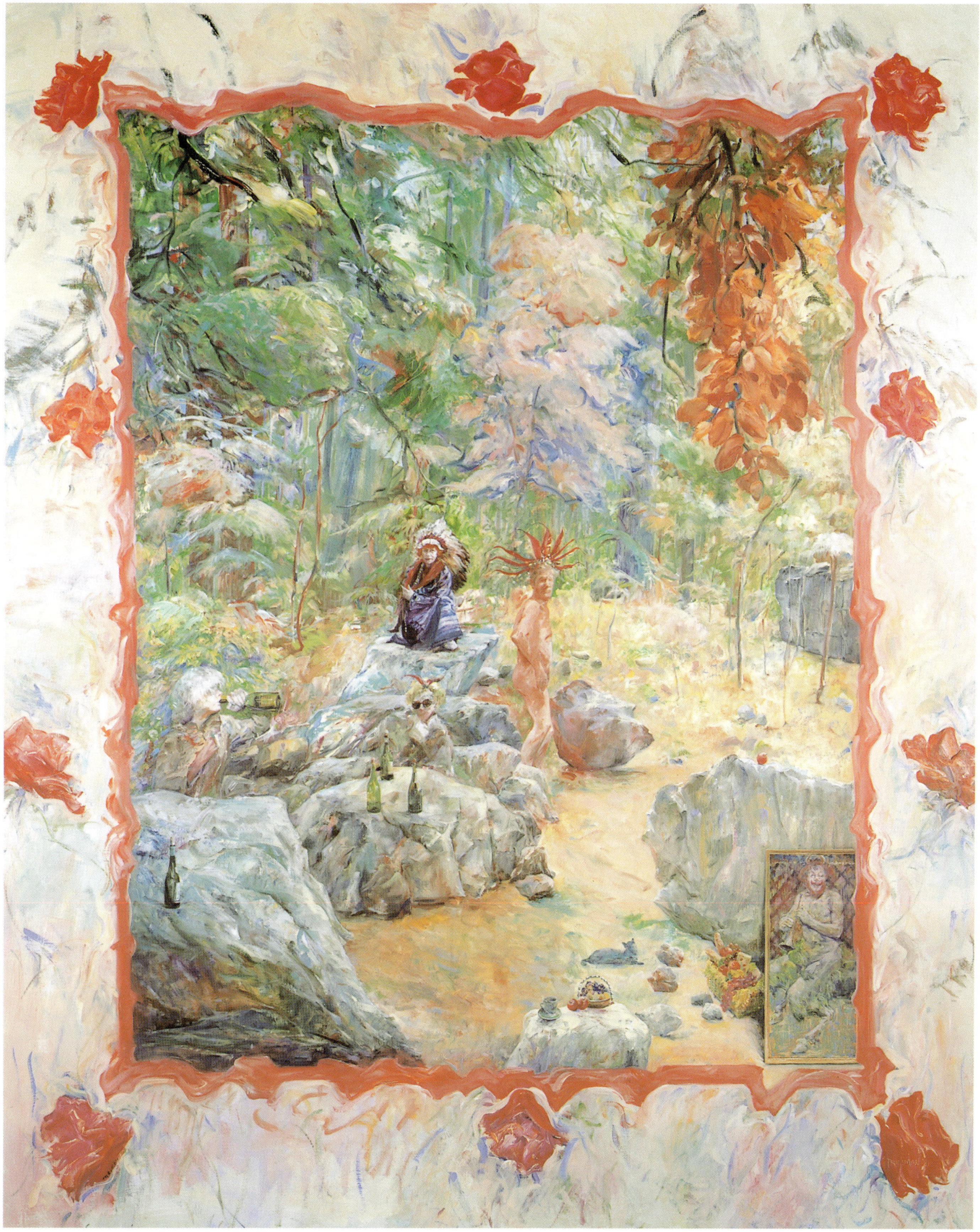

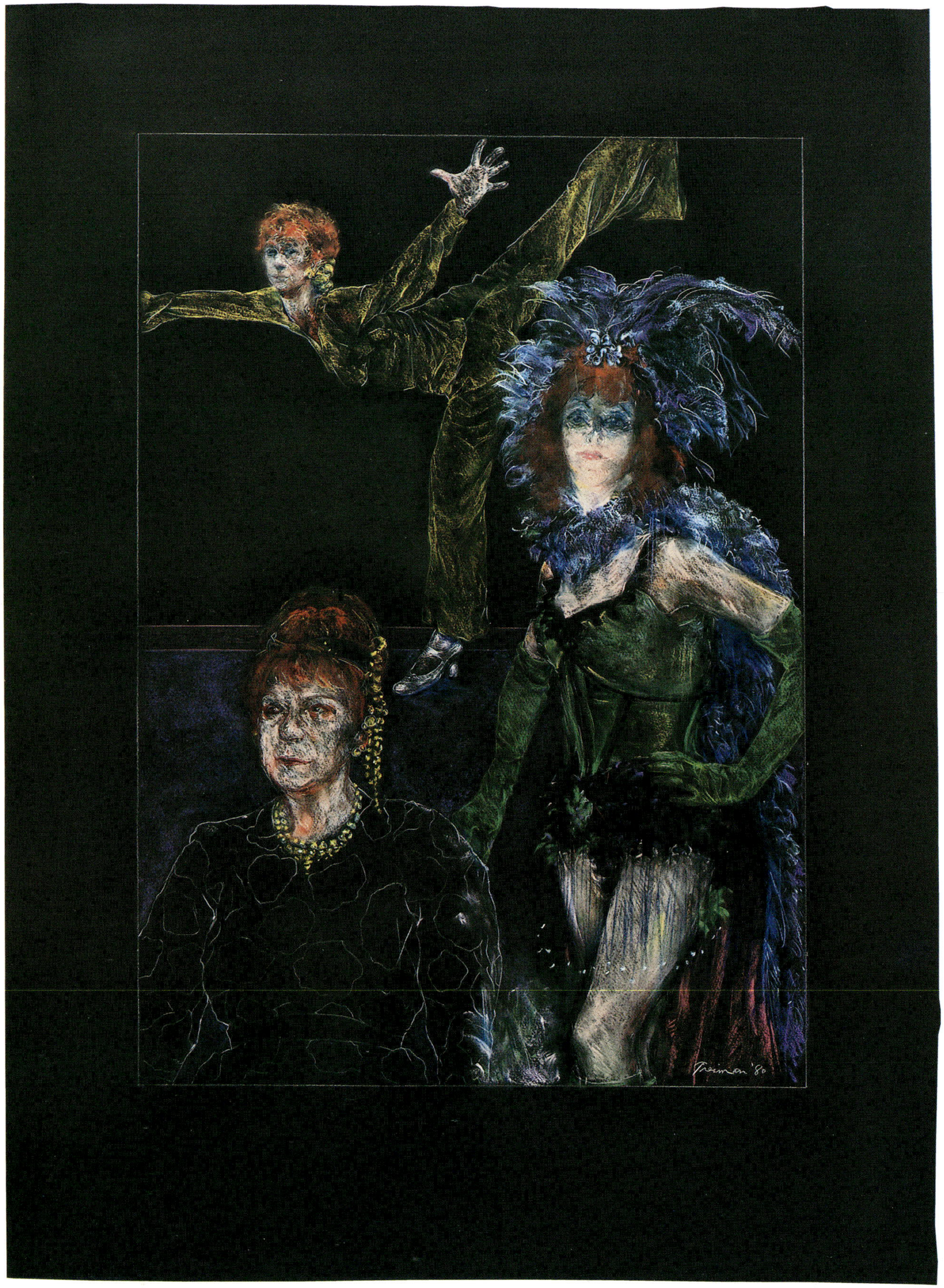

Three Redheads Including Rose
1980
pastel on paper
40 x 30 inches
Collection of Donald M. Treiman, Pacific Palisades, California

Tiepolo and Me
1981
oil on canvas
70 x 70 inches
Richard and Frances Luban

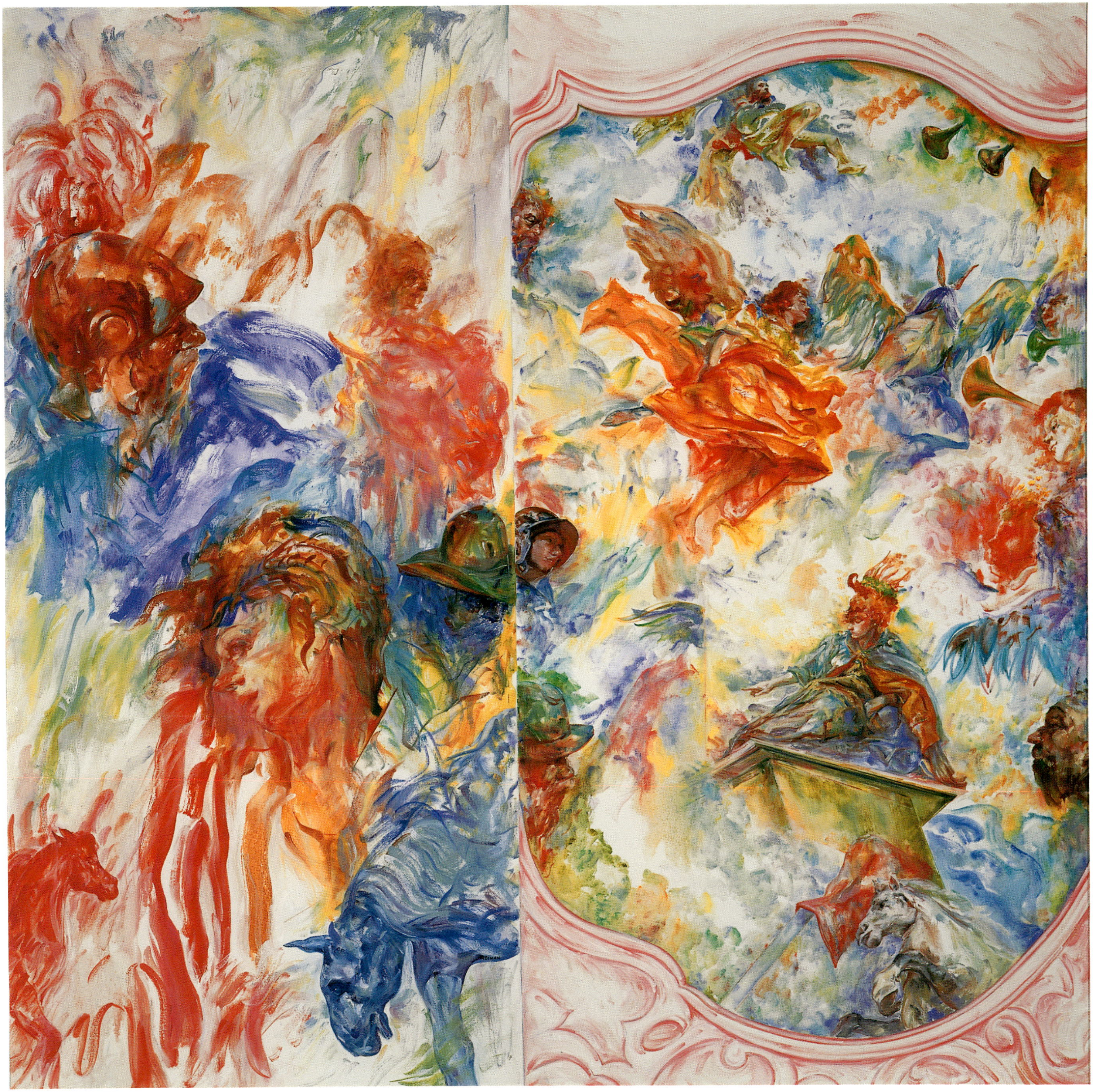

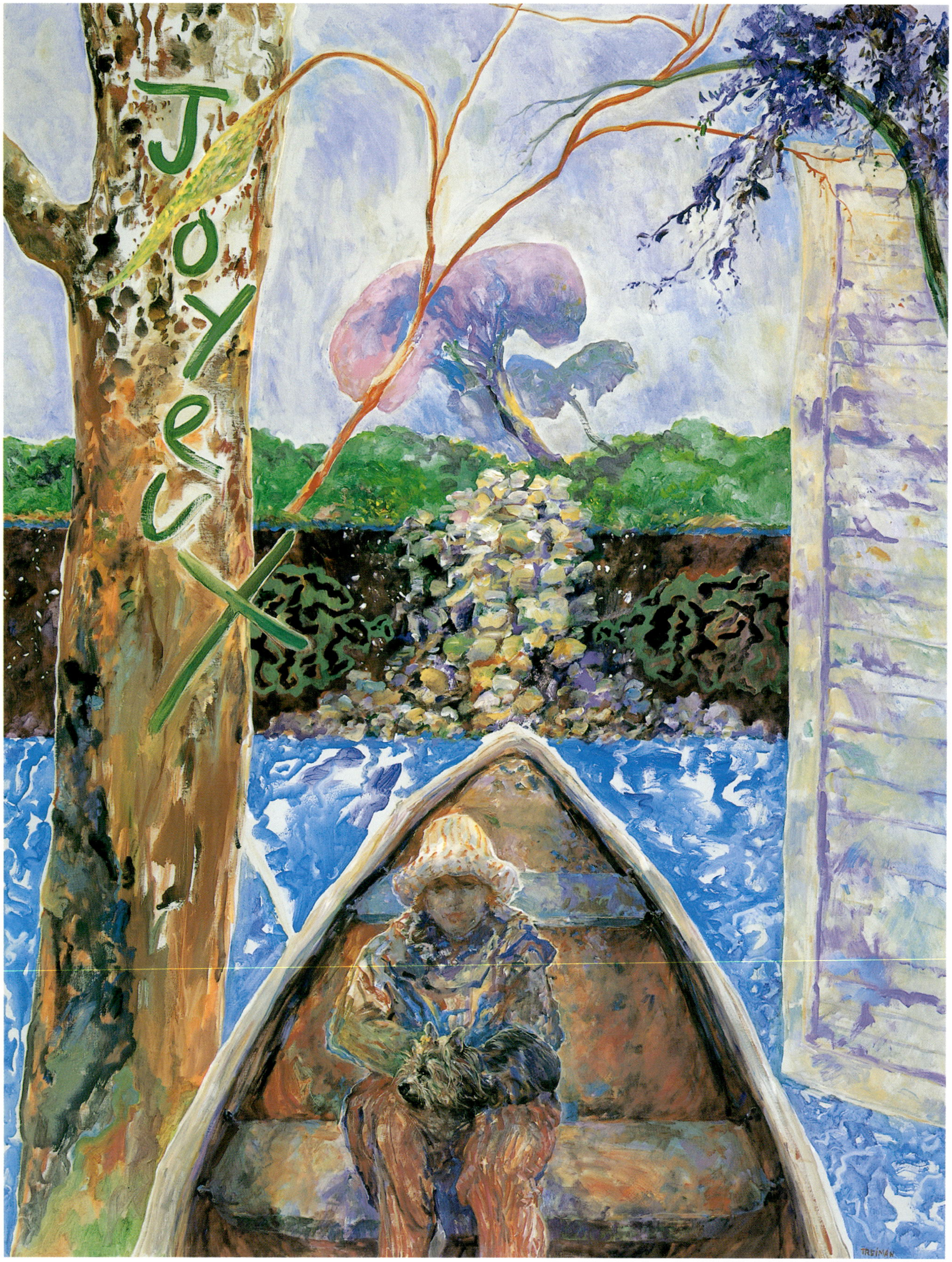

Joyeux
1981
oil on canvas
$81\frac{1}{4} \times 61\frac{1}{4}$ inches
Courtesy Schmidt Bingham Gallery, New York

The French Scarf
1982
oil on canvas
40 x 36 inches
Private collection, Los Angeles

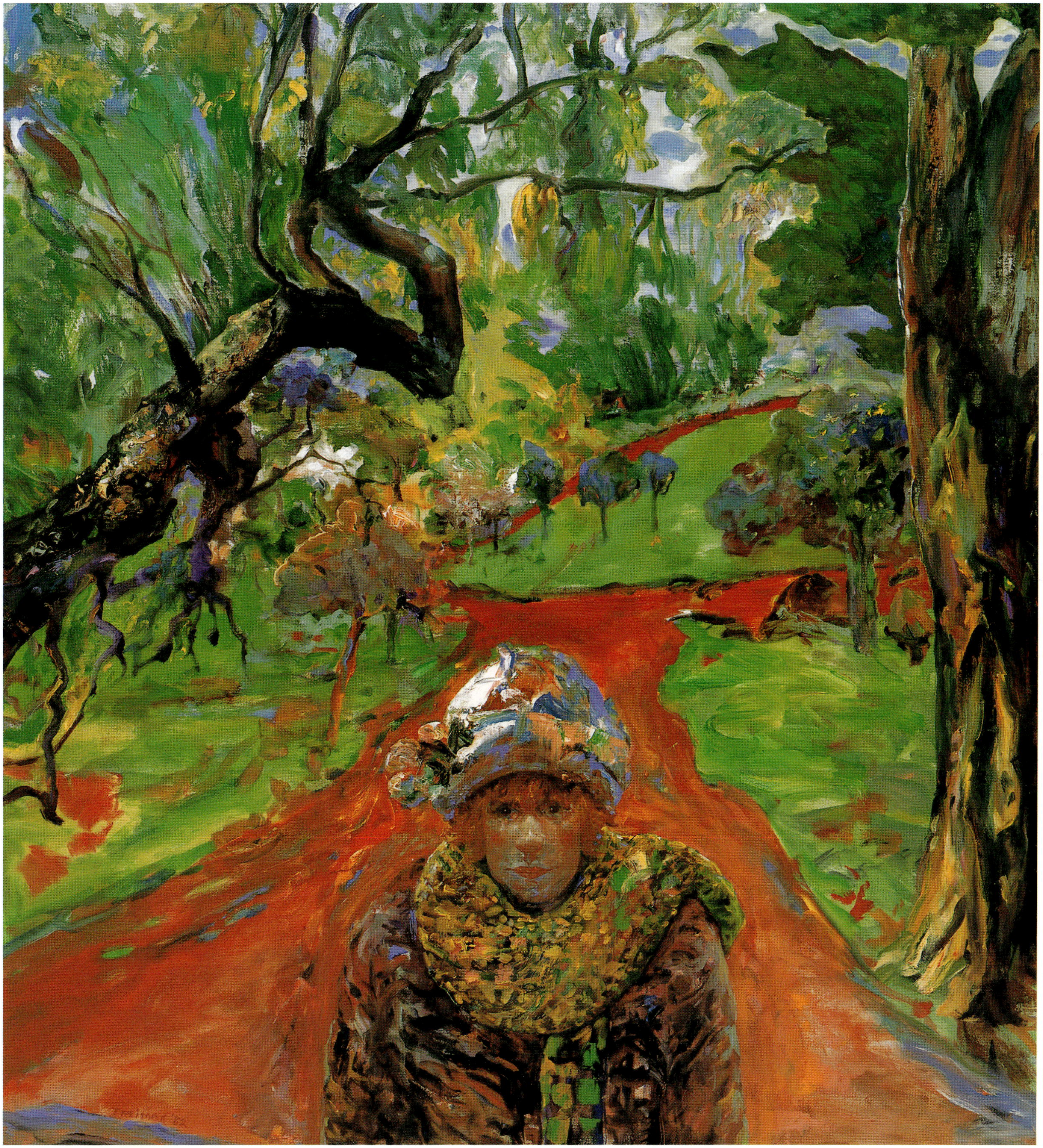

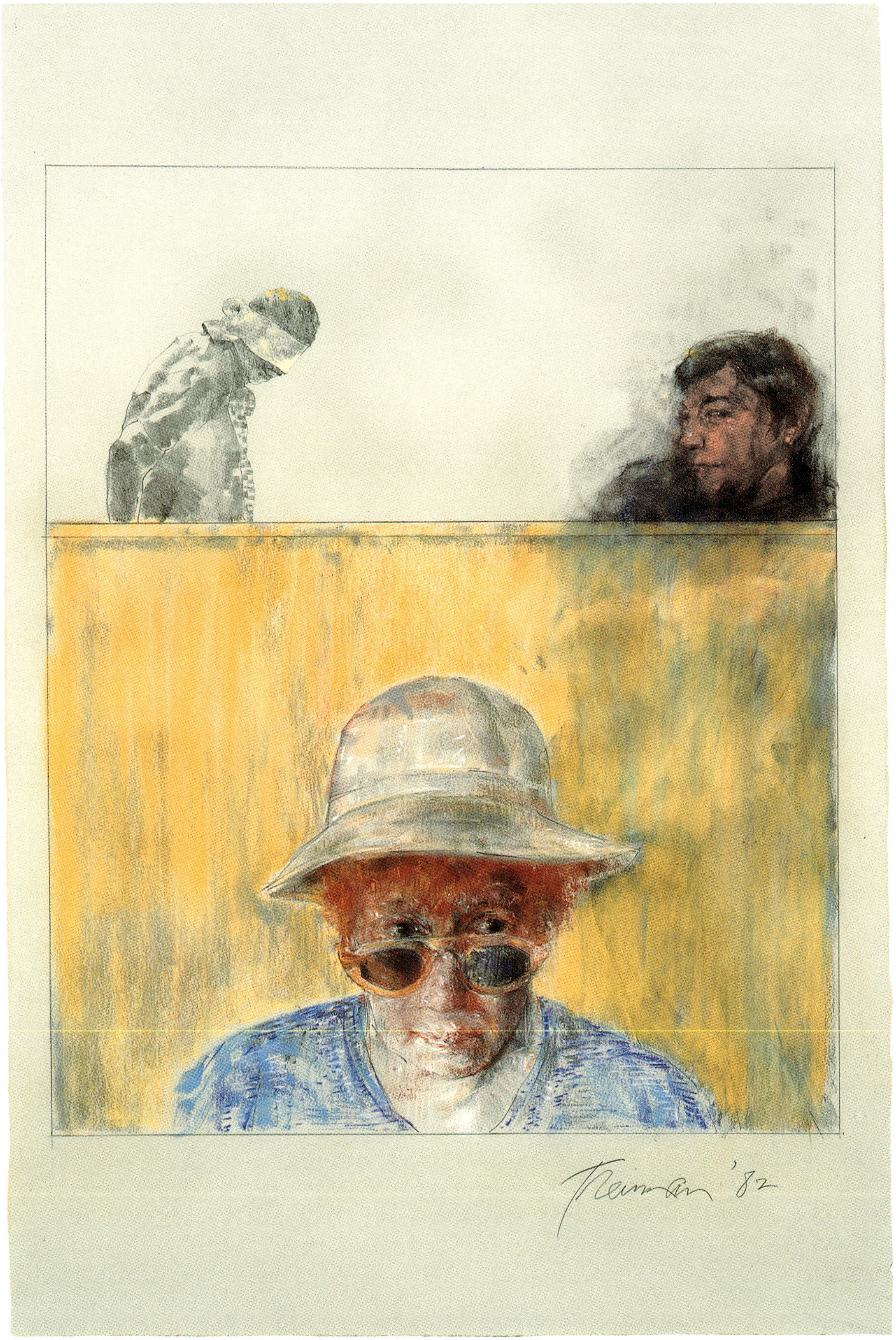

Self-Portrait in White Hat
1982
pastel and pencil on paper
30 x 20 inches
Private collection, Los Angeles

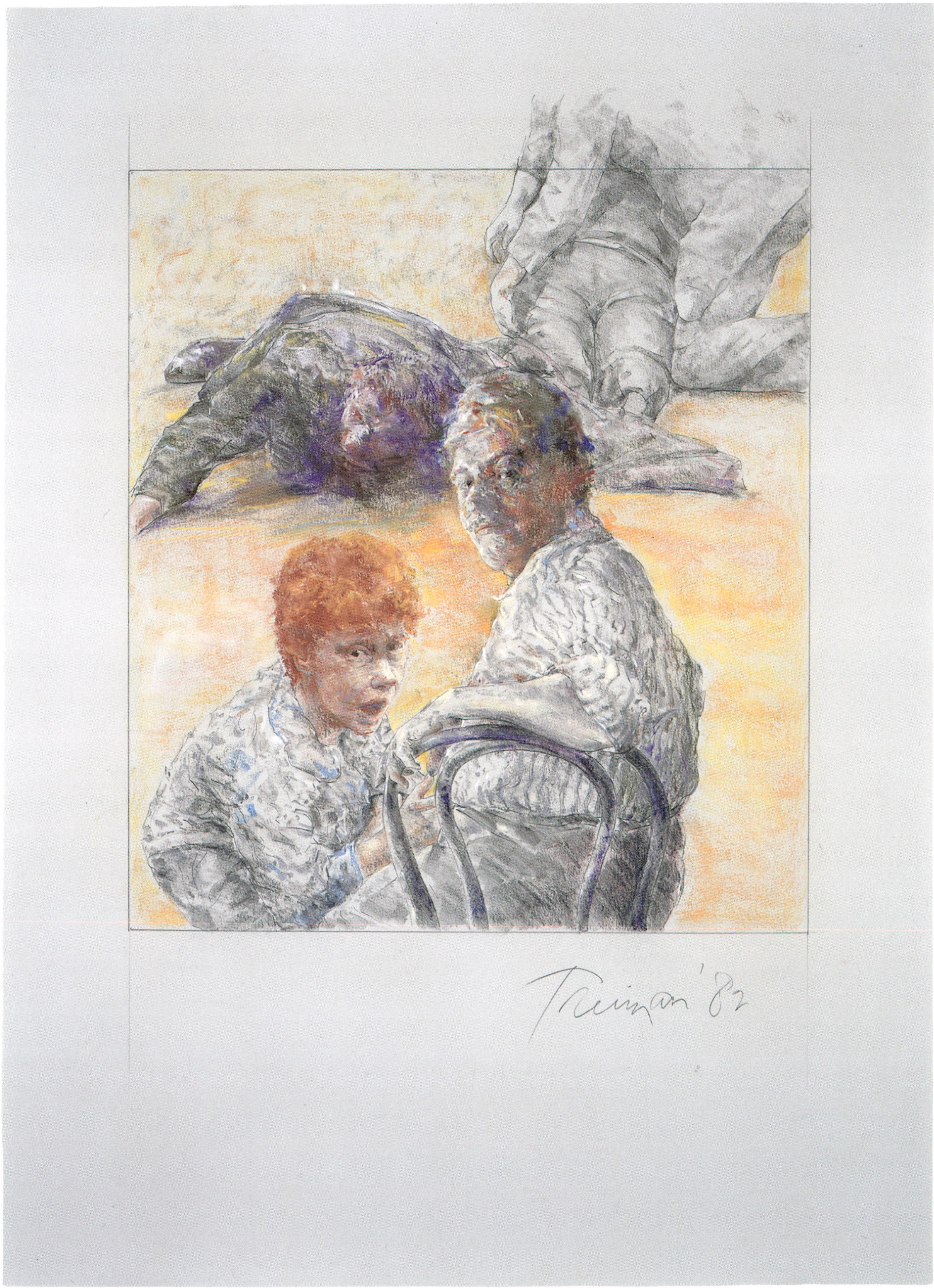

Untitled (The Observer)
1982
pastel and pencil on paper
$30\frac{1}{2} \times 22\frac{1}{8}$ inches
Hirshhorn Museum and Sculpture Garden, Smithsonian Institution, Gift of Donald M. Treiman, 1991

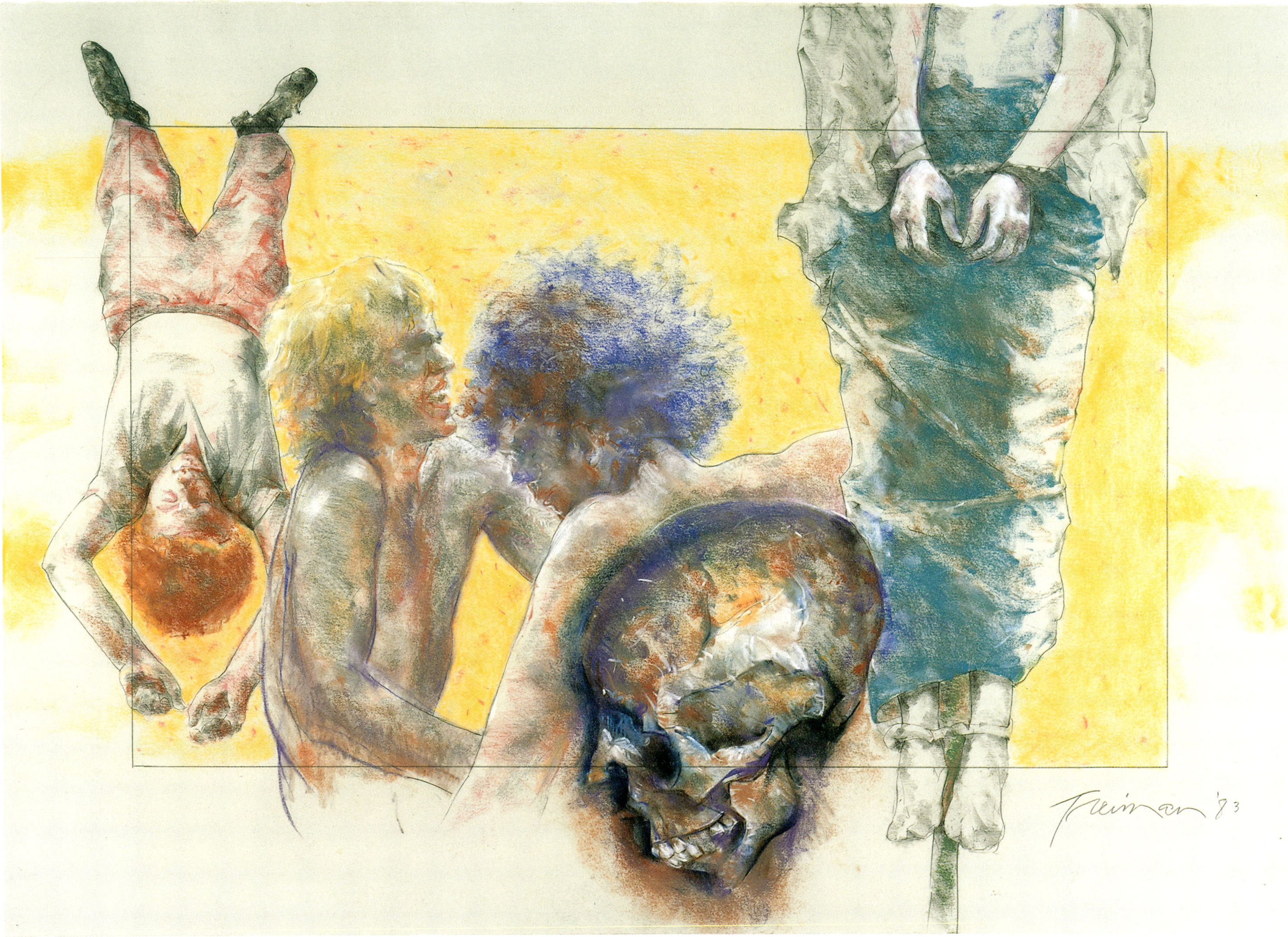

Fragments
1983
pastel and pencil on paper
20 × 28 inches
Collection of Alan Brodie

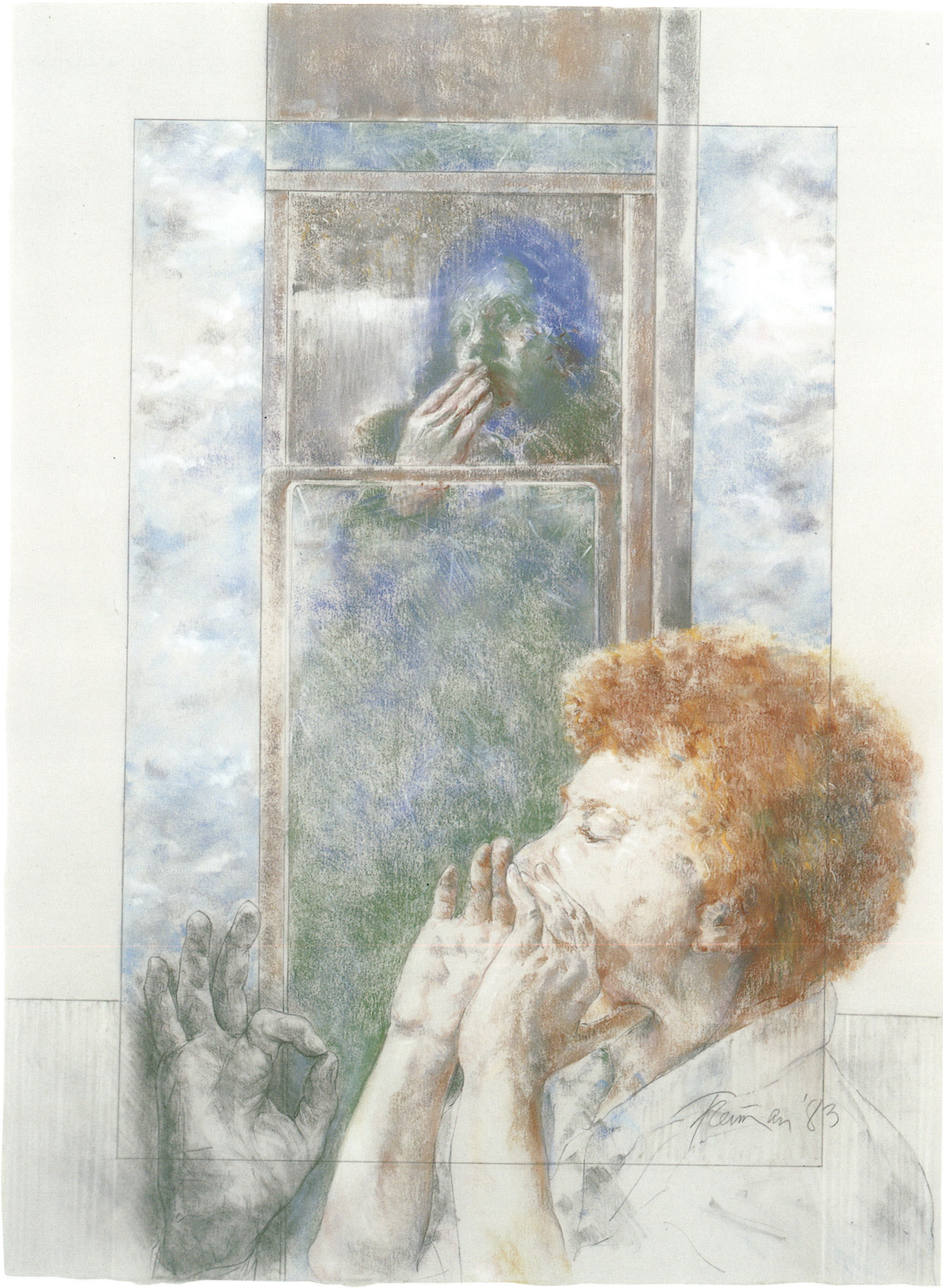

The Gray Hand
1983
pastel and pencil on paper
28 x 20½ inches
Abby and Alan D. Levy Collection

Hercules and the Arcadian Stag
1983
oil on canvas
70 x 70 inches
Private collection

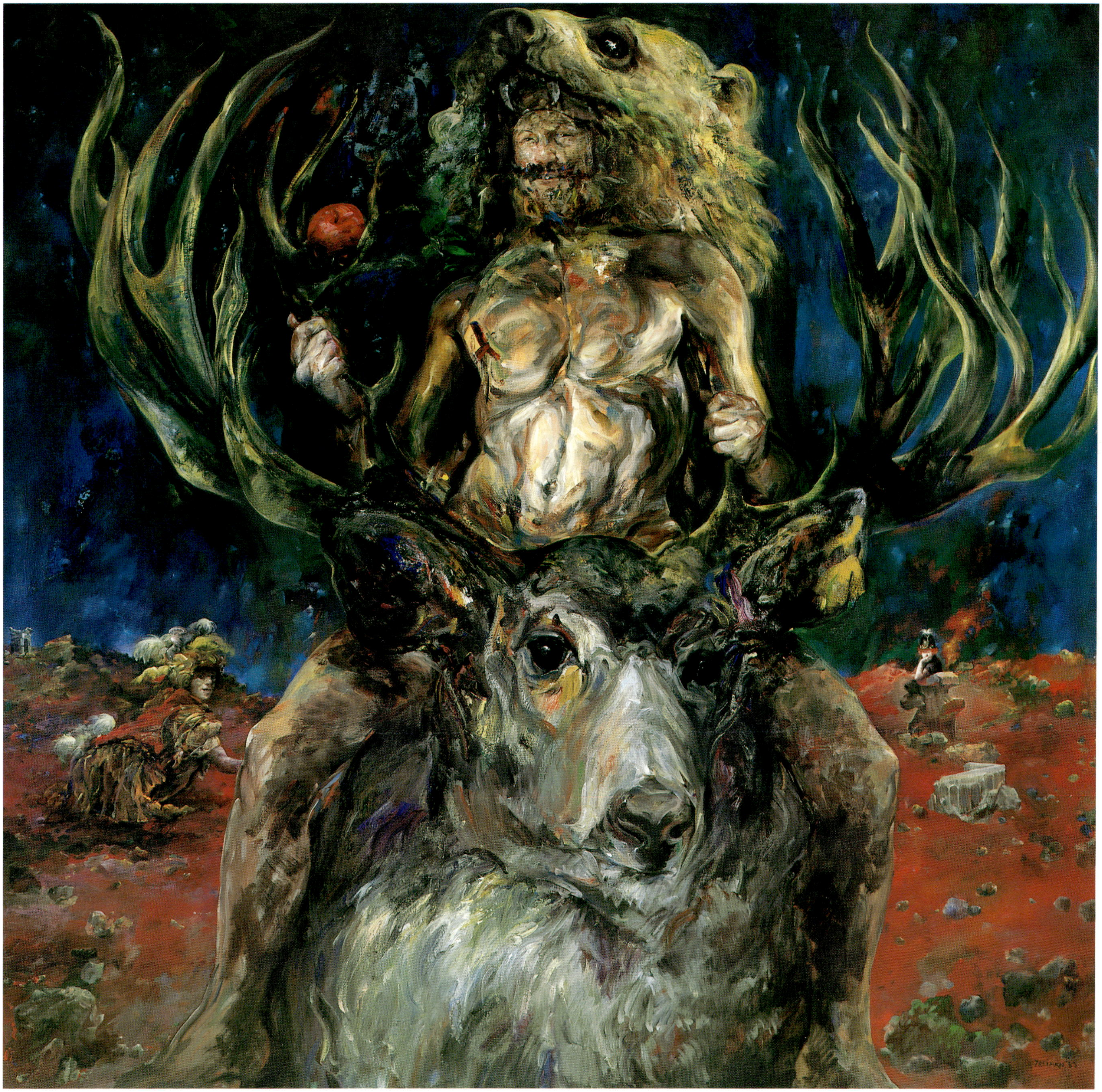

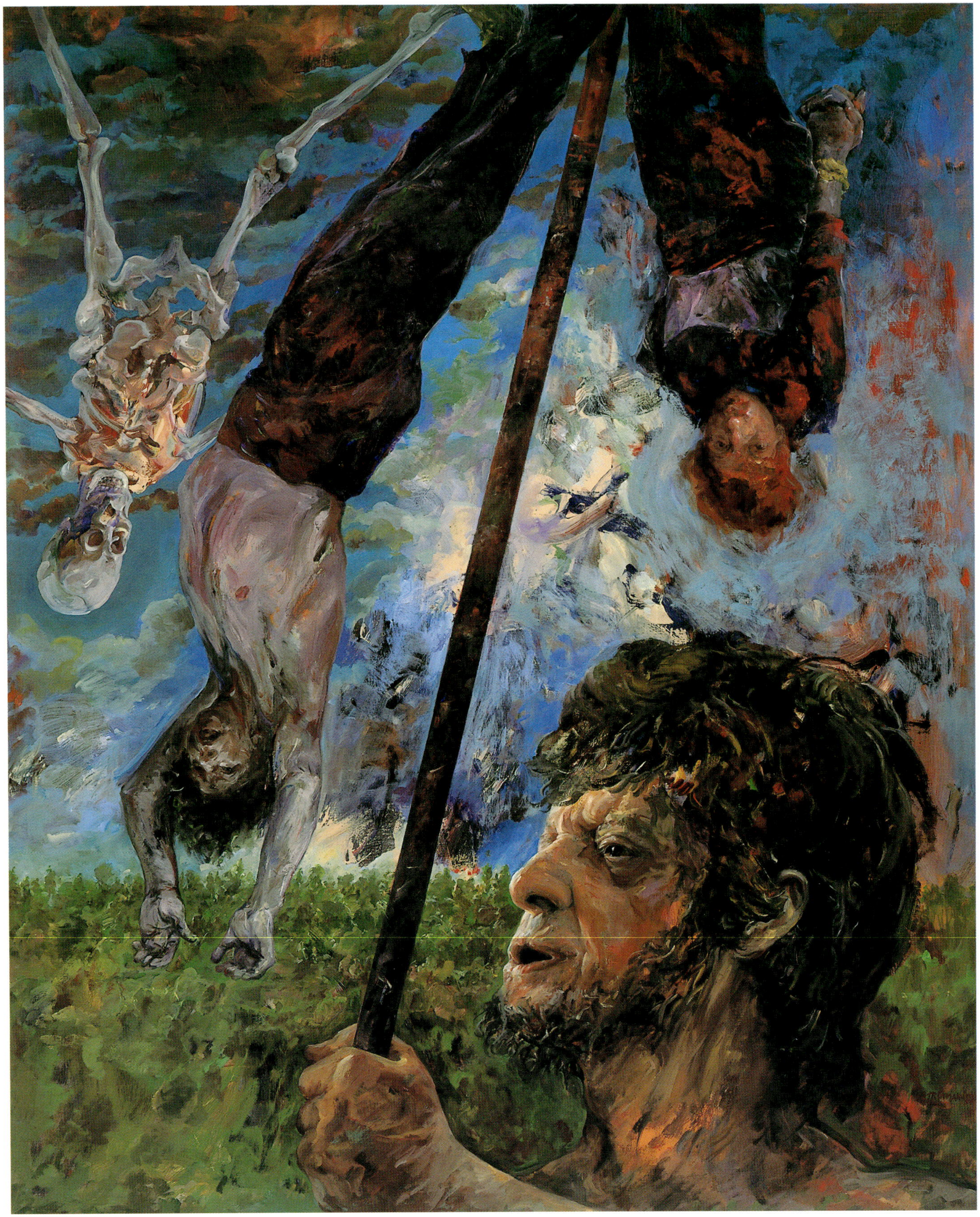

Hercules and Cercopes
1983
oil on canvas
60 x 48 inches
Courtesy Schmidt Bingham Gallery, New York

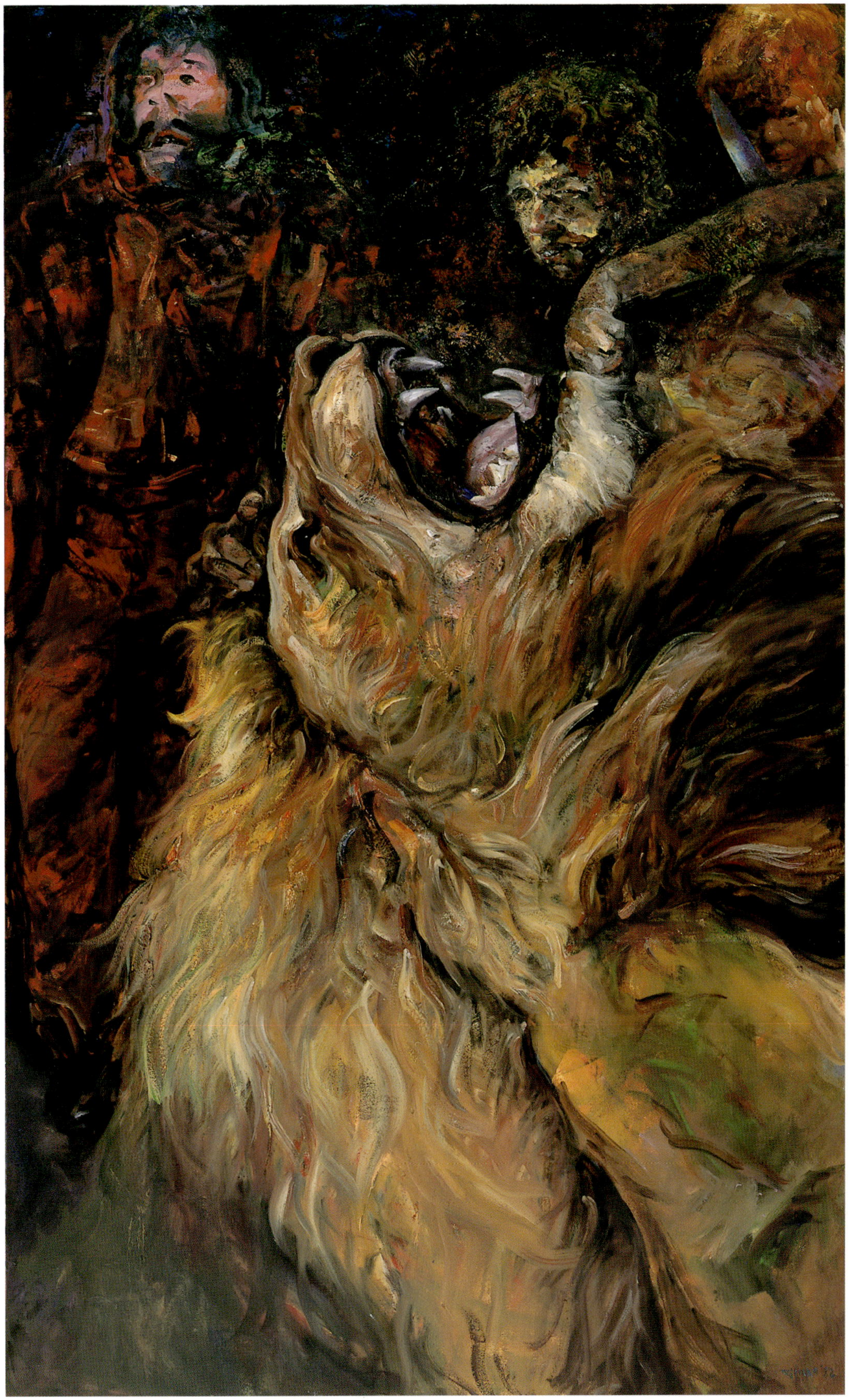

Hercules and the Nemean Lion
1982
oil on canvas
68 x 42 inches
Richard and Frances Luban

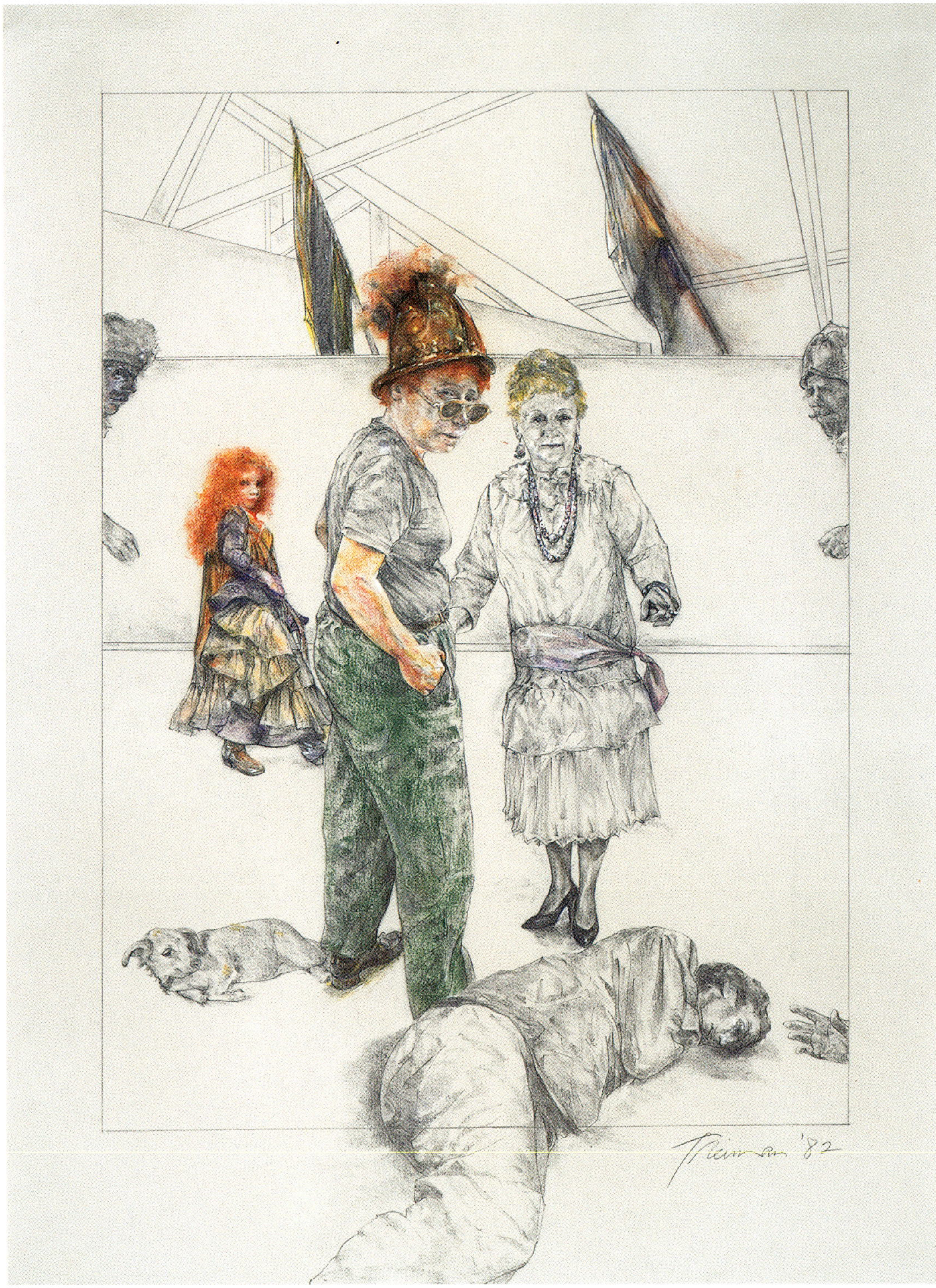

The Plumed Helmet: Study for "The Parting"
1982
pencil and pastel on paper
30¼ x 21¾ inches
Collection Memorial Art Gallery of the University of Rochester, Anonymous gift, 86.131

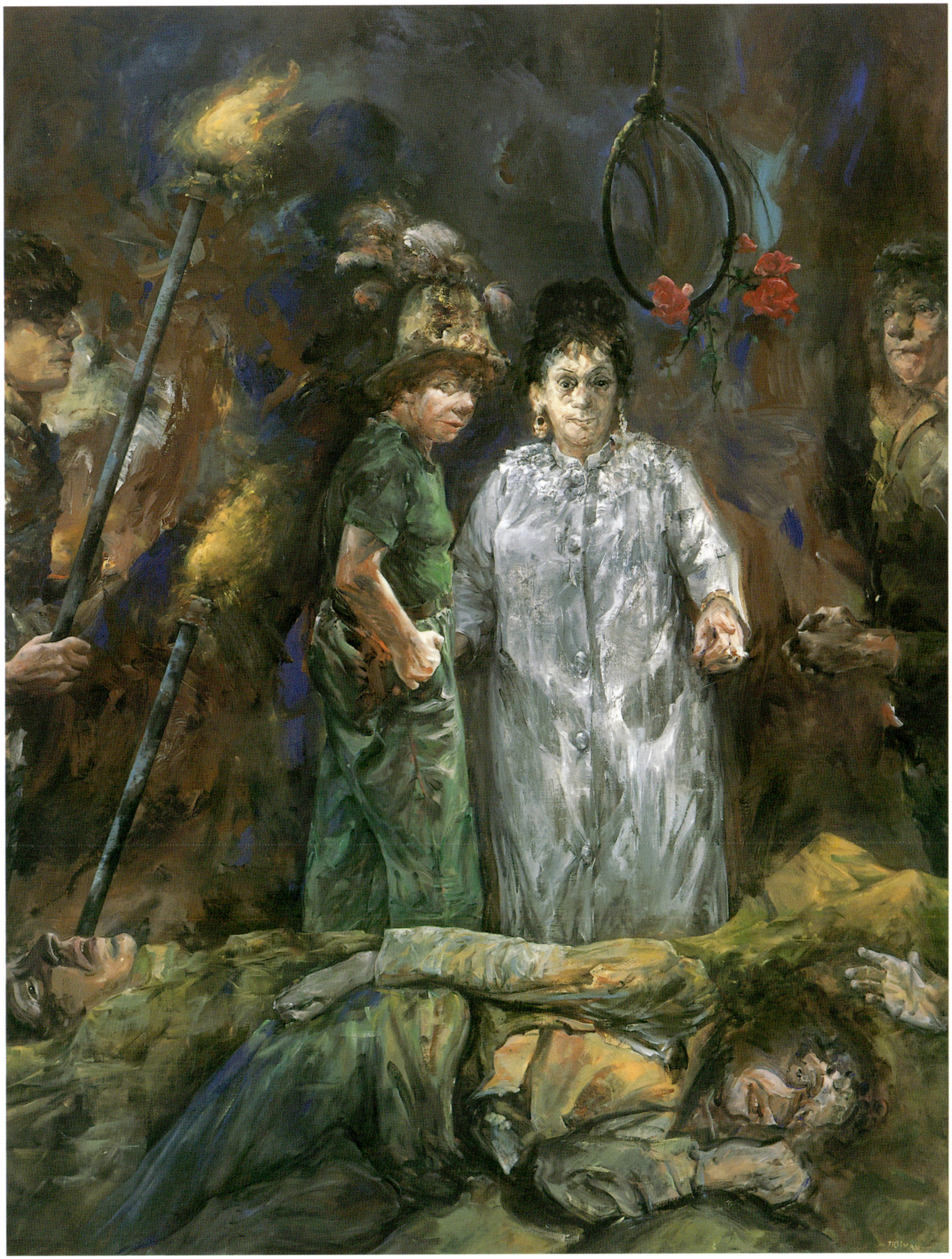

The Parting
1983
oil on canvas
80 x 60 inches
Memorial Art Gallery of the University of Rochester; Marion Stratton Gould Fund, 86.15

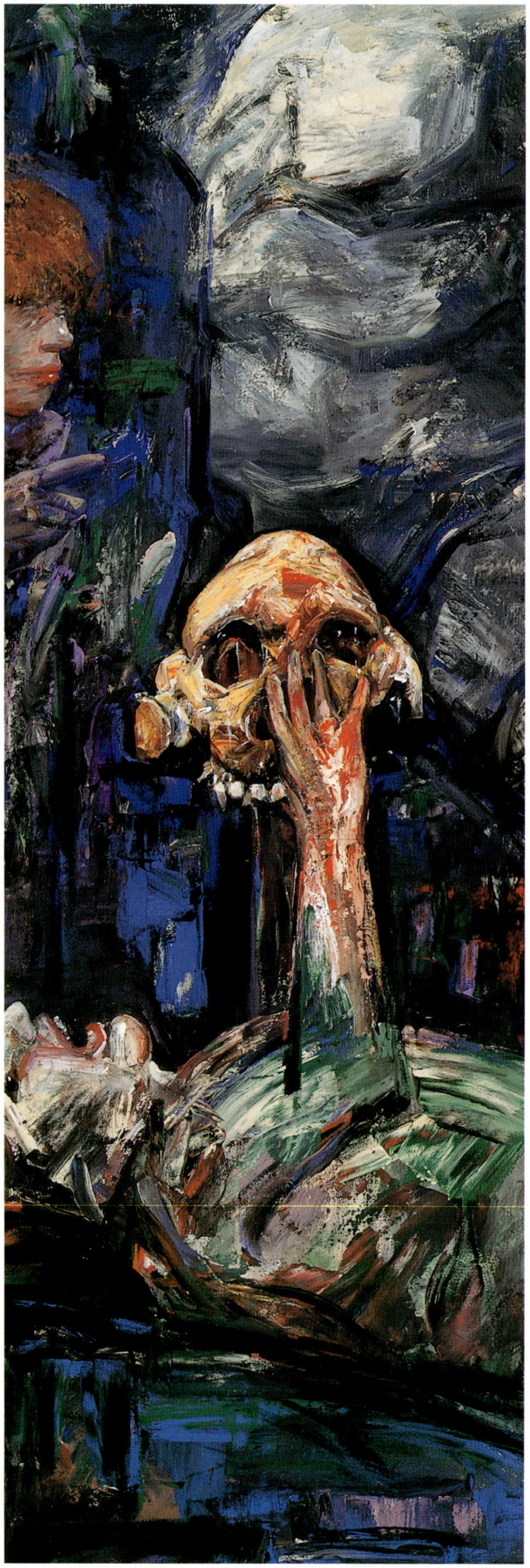

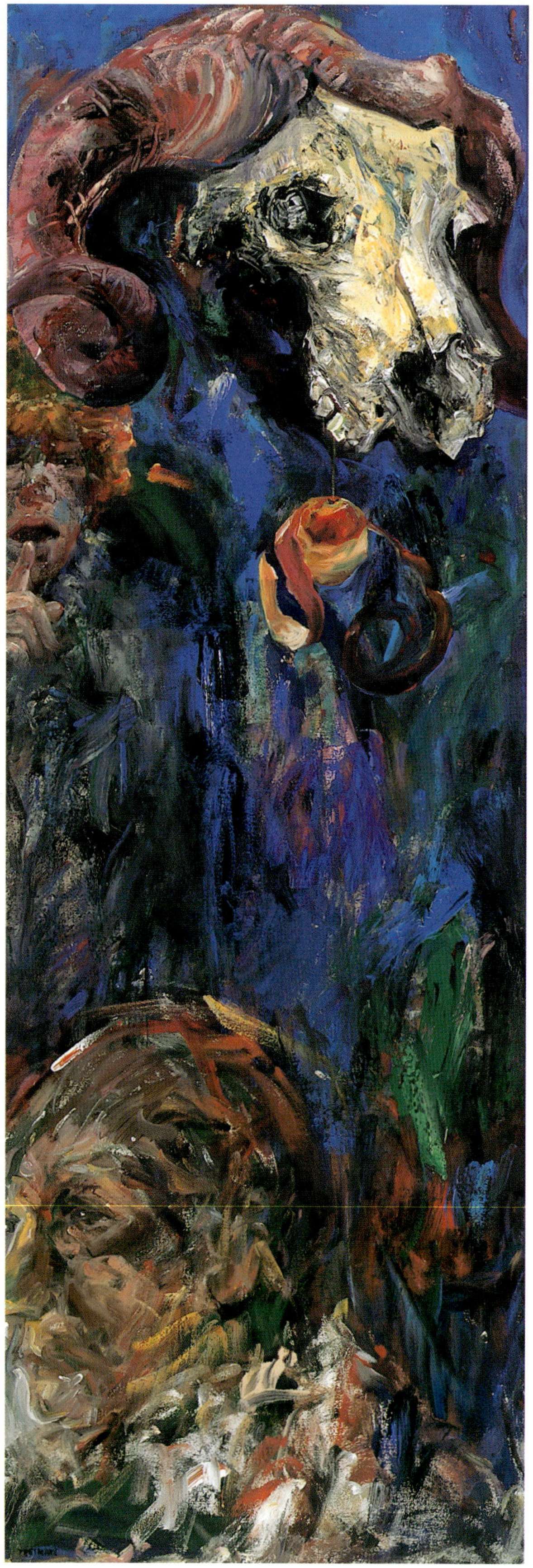

73.
◁◁ **The Torso**
1983
oil on canvas
77 x 31 inches
Courtesy Schmidt Bingham Gallery, New York

70.
◁ **The Ram**
1983
oil on canvas
77 x 31 inches
Courtesy Schmidt Bingham Gallery, New York

72.
The Smoker No. 21 ▷
1983
oil on canvas
77 x 31 inches
Courtesy Schmidt Bingham Gallery, New York

71.
Self-Portrait with Skull ▷▷
1983
oil on canvas
77 x 31 inches
Courtesy Schmidt Bingham Gallery, New York

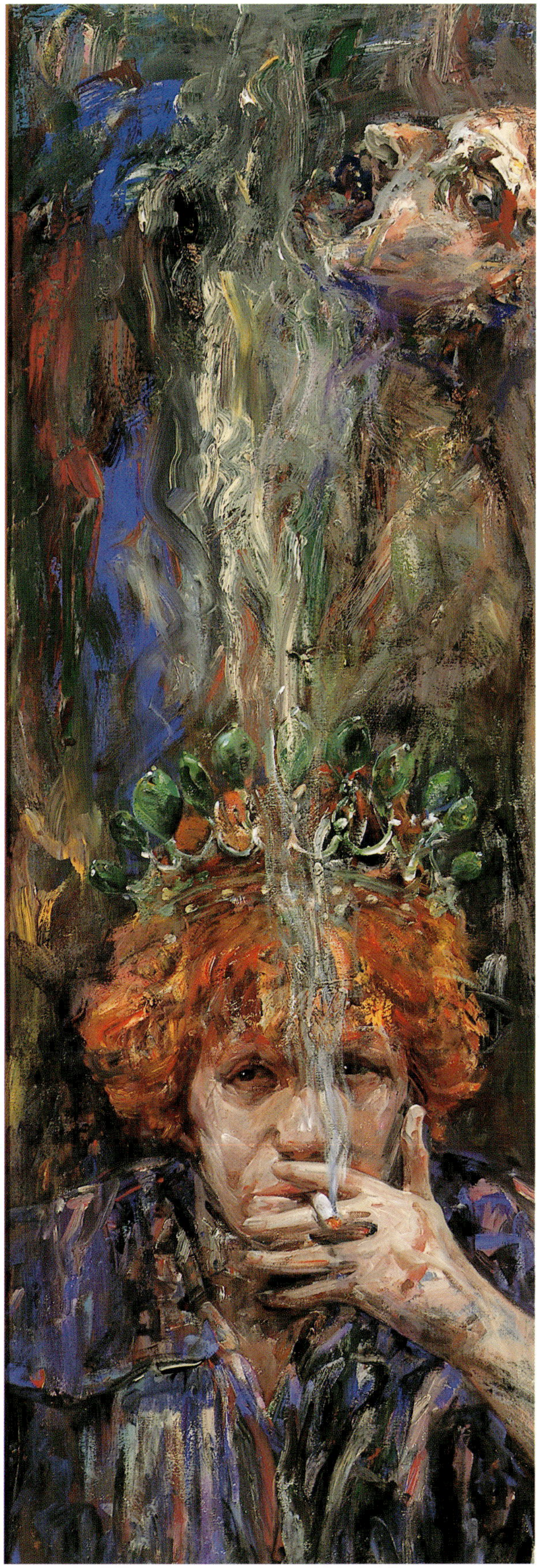
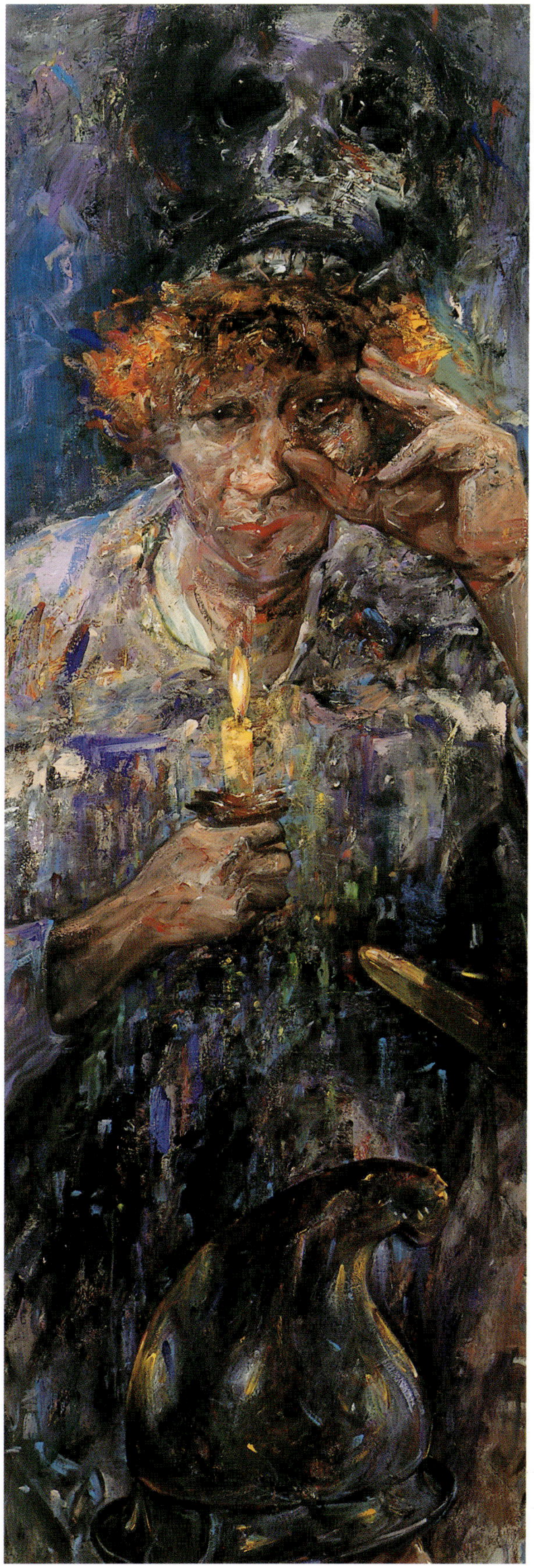

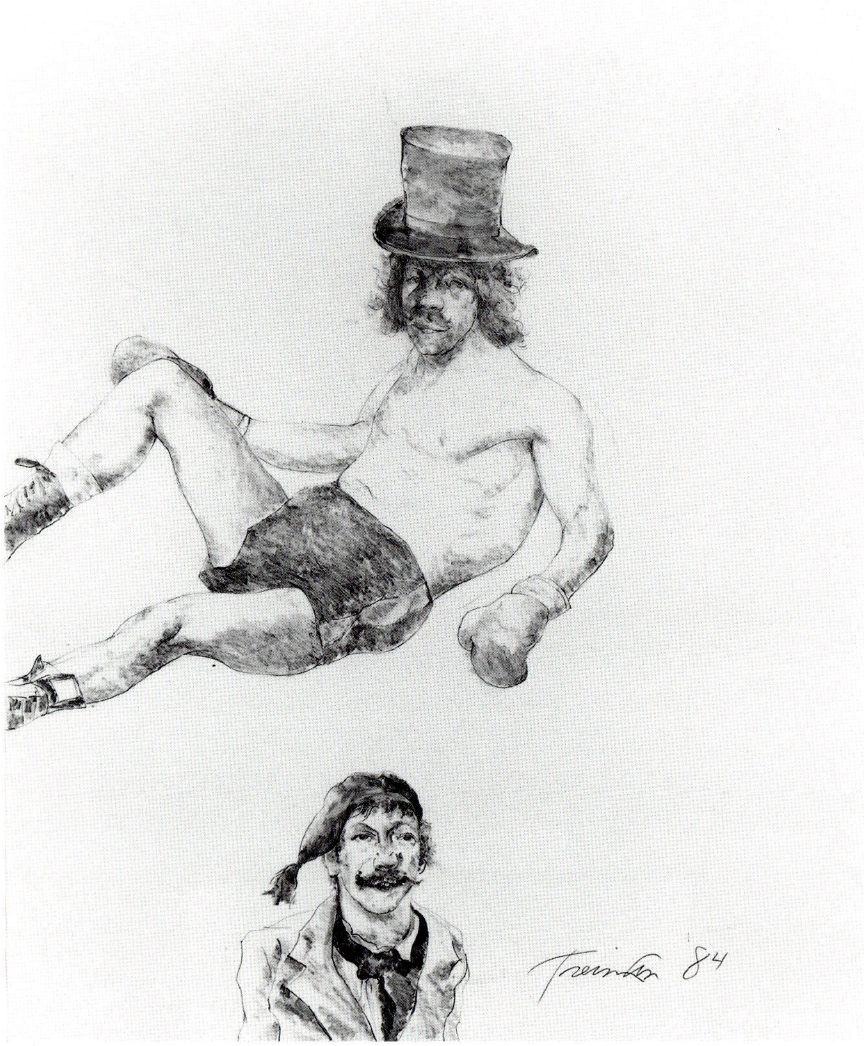

Untitled (Joker in Top Hat)
1984
pencil and colored pencil on paper
23¼ x 20¼ inches
Collection Donald M. Treiman, Pacific Palisades, California

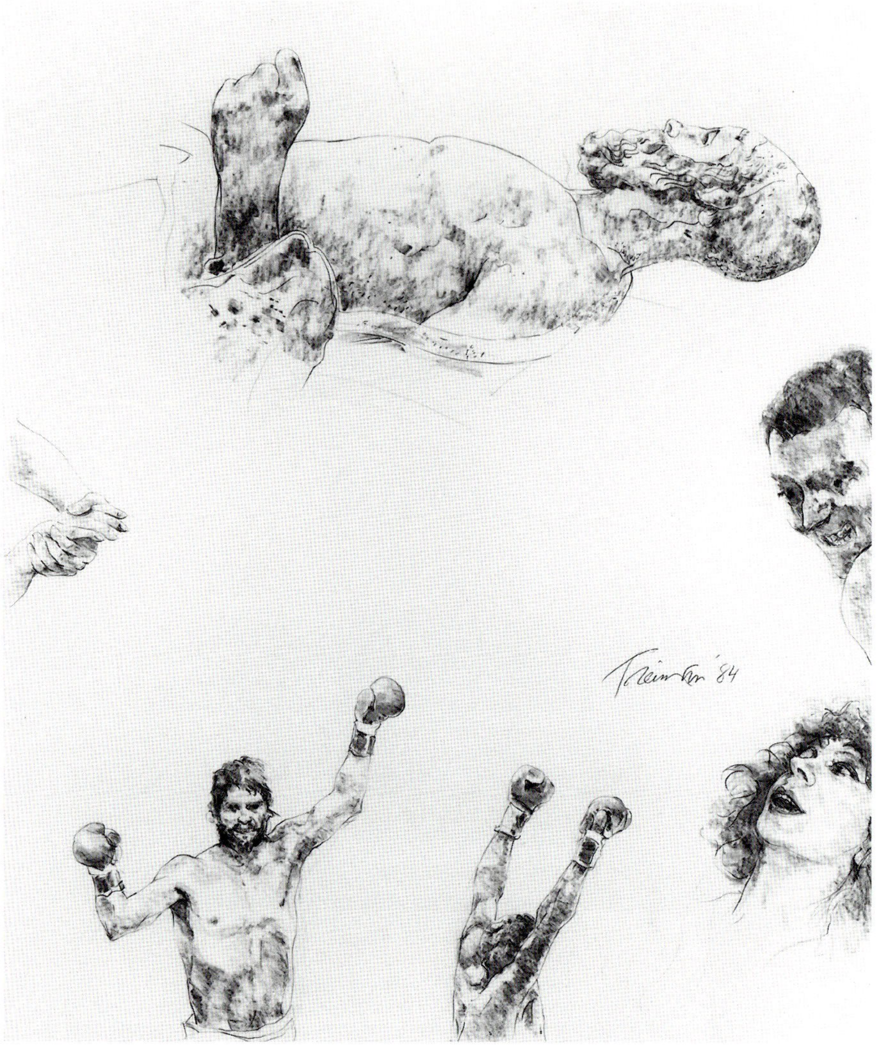

Untitled (Torso and Boxers)
1984
pencil and colored pencil on paper
24 x 21 inches
Courtesy Schmidt Bingham Gallery, New York

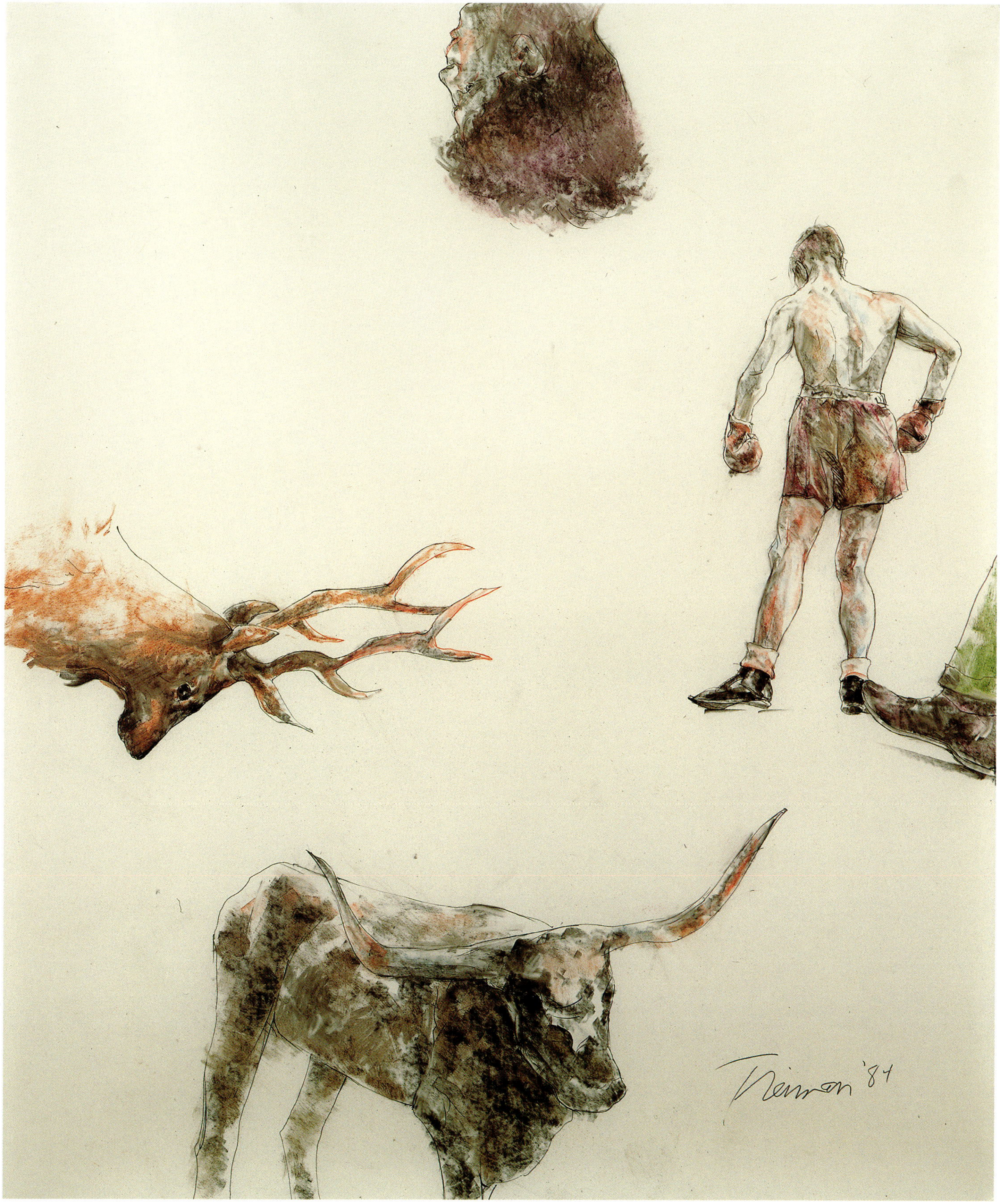

Boxer with Upside-down Head
1984
colored pencil on paper
17 x 14 inches
Stephens Inc., Little Rock, Arkansas

Self-Portrait in Titus's Hat
1983
oil on canvas
78 x 40 inches
Collection Donald M. Treiman,
Pacific Palisades, California

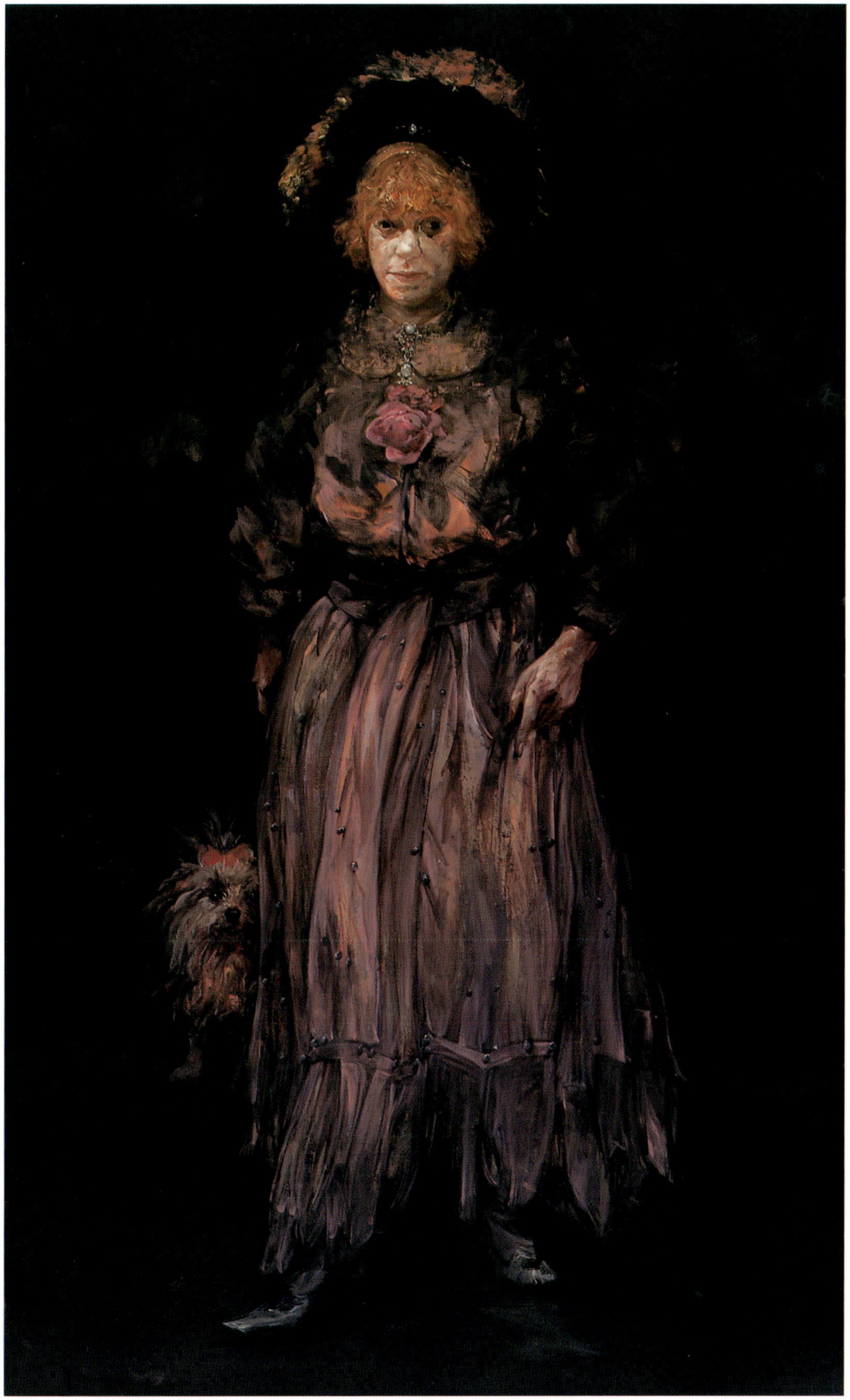

Thanatopsis
1983
oil on canvas
70 x 70 inches
Santa Barbara Museum of Art,
Gift of Harry W. Saunders, 1991.159

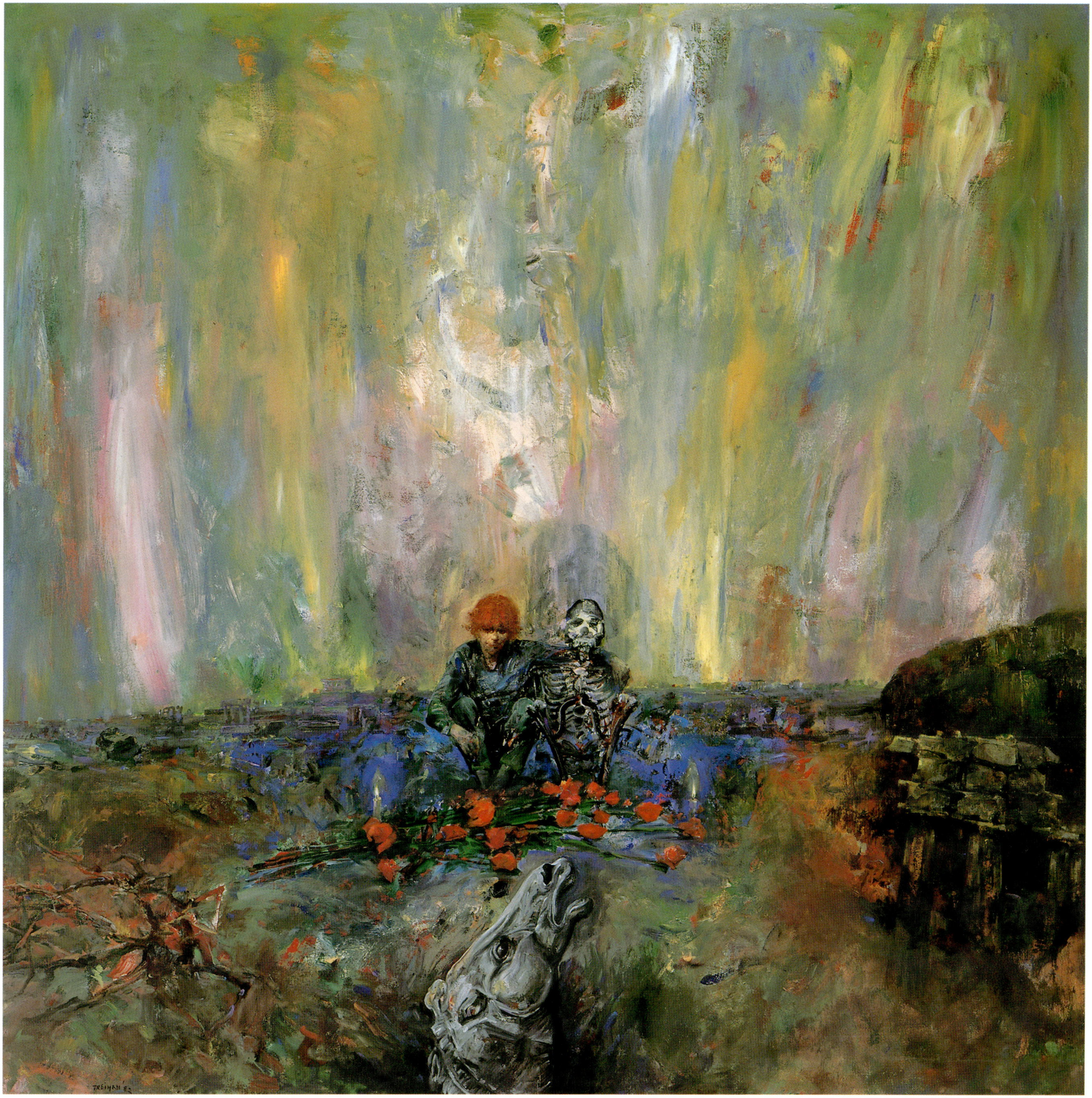

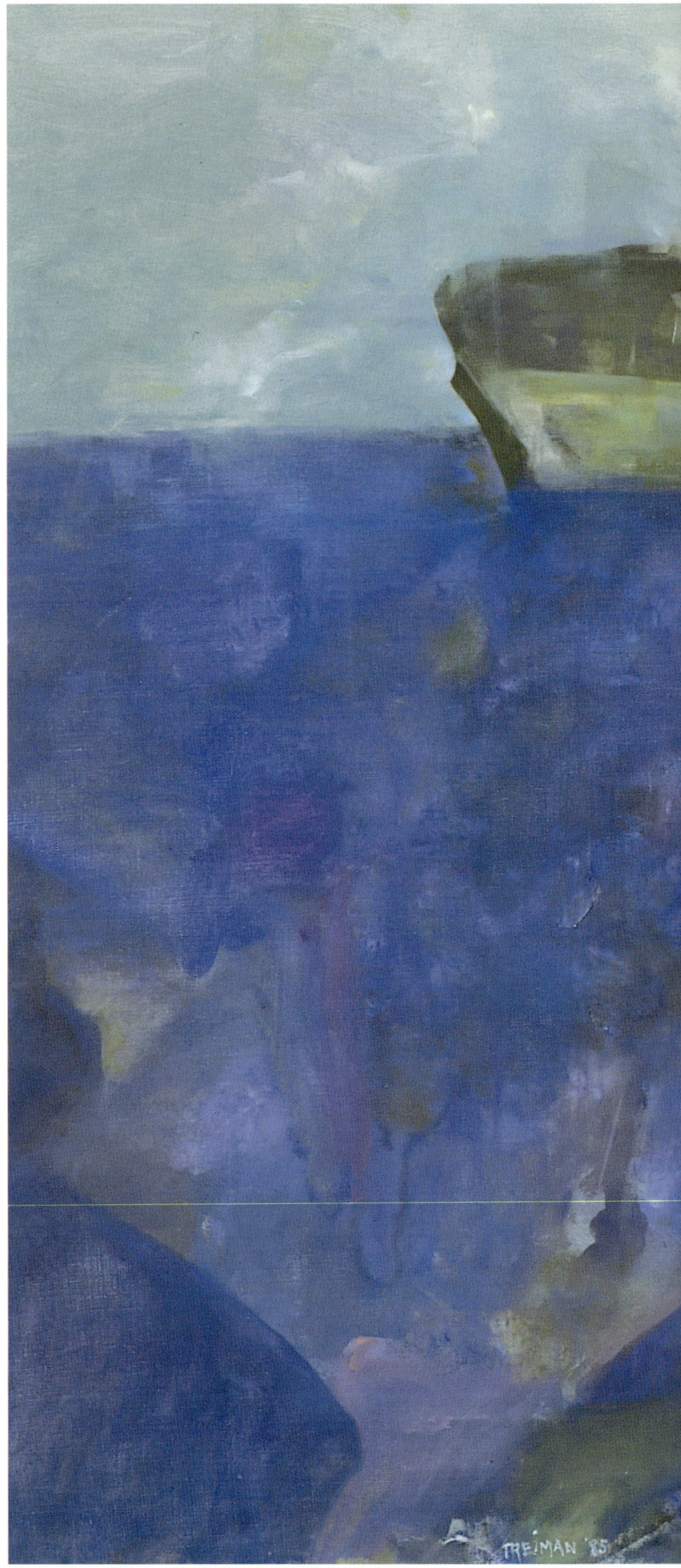

Mysterious Voyage
1985
oil on canvas
30 x 48 inches
Collection Donald M. Treiman, Pacific Palisades, California

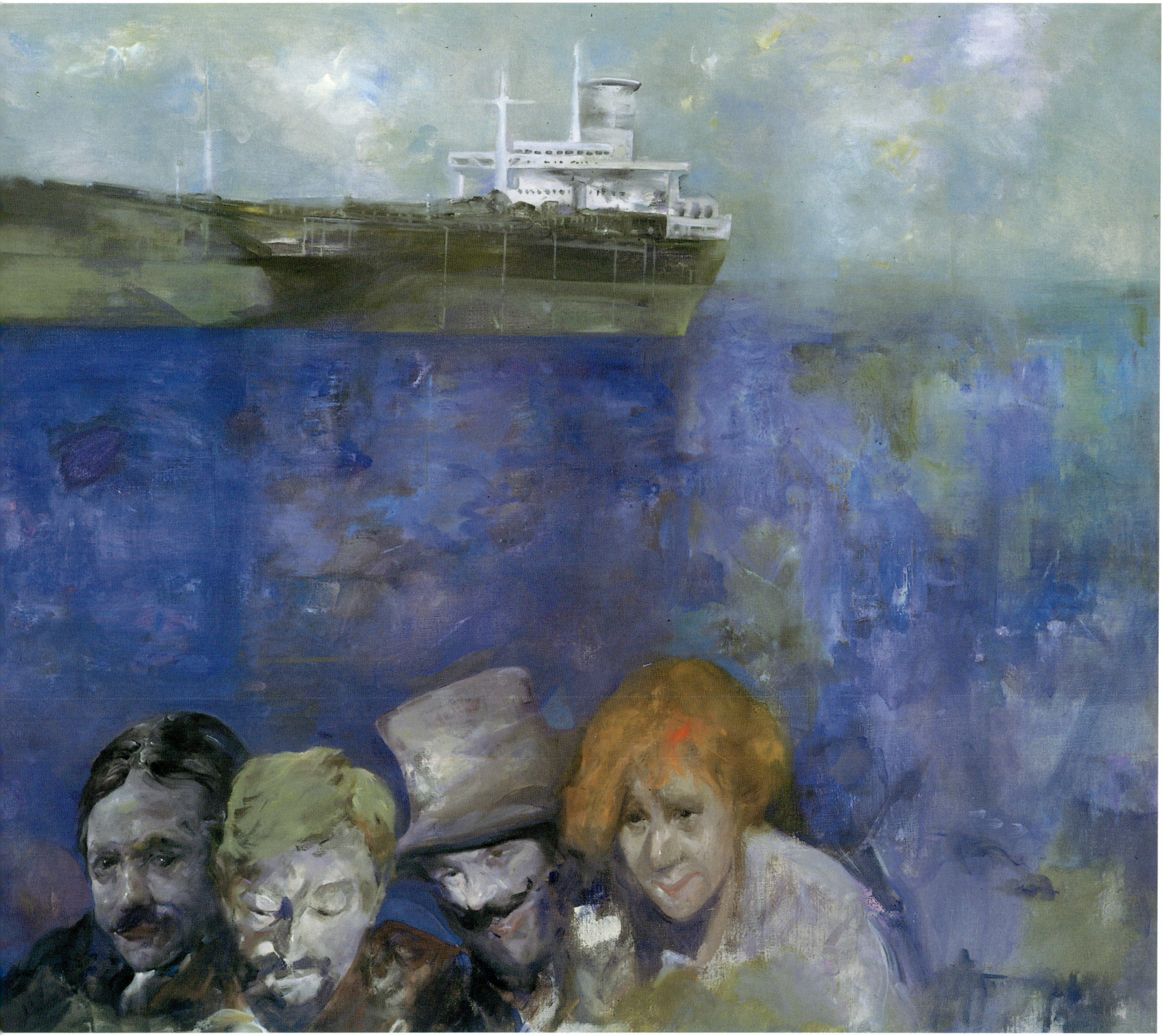

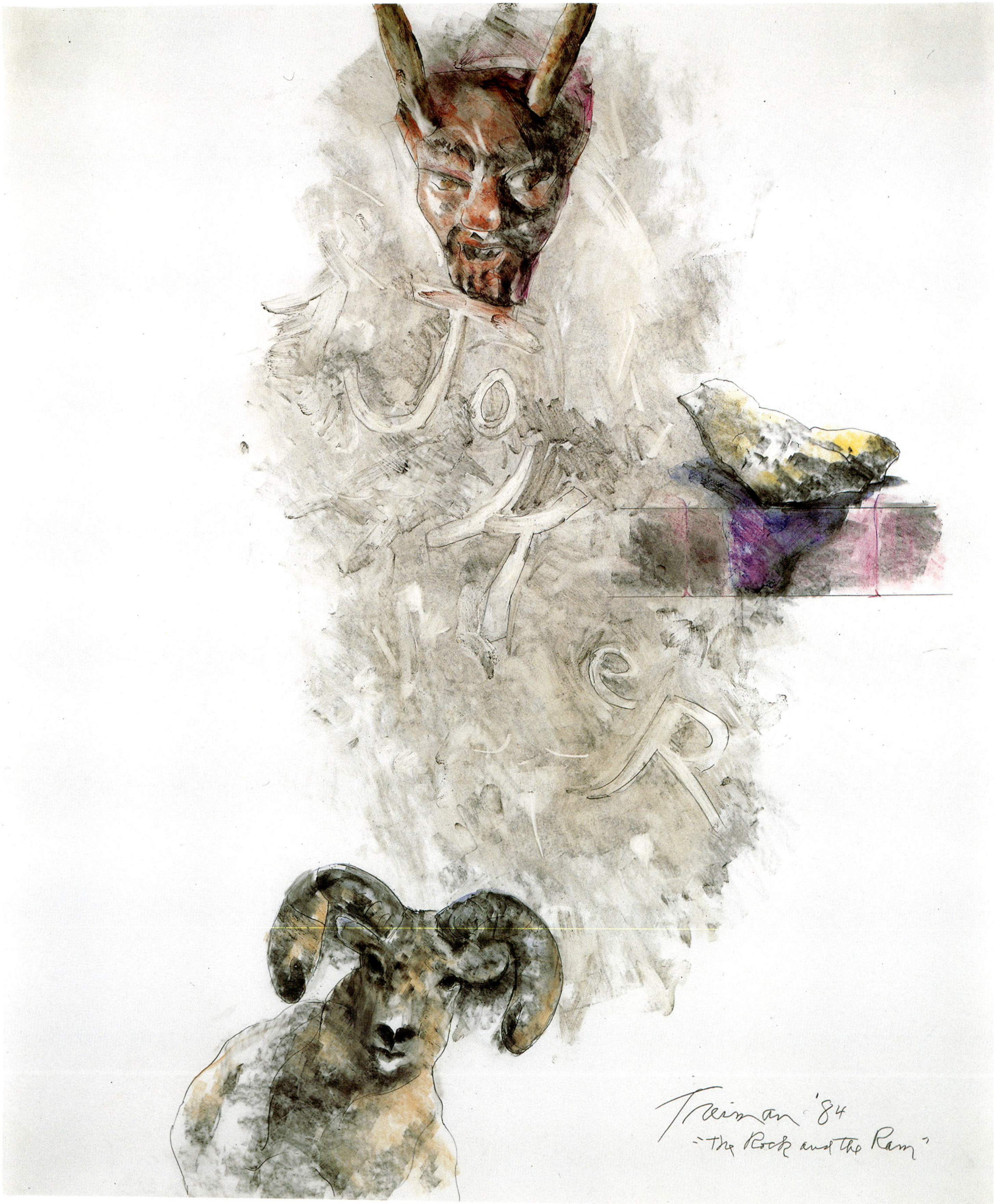

The Rock and the Ram
1984
charcoal, pencil, pastel, and colored pencil on paper
17 x 14 inches
Collection Donald M. Treiman, Pacific Palisades, California

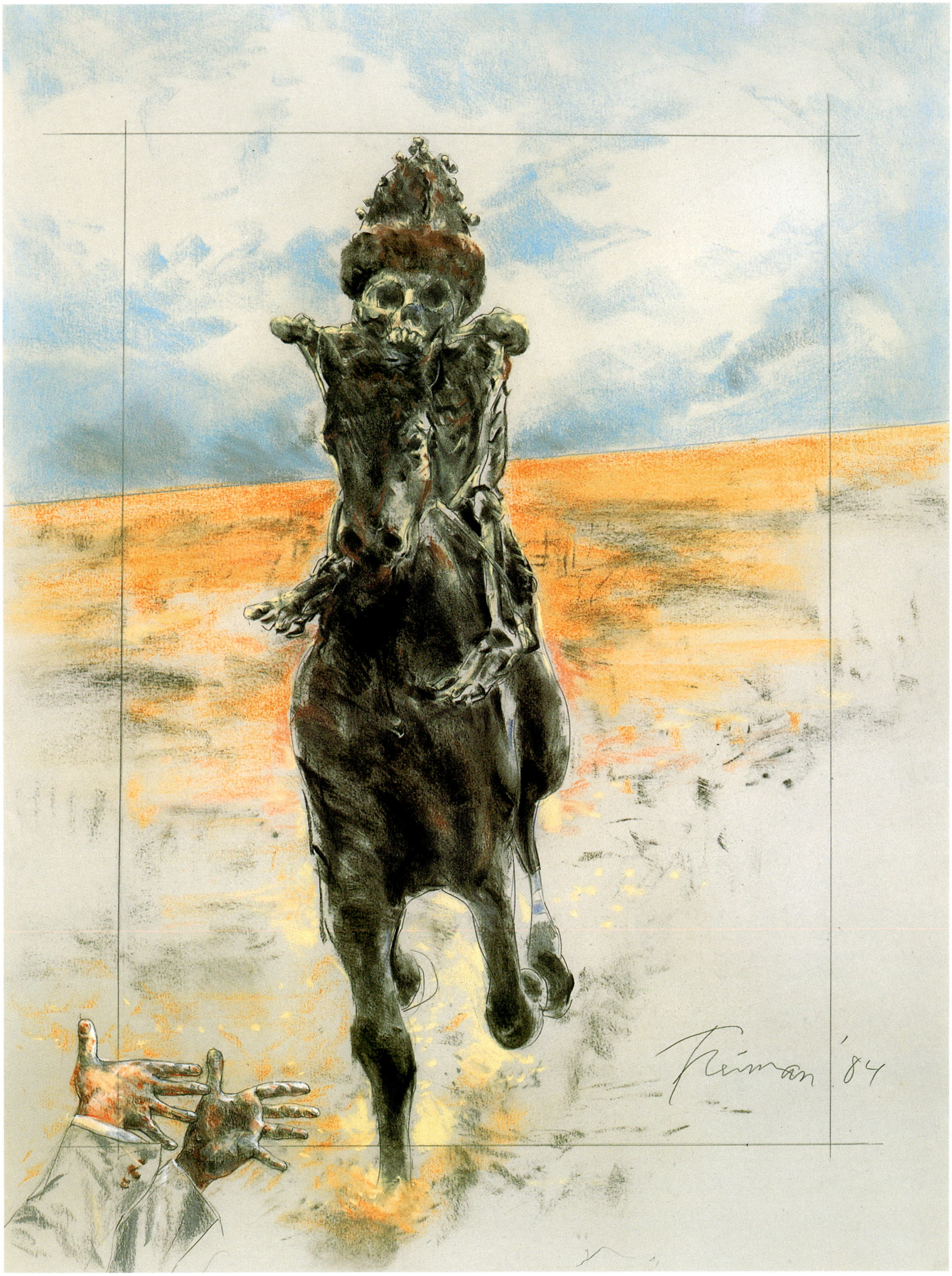

Untitled (The Rider)
1984
pastel and pencil on paper
30 x 22½ inches
Collection Judd Hammack, Santa Monica

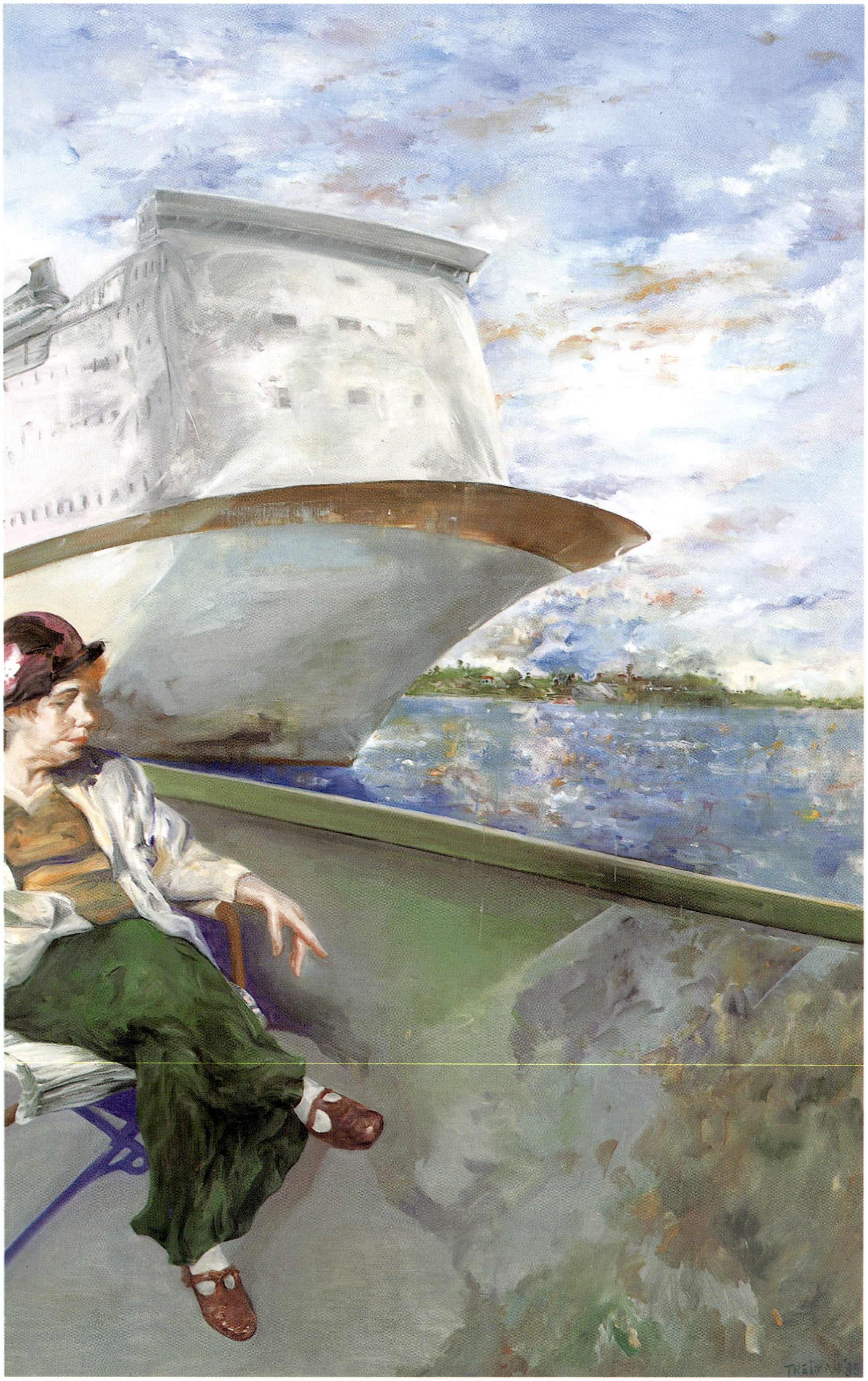

Me and Big Ship
1985
oil on canvas
48 x 30 inches
Courtesy Schmidt Bingham Gallery, New York

Seated Self-Portrait with Joker
1985
oil on canvas
42 x 42 inches
Collection of Harry Saunders

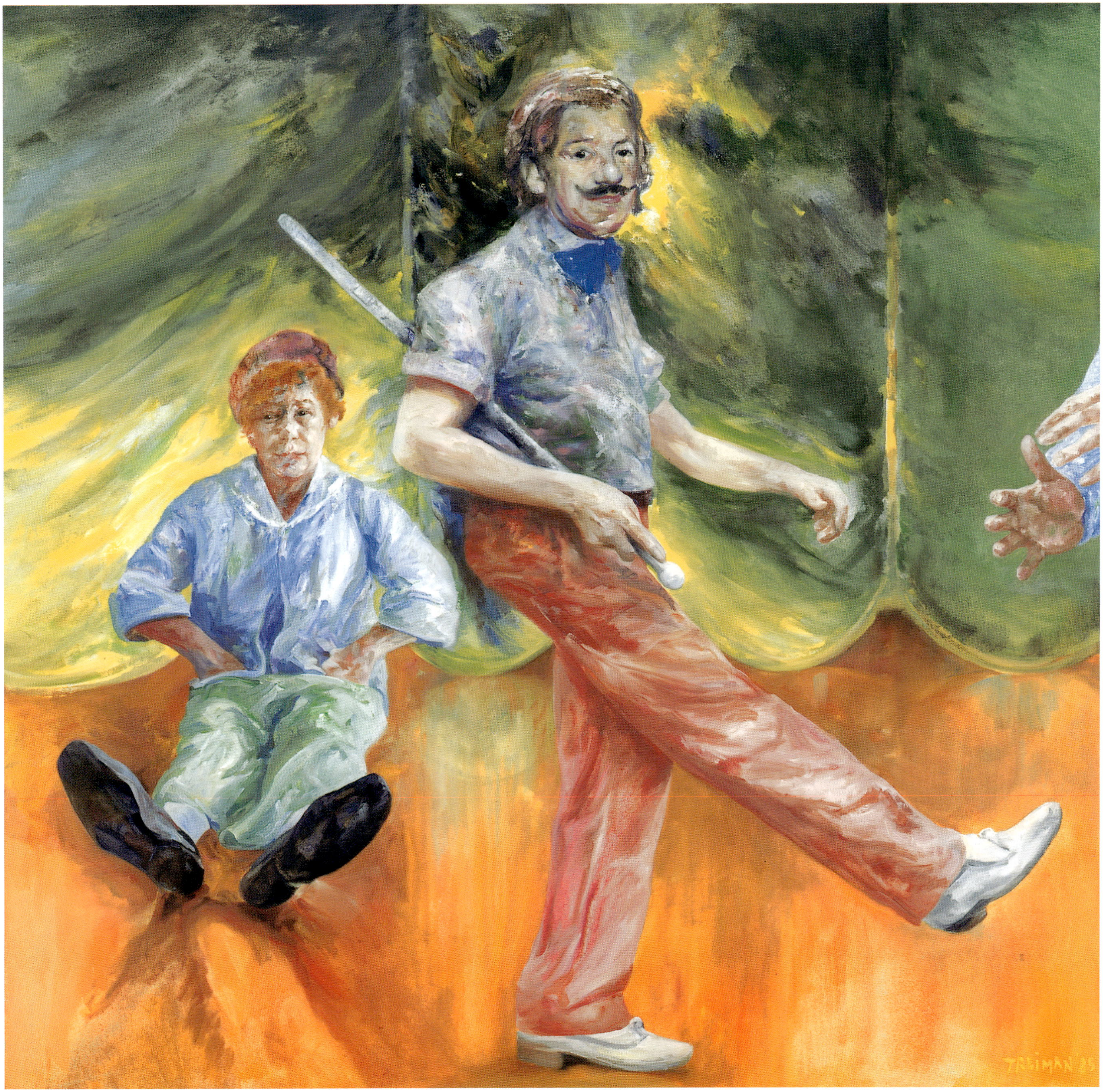

Sailing Away
1985
oil on canvas
48 x 30 inches
Martin and Sharleen Cohen

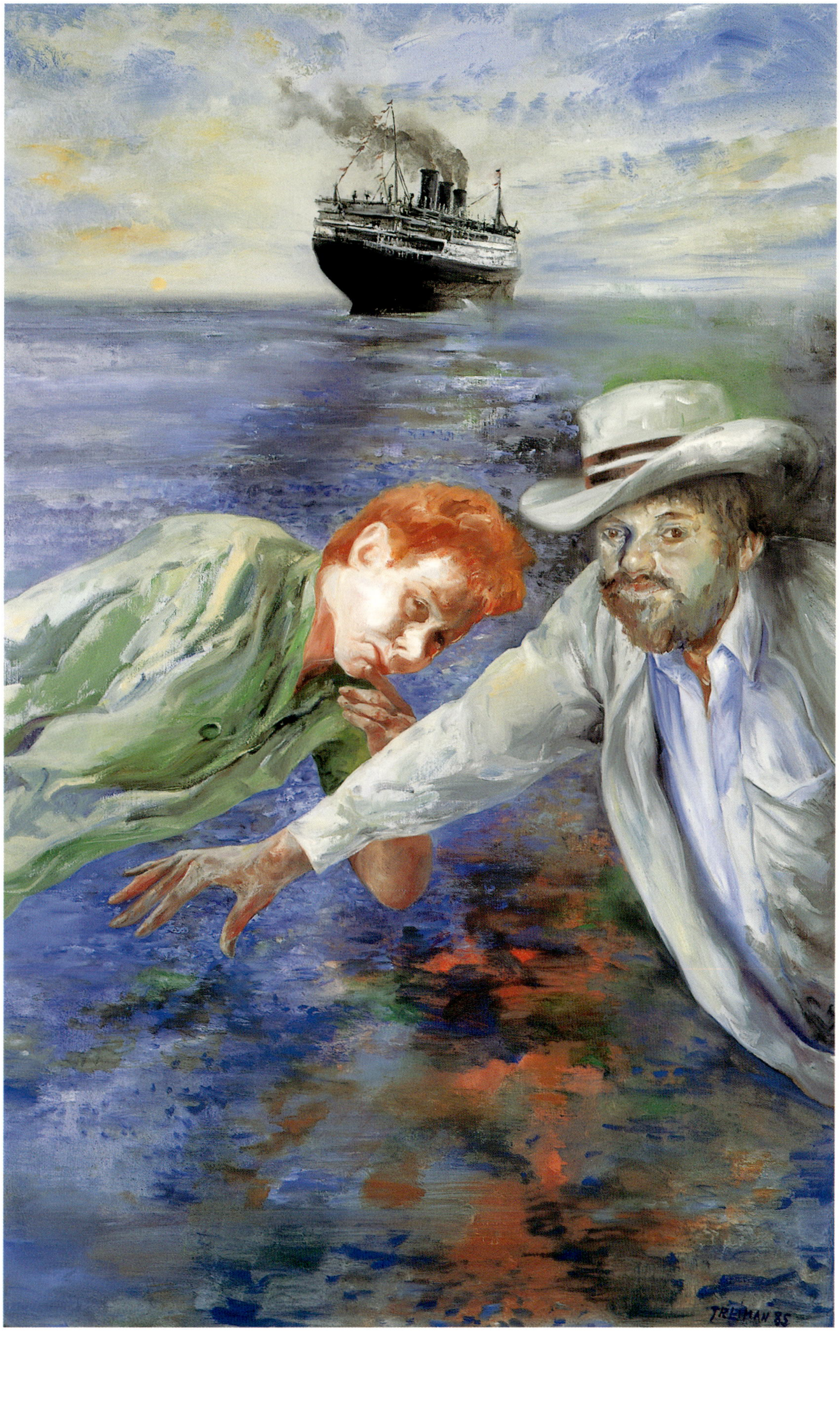
TREIMAN 85

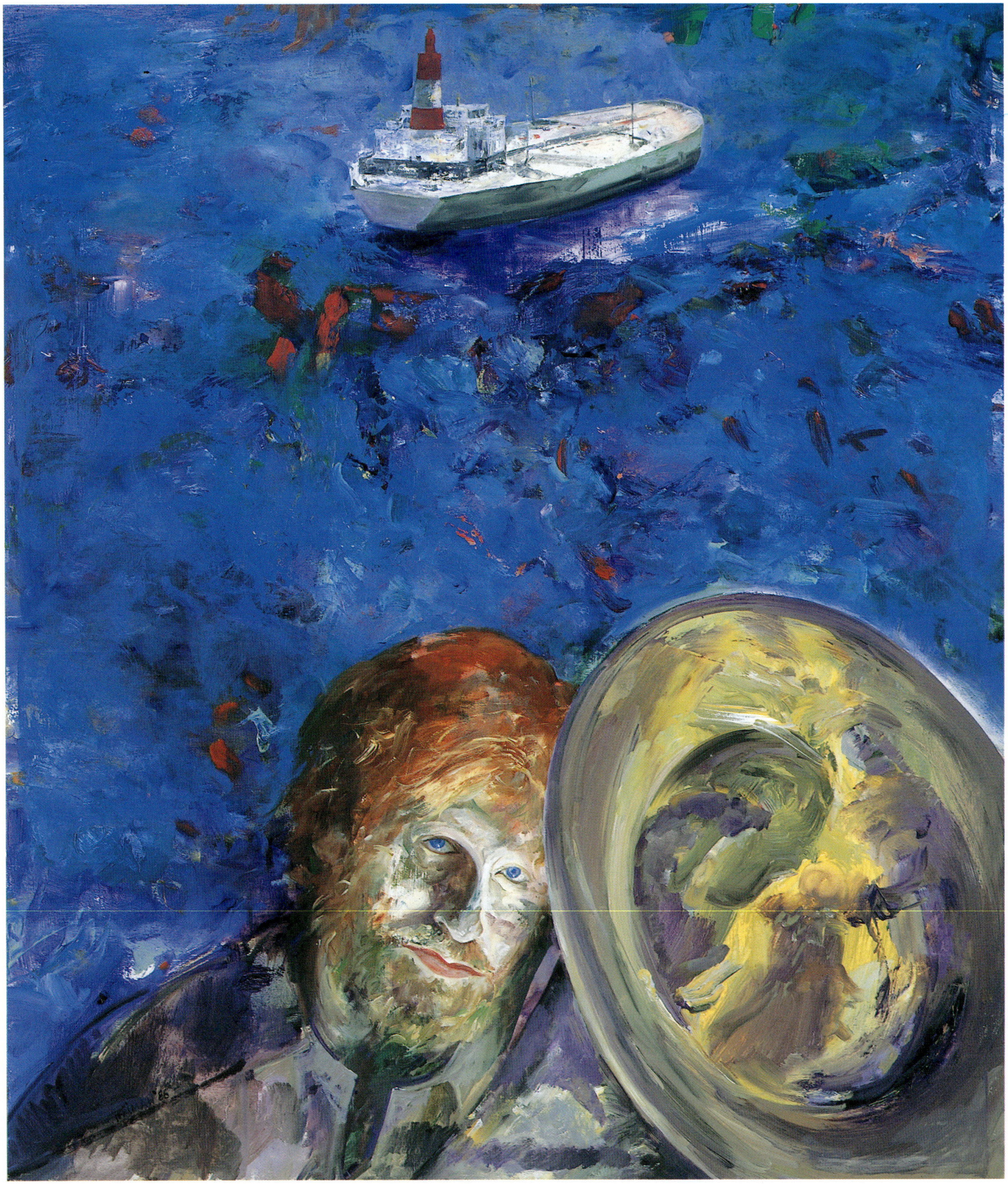

Horn, Stranger, and Ship
1986
oil on wood
32 x 26½ inches
Collection Donald M. Treiman,
Pacific Palisades, California

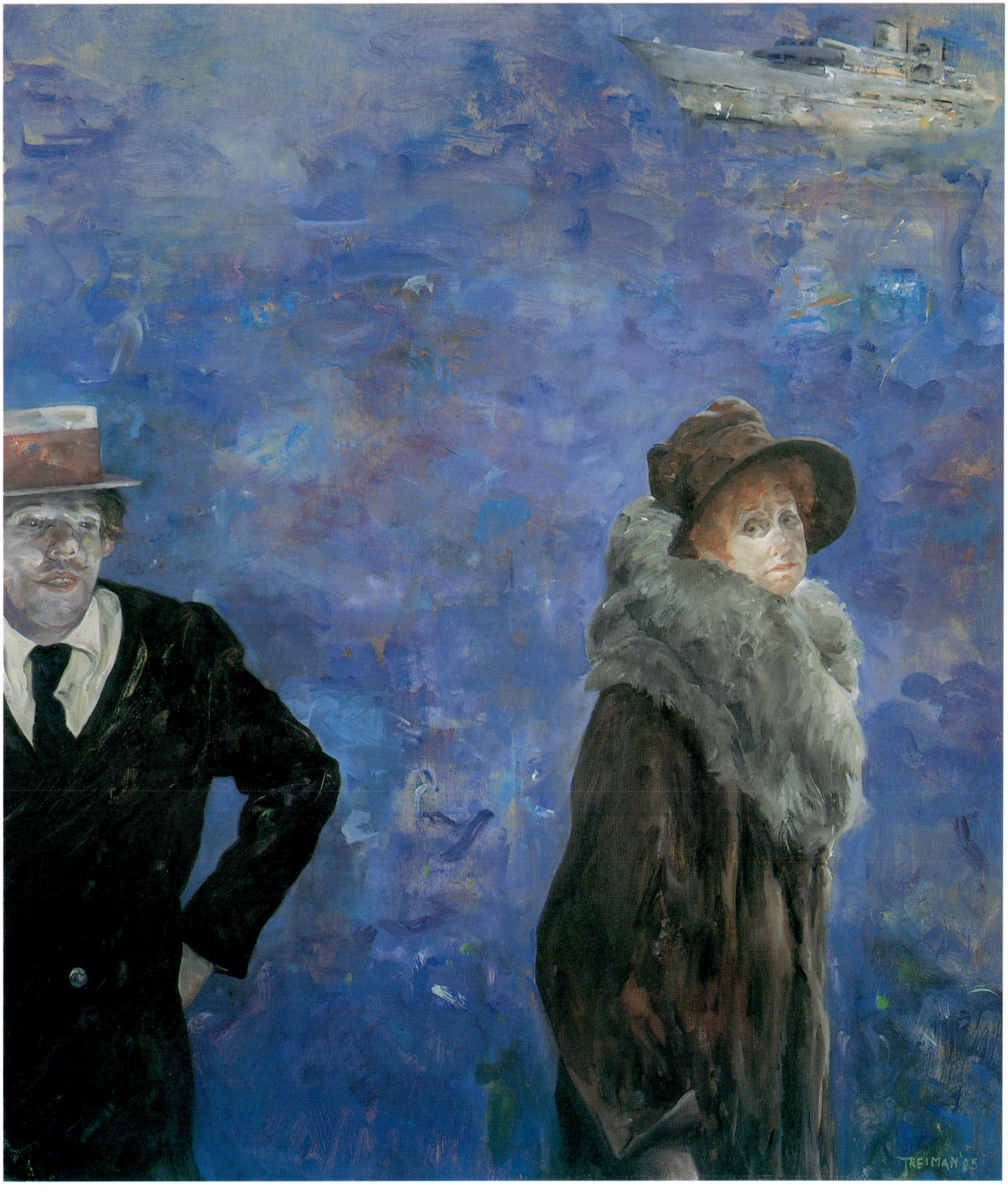

Joker, Me, and Ship
1986
oil on canvas
26 x 22 inches
Private collection, Los Angeles, California

The Rose, the Joker, and Me
1986
oil on canvas
30 x 48 inches
Mrs. Charlene and Dr. S. Sanford Kornblum

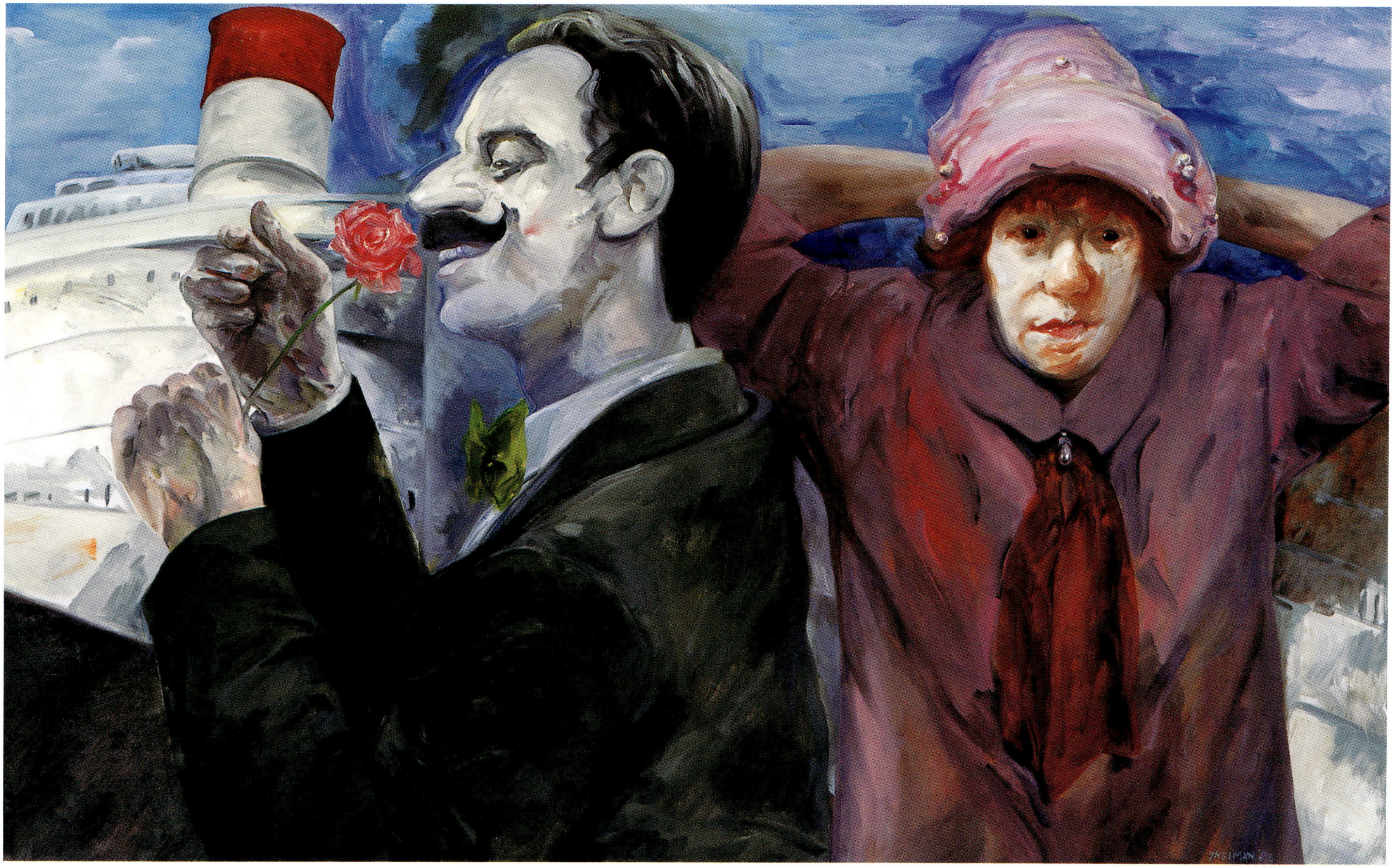

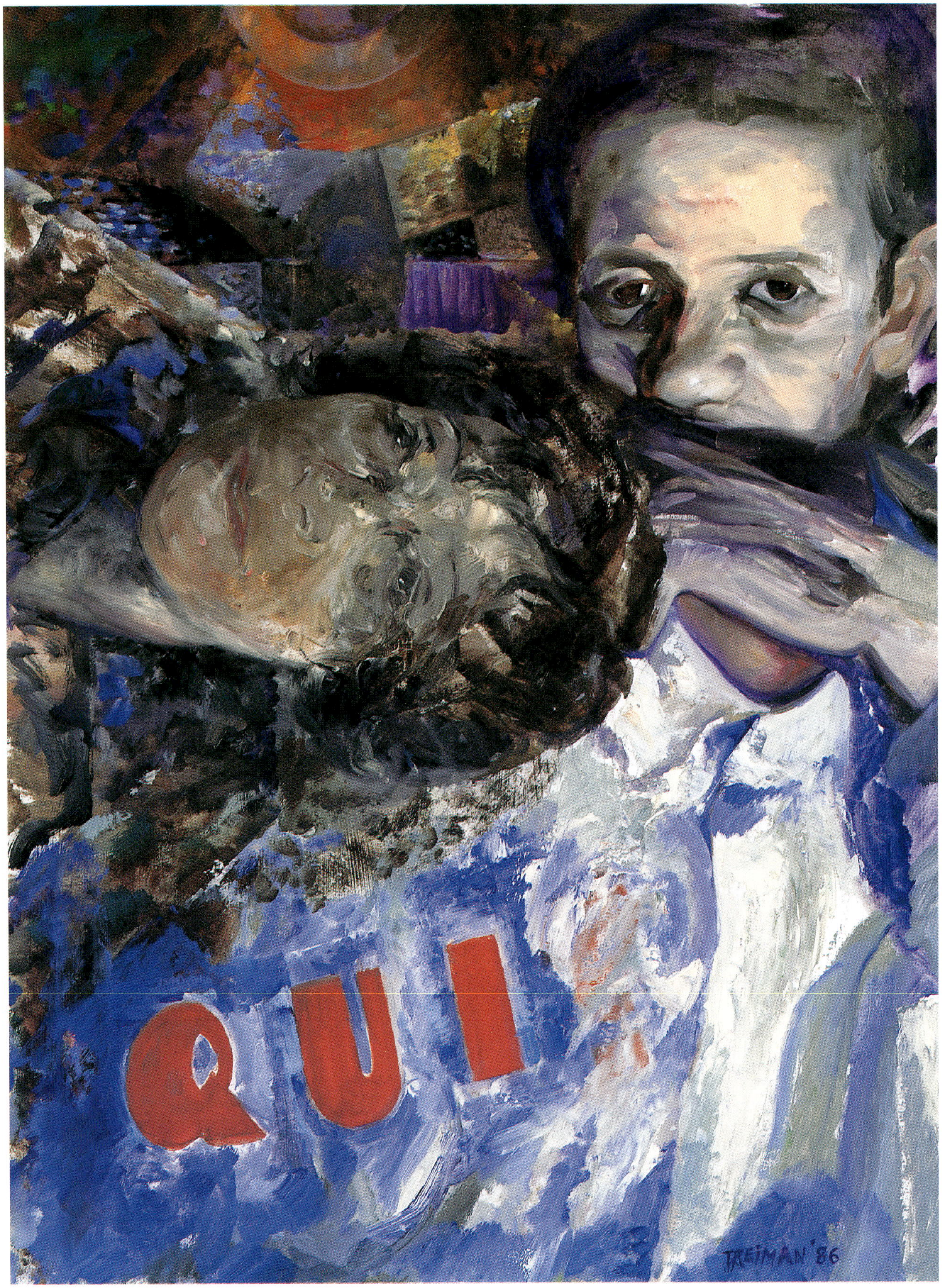

Stranger without Me
1986
oil on wood
22 x 16 inches
Collection Donald M. Treiman,
Pacific Palisades, California

Wits End and Rose
1986
oil on canvas
76 x 70 inches
Nancy Cooper Federman and
the late Ronald Harrison Cooper

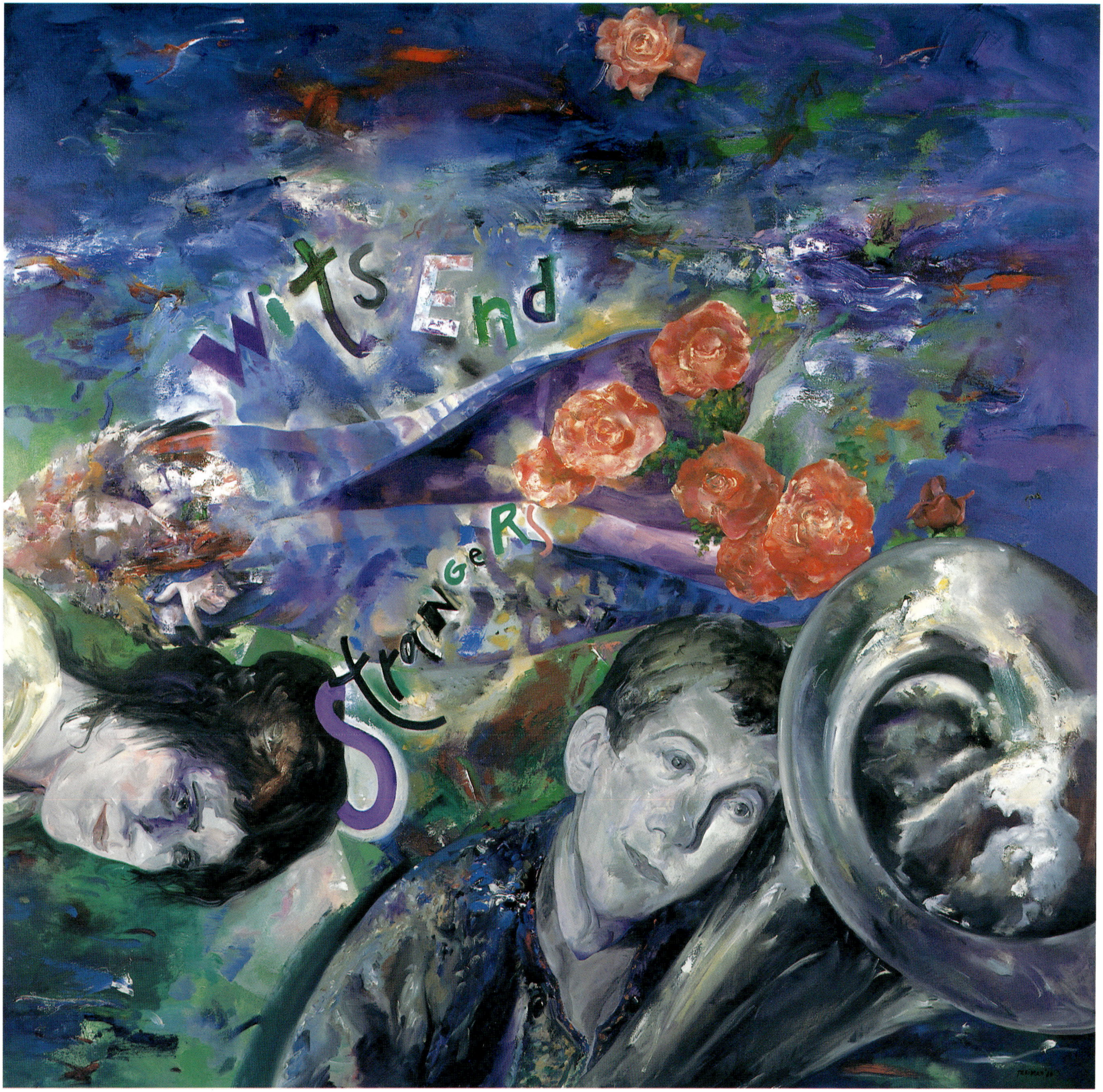
Wits End
Strangers

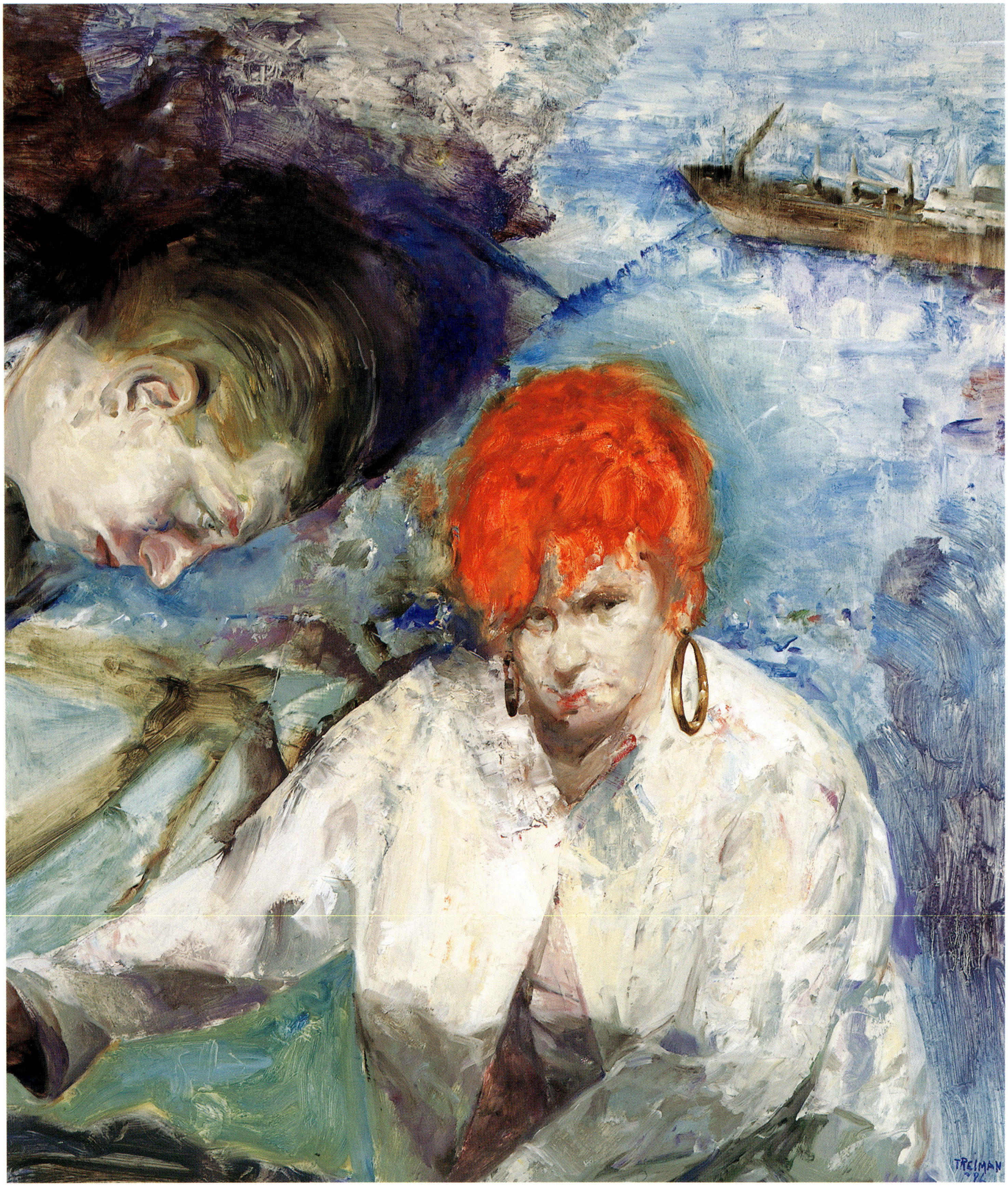

Joker Looking Down and Me
1986
oil on board
25 1/2 x 21 inches
Collection of Lizard/Harp

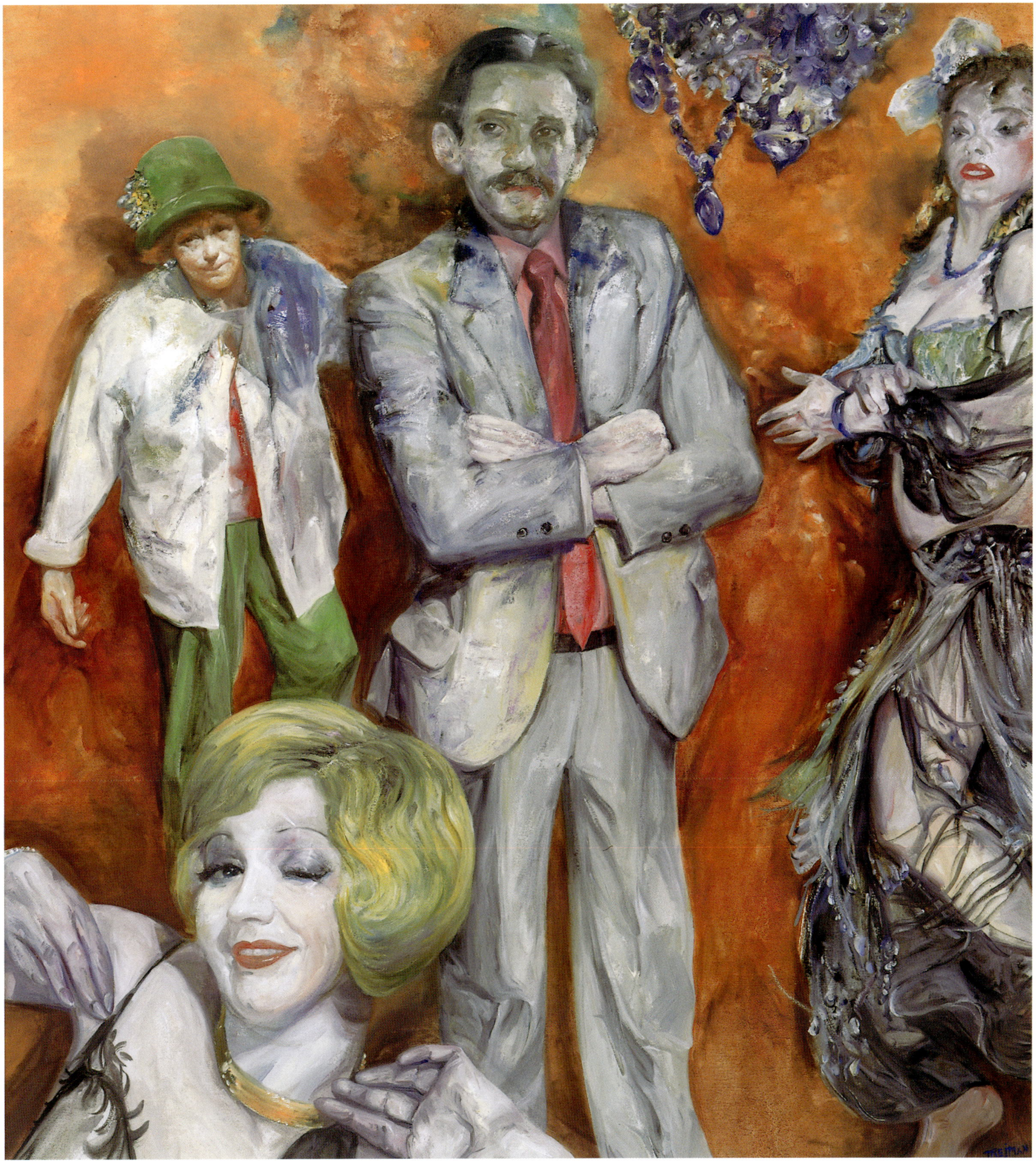

Winking Woman, Joker, and Me
1986
oil on canvas
48 x 42 inches
Abby and Alan D. Levy Collection

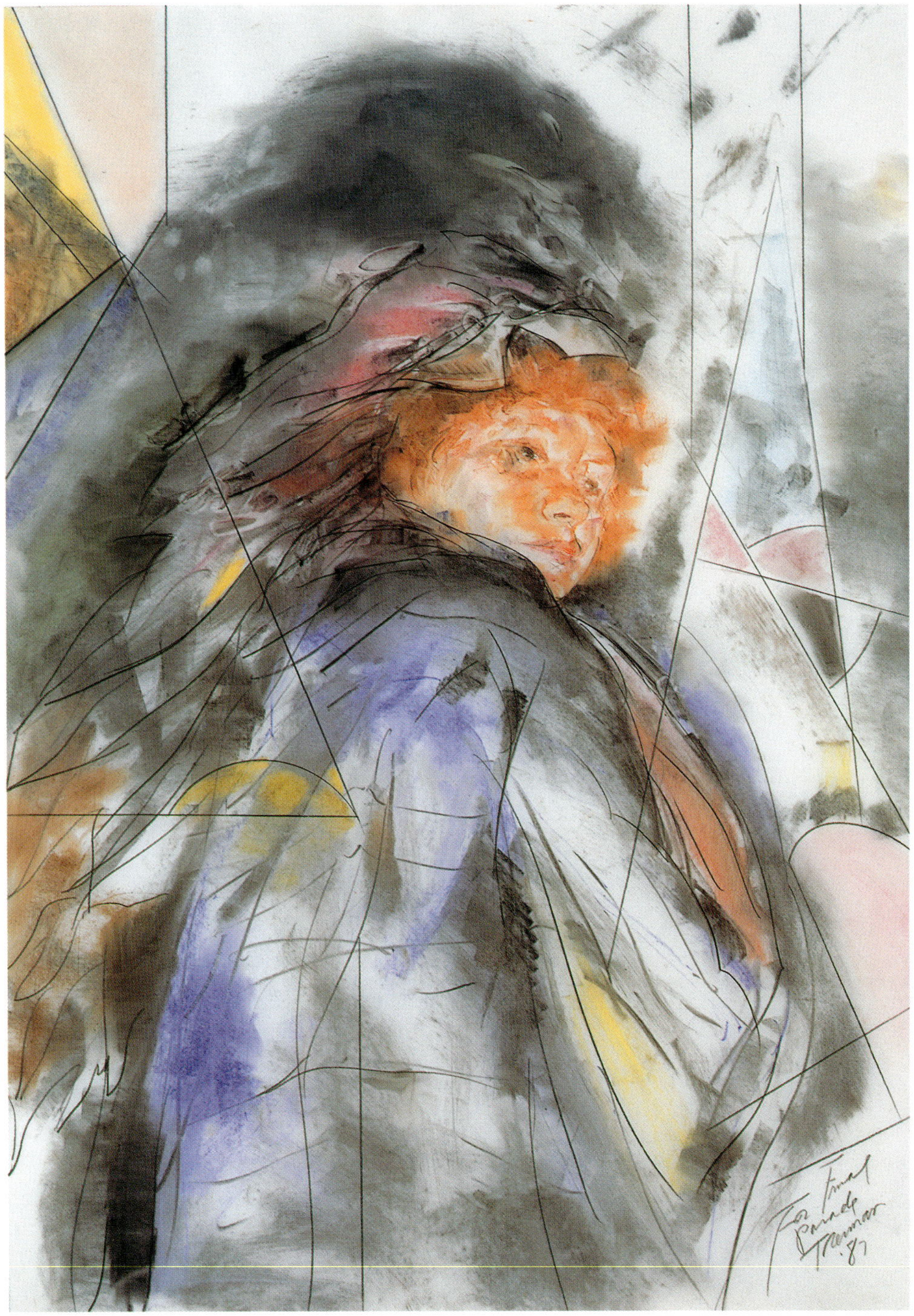

For Final Parade
1987
pastel, pencil, and colored pencil on paper
30 x 20 inches
Collection of ARAMARK, Philadelphia

The Lost Parade
1987
oil on canvas
70 x 70 inches
The Metropolitan Museum of Art, New York,
Anonymous Gift, 1989 (1989.393)

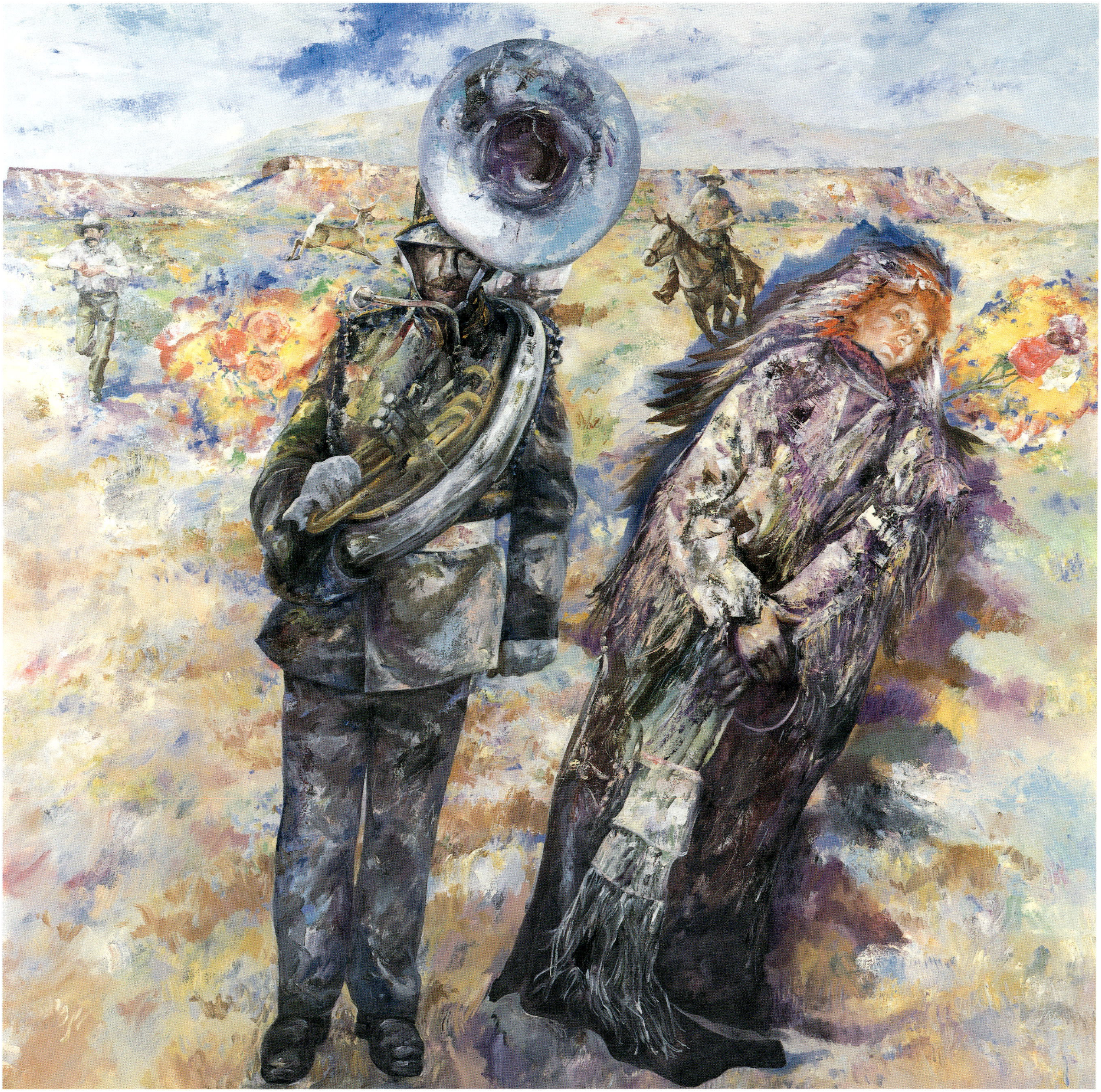

Friends and Strangers
1987
oil on canvas
70 x 70 inches
Pritzker Collection

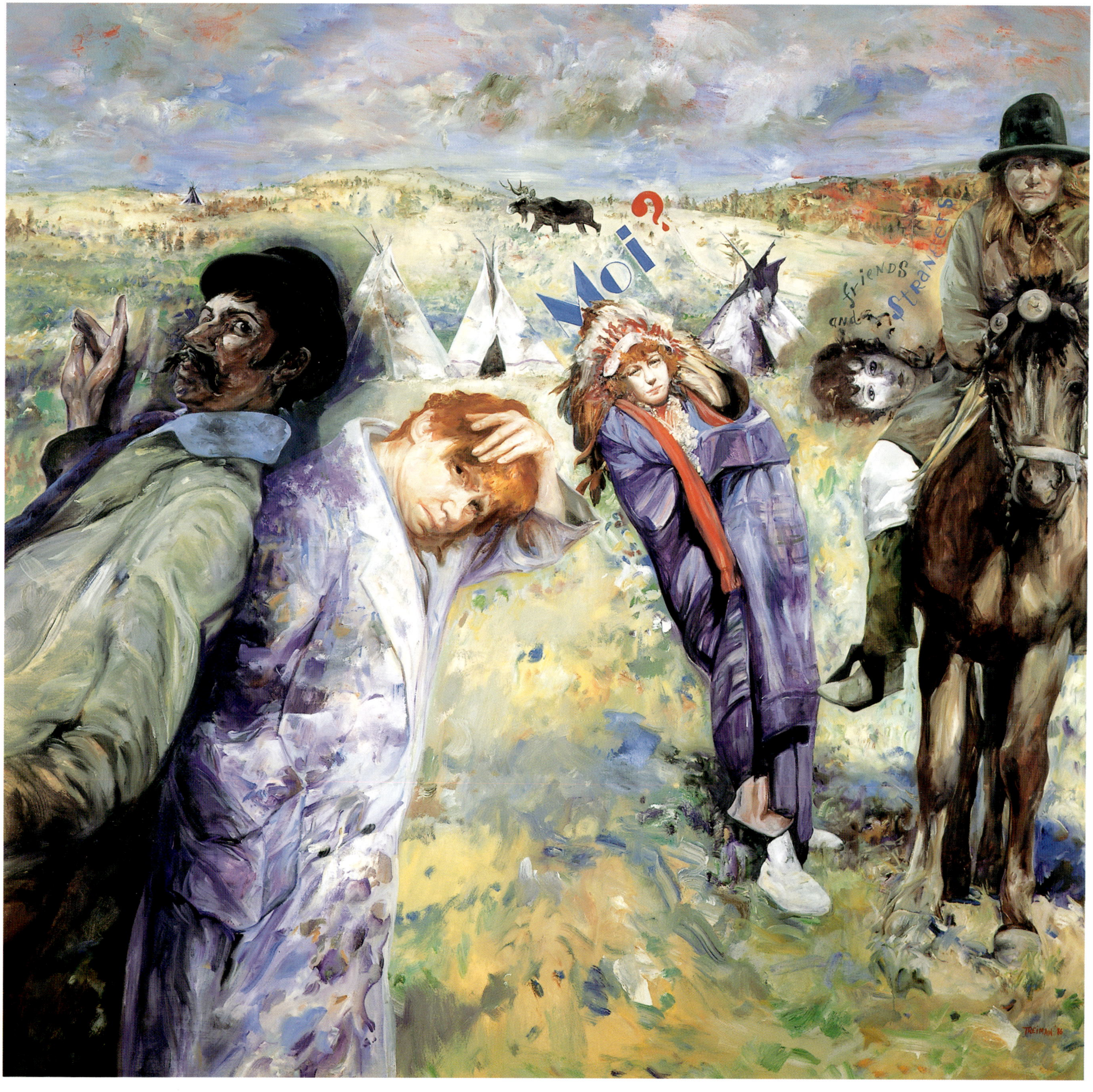
Moi?
friends and Strangers

The Nude Out West
1987
oil on canvas
70 x 70 inches
Lisa and John Pritzker

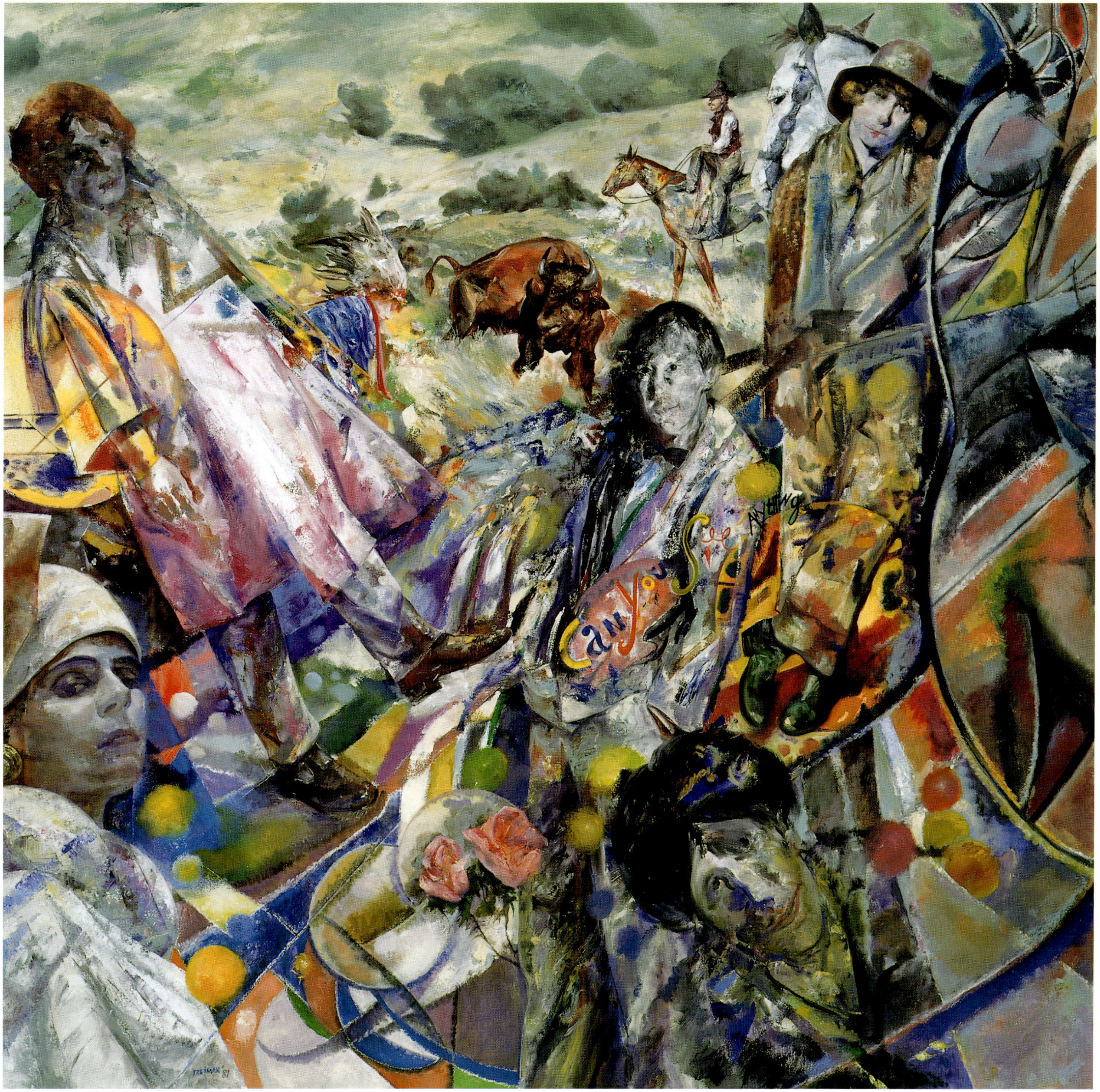
Can You

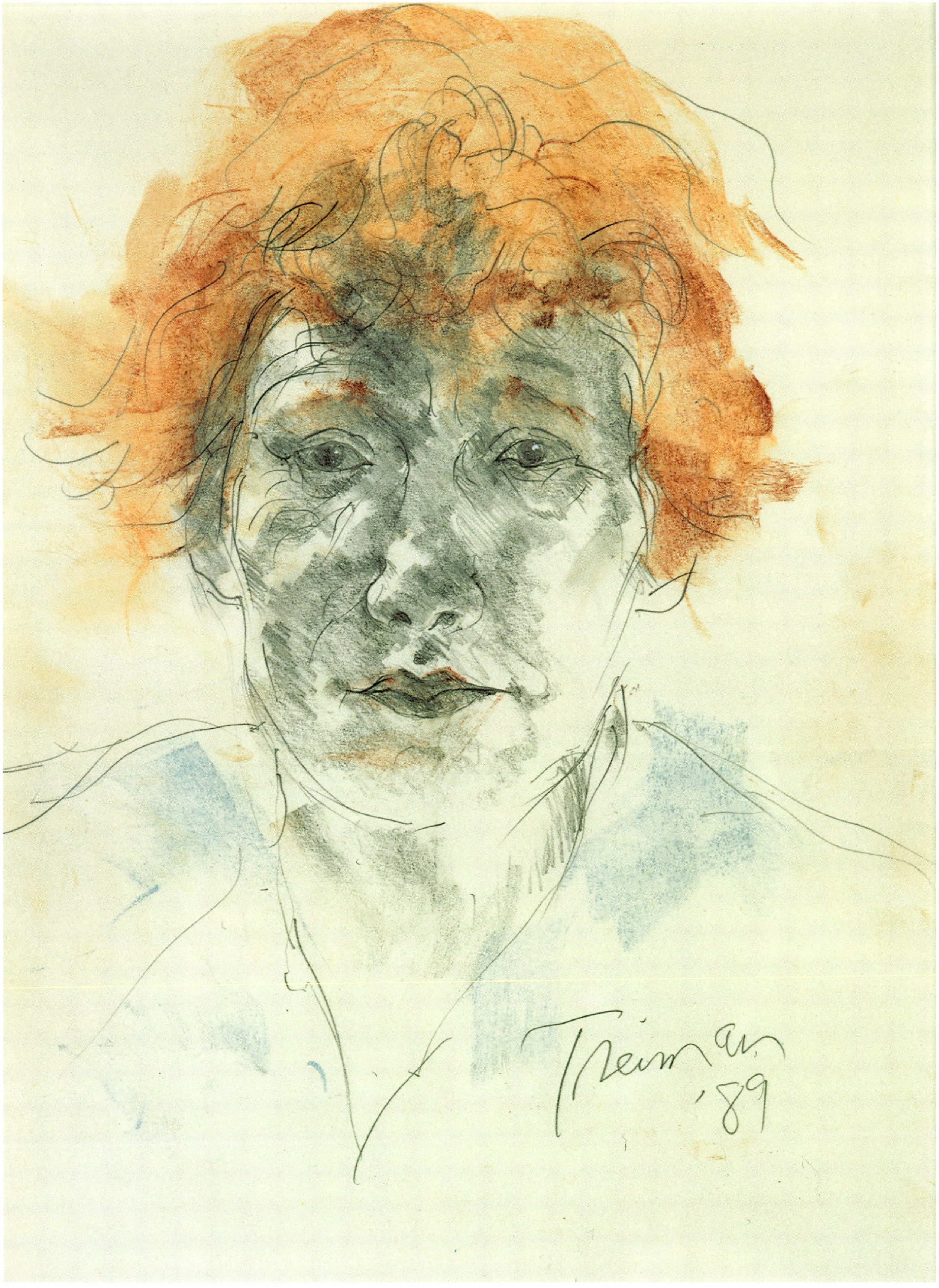

Self-Portrait
1989
charcoal, pencil, and pastel on paper
$11^{3}/_{8} \times 8^{1}/_{2}$ inches
Philip L. Brewer, M.D.

Six Self-Portraits
1987
oil on canvas
$25^{3}/_{4} \times 29$ inches
Private collection

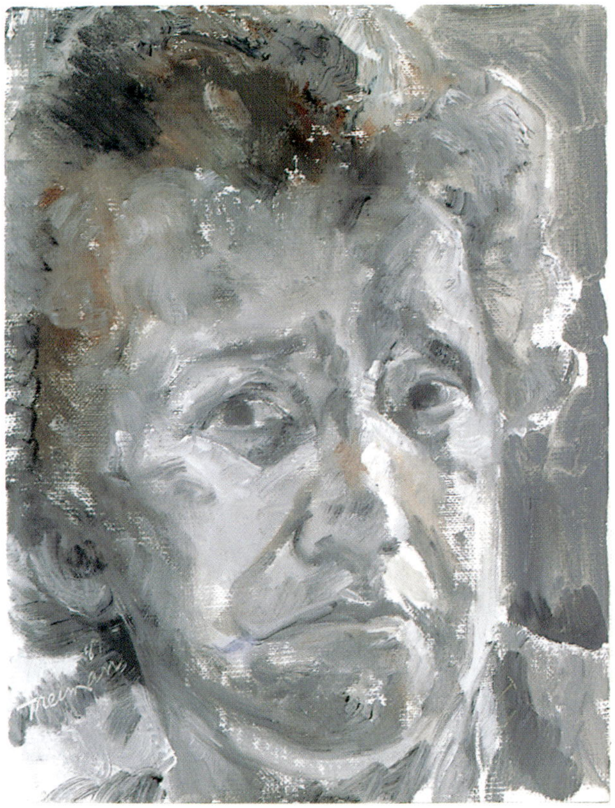

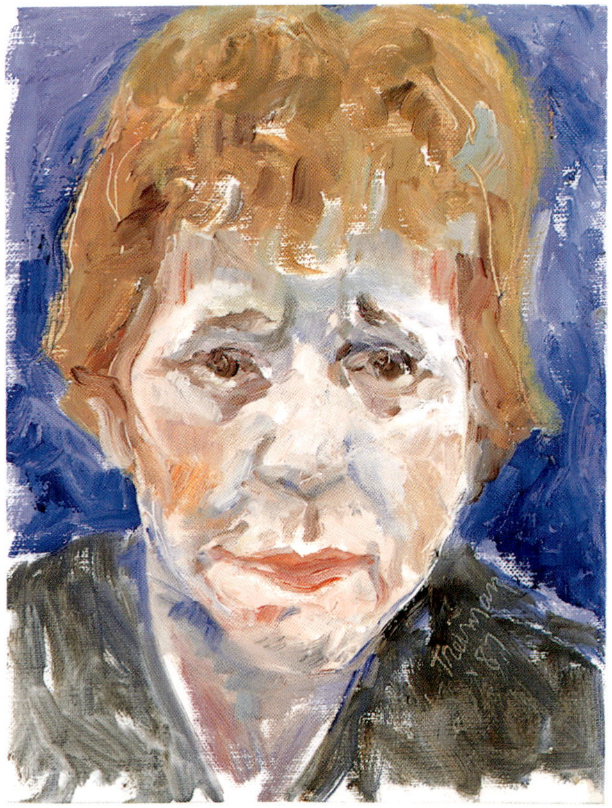

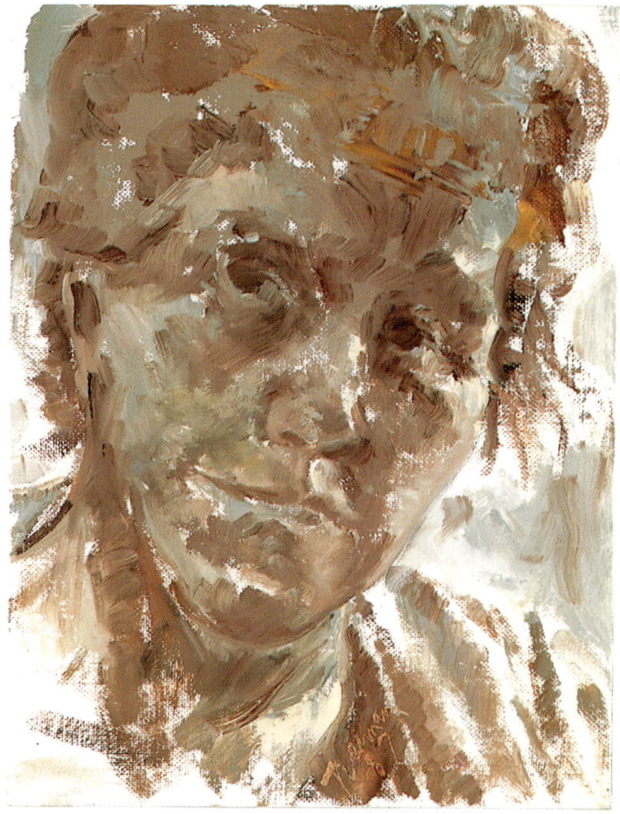

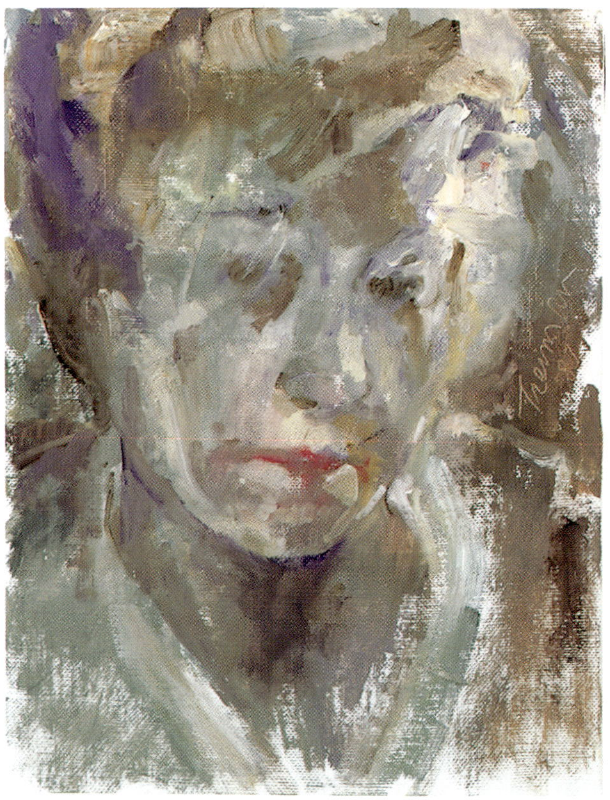

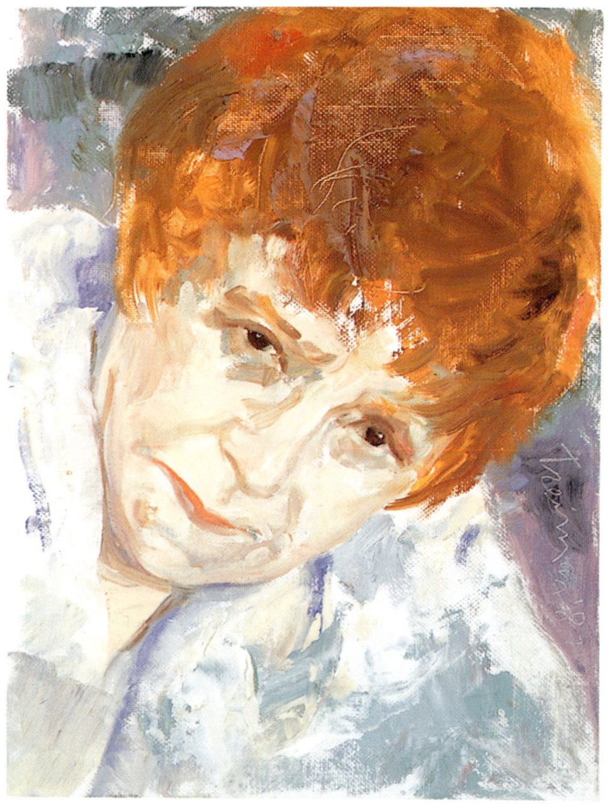

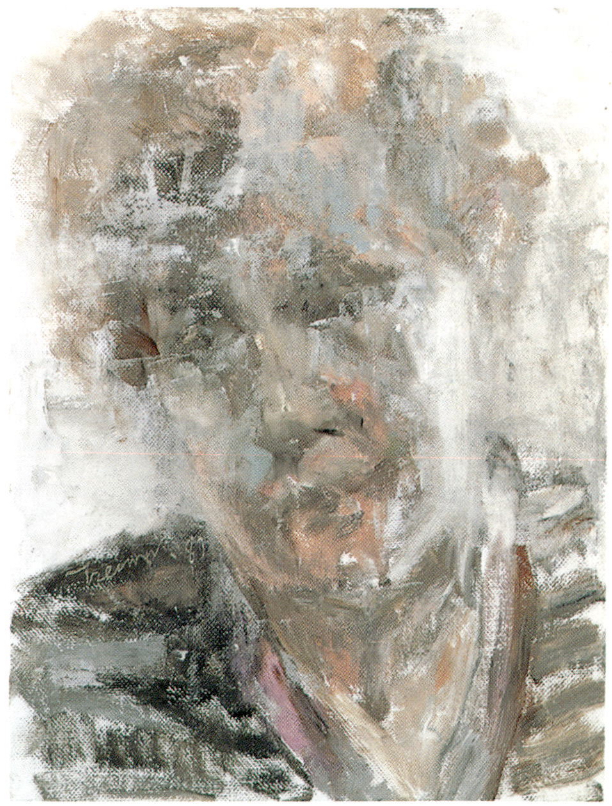

The Witness
1987
oil on canvas
70 × 70 inches
Collection of ARAMARK, Philadelphia

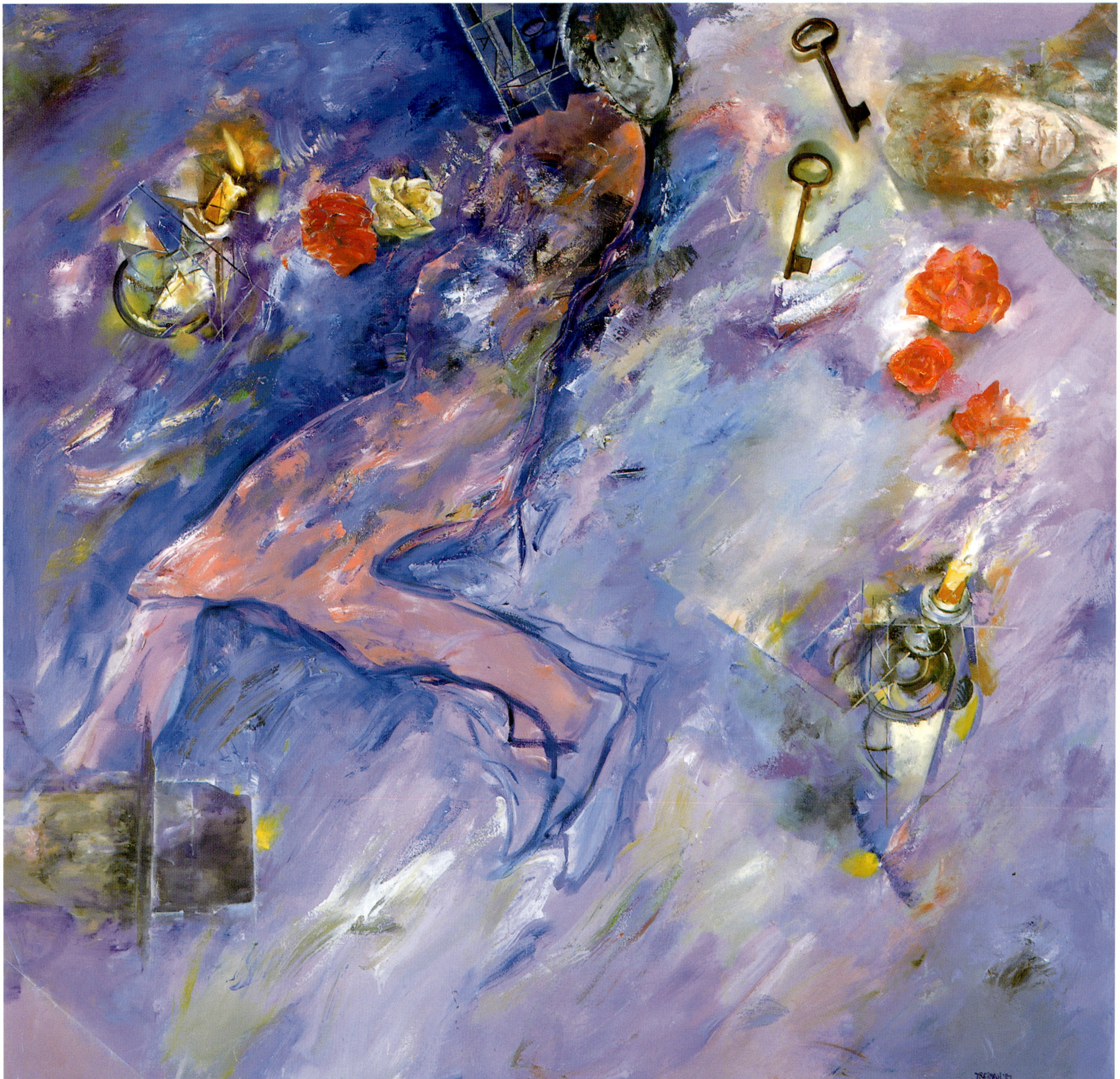

Uphill
1988
oil on canvas
70 × 70 inches
Collection Donald M. Treiman,
Pacific Palisades, California

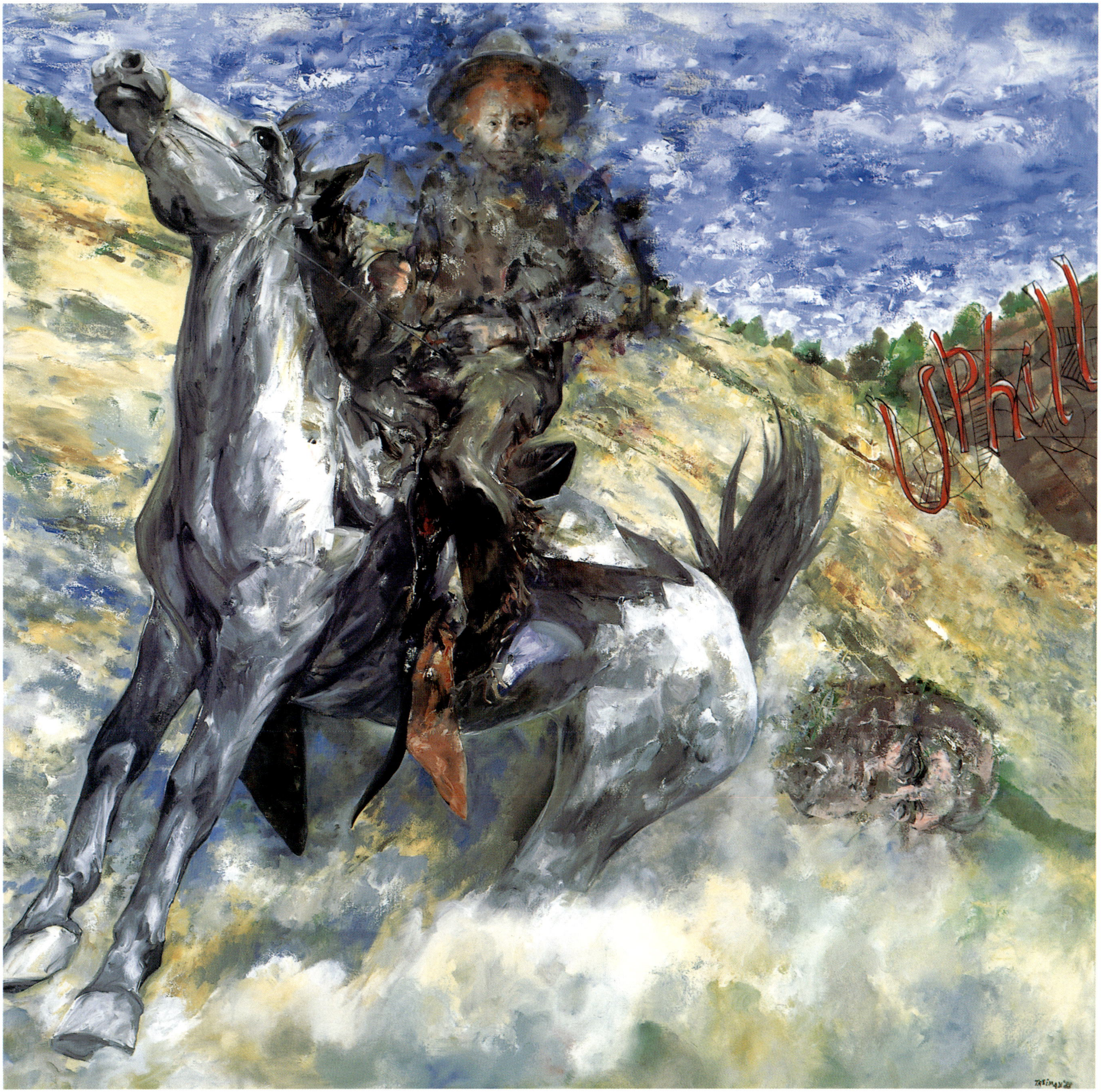
UPhill

Camouflage
1989
oil on canvas
70 x 70 inches
Collection Donald M. Treiman,
Pacific Palisades, California

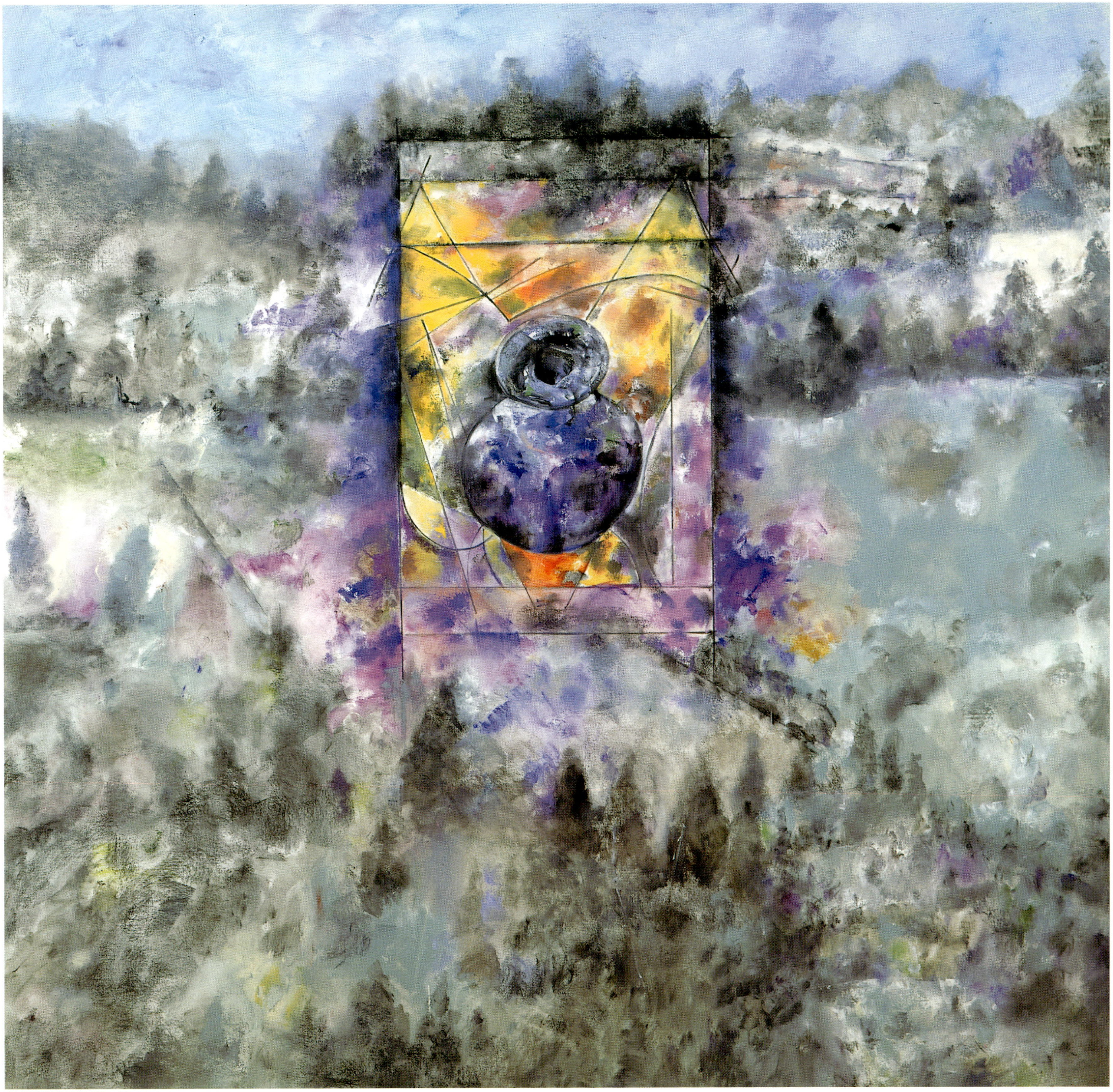

Much Madness
1989
oil on canvas
71 1/2 x 71 1/2 inches
Collection Donald M. Treiman, Pacific Palisades, California

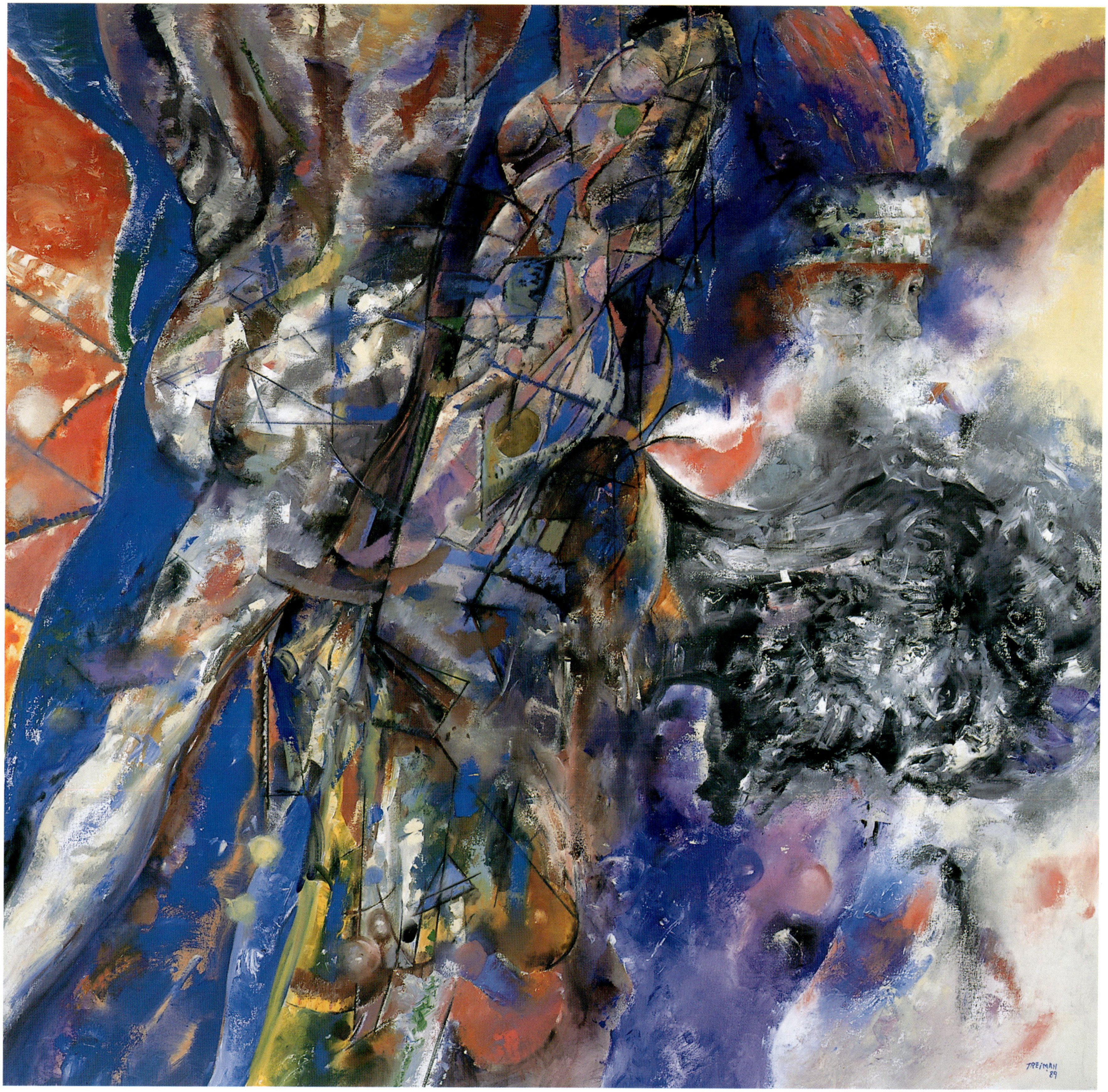
TREISMAN
89

Leaden Echo
1989
oil on canvas
70 x 70 inches
Collection Donald M. Treiman,
Pacific Palisades, California

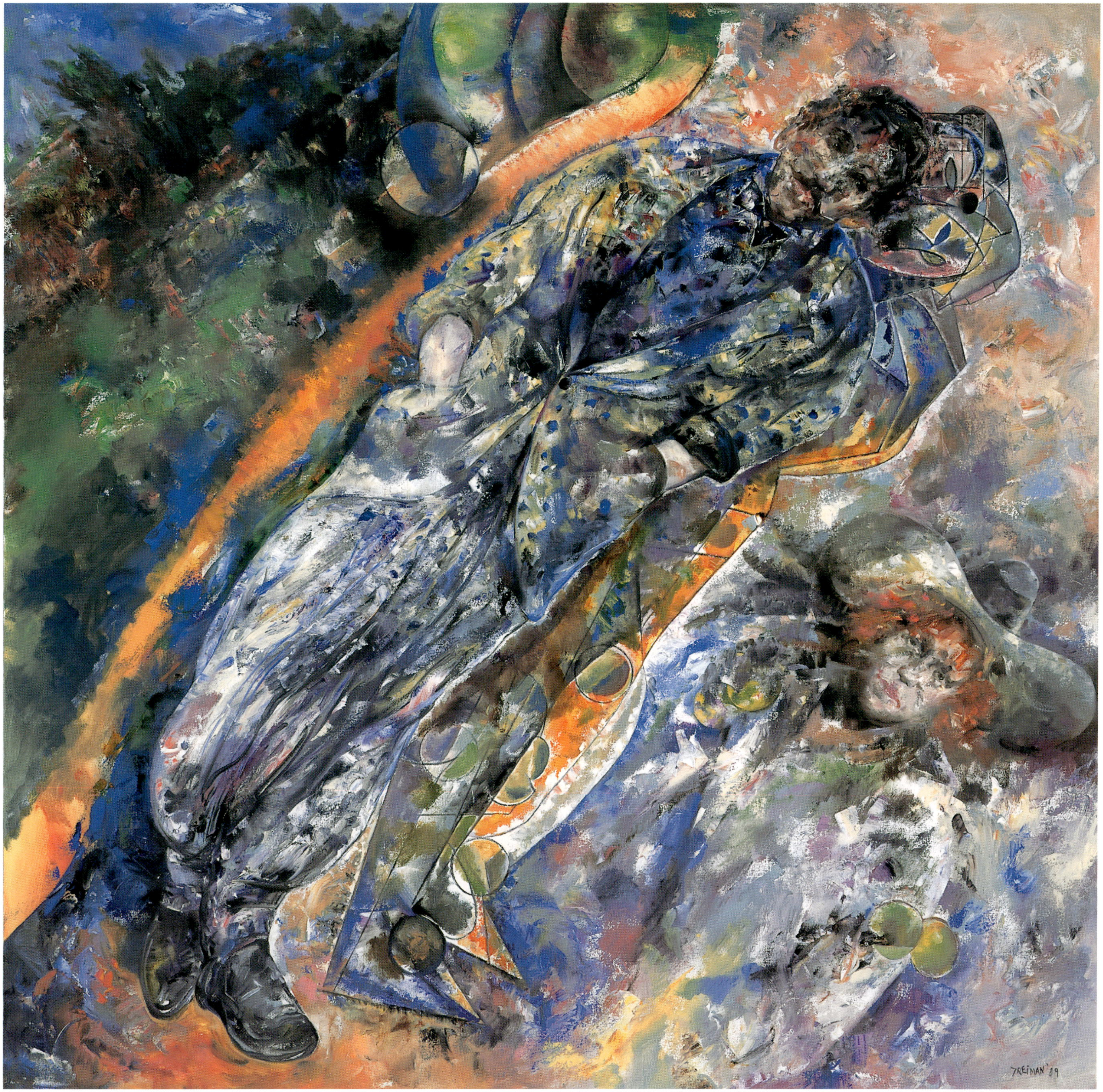
TREIMAN '89

Roses and Vase
1991
pastel on paper
14 x 11 inches
Collection of Kirby and Priscilla Smith

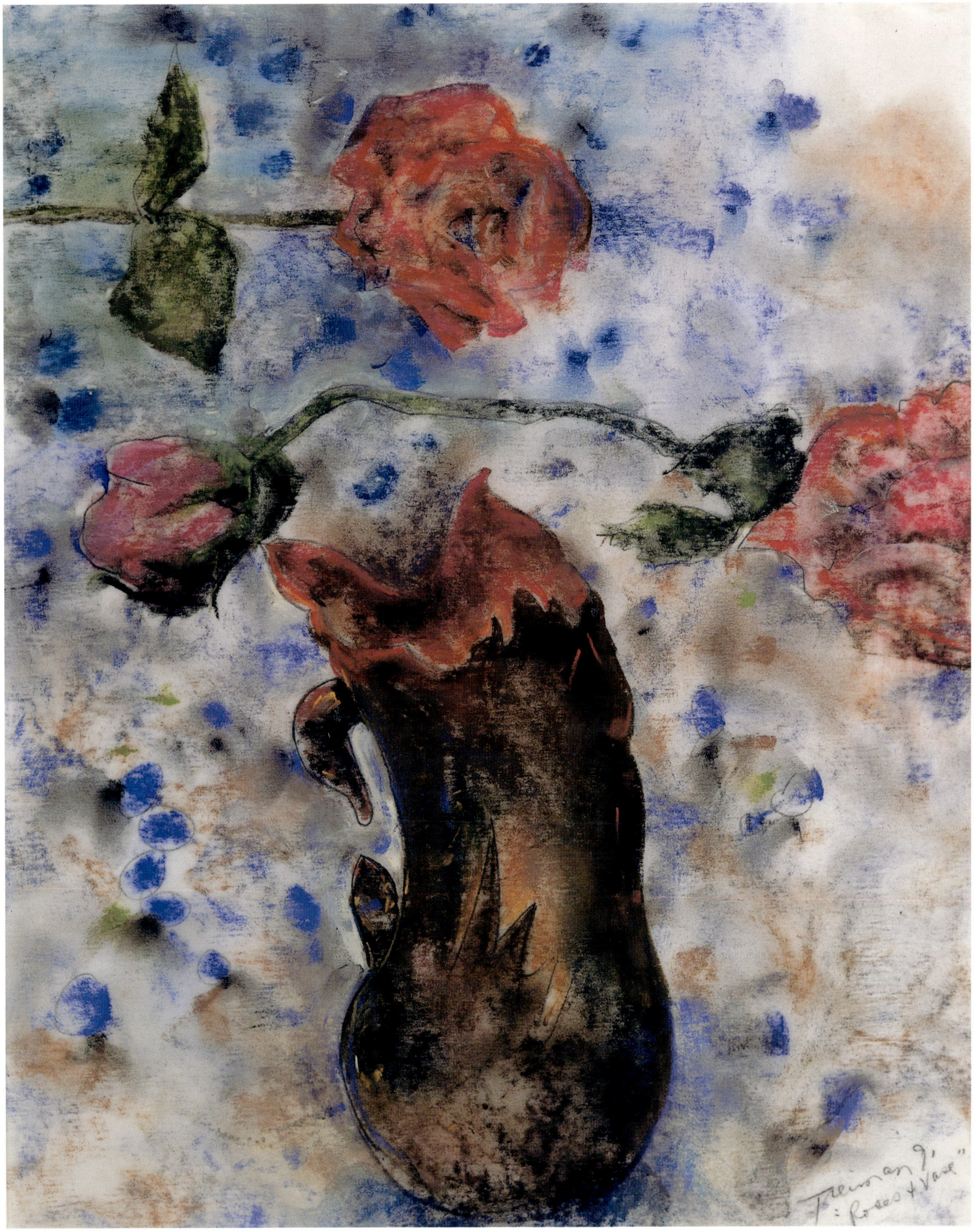

Indian Self-Portrait
1990
pastel on paper
24 x 19 inches
Mr. and Mrs. Joseph Niciforo

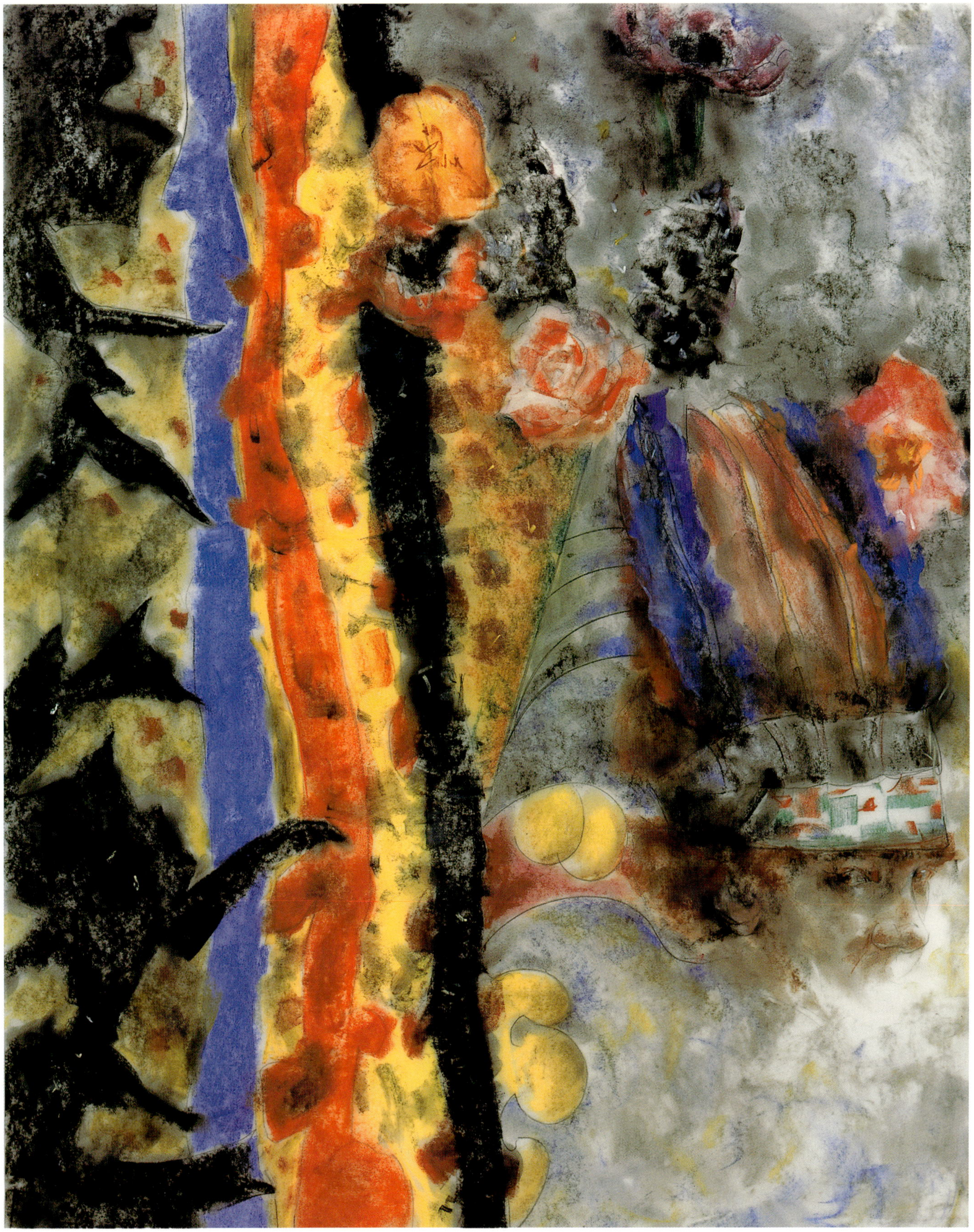

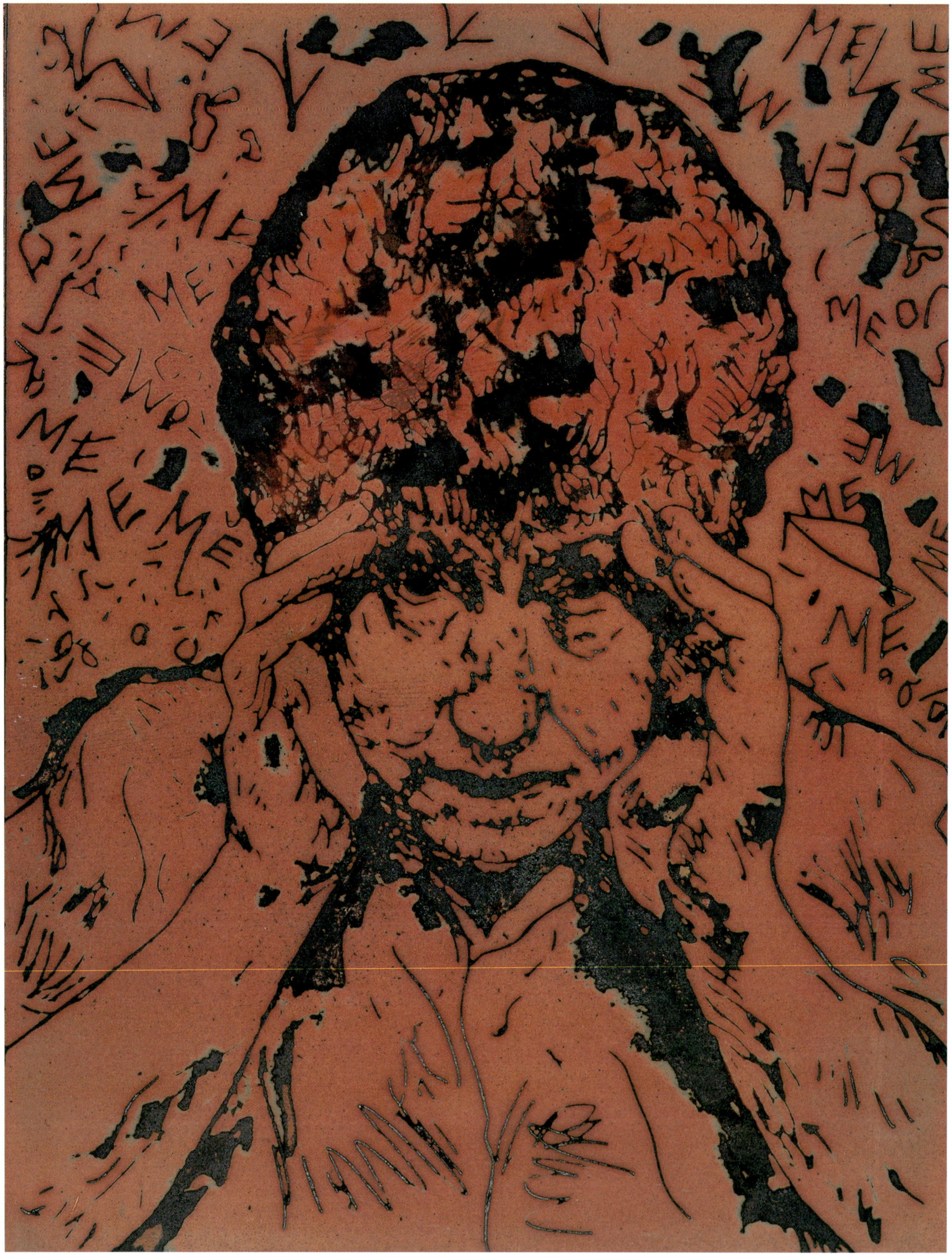

Self-Portrait
n.d.
enamel on copper etching plate
12 x 9 inches
Courtesy Schmidt Bingham Gallery, New York

CHRONOLOGY

1922 May 29, born in Evanston, Illinois, to René and Rose Wahl, the youngest of three children

1929 Summer, travels to Europe

1939–41 Attends Stephens College, Columbia, Missouri, earns Associate in Arts

1941–43 Attends State University of Iowa, earns B.F.A.

1943 Graduate Fellowship, State University of Iowa

1943–46 Works in Chicago at publishing companies

1945 Marries Kenneth Treiman

1950 Son, Donald M., is born

1955 Summer, travels to Paris and Italy

1955–59 Teaches at Winnetka, Illinois, Community House

1960 Moves with family to Los Angeles

1961 Teaches at University of California, Los Angeles

1964 Summer, travels to Middle East

1967 Travels to Europe; lectures at University of California, Los Angeles

1968 Visiting Professor, Art Center School, Los Angeles; travels to Europe

1969 Travels to Europe; Visiting Professor, San Fernando State University; Visiting Lecturer, University of California, Los Angeles (1969–70)

1971 Visiting Professor, California State University, Northridge

1977 Visiting Professor, California State University, Long Beach

1983 November, diagnosed with lung cancer

1991 June 2, dies in Los Angeles

AWARDS

1940 Deering Award, Stephens College, Columbia, Missouri

1947 Louis Comfort Tiffany Foundation Fellowship

1948 Old Northwest Territory Prize, Illinois State Museum, Springfield

Purchase Prize, Denver Art Museum

1949 Armstrong Prize, The Art Institute of Chicago

1950 Bartels Prize, The Art Institute of Chicago

First Prize, Artists of Chicago and Vicinity, The Art Institute of Chicago

1951 Logan Prize and Purchase, The Art Institute of Chicago

1953 Pauline Palmer Prize, The Art Institute of Chicago

Festival of Art Exhibition Prize, Highland Park, Illinois

Magnificent Mile Exhibition Prize, Chicago

1955 Tupperware Art Fund Fellowship

1959 Martin B. Cahn Prize, Sixty-second Annual American Exhibition, Painting and Sculpture, The Art Institute of Chicago

Sarasota (Florida) American Painting Exhibition Award

1960 Martin B. Cahn Prize, Sixty-third Annual American Exhibition, Painting and Sculpture, The Art Institute of Chicago

Ford Foundation Purchase Prize

1961 Purchase Prize, American Painting, Ball State University, Muncie, Indiana

Tamarind Lithography Fellowship

1962 La Jolla (California) Museum Prize

Pasadena (California) Museum Prize

1963 All-City Exhibition Prize, Municipal Art Gallery, Barnsdall Park, Los Angeles

Ford Foundation, Artist-in-Residence Grant at Tamarind Lithography Workshop, Los Angeles

1964 All-City Exhibition Prize, Municipal Art Gallery, Barnsdall Park, Los Angeles

Woman of the Year citation from *Who's Who in America*

1965 *Los Angeles Times* Woman of the Year (for Art)

All-City Exhibition Prize, Municipal Art Gallery, Barnsdall Park, Los Angeles

1972 Purchase Prize, Long Beach (California) Museum of Art

1985 Honoree, National Women's Caucus for Art Conference, Outstanding Achievement in the Visual Arts, Los Angeles

1987 Nominated, American Institute of Arts and Letters

1989–90 National Endowment for the Arts—Visual Arts Fellowship Grant

1990 Elected to National Academy of Design, New York

1991 Woman of the Year Award, Women's Committee of the Palm Springs Desert Museum, California

SOLO EXHIBITIONS

(* denotes publication of an exhibition catalogue or brochure)

1942 Paul Theobald Gallery, Chicago

1945 John Snowden Gallery, Chicago

1947 Chicago Room, The Art Institute of Chicago

North Shore Country Day School, Winnetka, Illinois

1950 Edwin Hewitt Gallery, New York

Fairweather-Garnett Gallery, Evanston, Illinois

1952 Palmer House Galleries, Chicago

1953 Elizabeth Nelson Gallery, Chicago

Glencoe Library, Glencoe, Illinois

1955 Charles Feingarten Gallery, Chicago*

Cliff Dwellers' Club, Chicago

Fairweather Hardin Gallery, Chicago

1958 Fairweather Hardin Gallery, Chicago

1960 Willard Gallery, New York*

1961 Felix Landau Gallery, Los Angeles*

1962 Fairweather Hardin Gallery, Chicago

1963 Forum Gallery, New York*

1964 Fairweather Hardin Gallery, Chicago*

Felix Landau Gallery, Los Angeles*

1966 Forum Gallery, New York*

1969 Adele Bednarz Gallery, Los Angeles

1970 Forum Gallery, New York

1971 Adele Bednarz Gallery, Los Angeles

Forum Gallery, New York

1972 Paintings, 1961–1972, traveling exhibition: La Jolla Museum of Contemporary Art, California; Fairweather Hardin Gallery, Chicago; Telfair Academy of Arts and Sciences, Savannah, Georgia*

1973 Fairweather Hardin Gallery, Chicago

1974 Joyce Treiman: Portraits and Gardens, Adele Bednarz Gallery, Los Angeles

1975 Forum Gallery, New York

1976 Adele Bednarz Gallery, Los Angeles

1977 Joyce Treiman: The Model in the Studio, traveling exhibition: Palos Verdes Art Center; University of California, Santa Cruz; Malone Art Gallery, Loyola Marymount University, Los Angeles; California State University, Long Beach*

1978 James Willis Gallery, San Francisco

Joyce Treiman Retrospective, 1947–1977, Los Angeles Municipal Art Gallery, Barnsdall Park; James Willis Gallery, San Francisco; Fairweather Hardin Gallery, Chicago; Tortue Gallery, Santa Monica, California*

1979 Drawings, The Art Institute of Chicago*

Thirty Monotypes, The Grunwald Center of the Graphic Arts, University of California, Los Angeles*

Recent Paintings, Tortue Gallery, Santa Monica, California

1981 Forum Gallery, New York*

Tortue Gallery, Santa Monica, California

1982 French Journal, Fairweather Hardin Gallery, Chicago

Joyce Treiman, Pierce College Art Gallery, Woodland Hills, California

Monotypes by Joyce Treiman, Portland Art Museum, Oregon

Self-Portraits, California State University, San Jose

1983 Recent Paintings, Tortue Gallery, Santa Monica, California*

1984 Fairweather Hardin Gallery, Chicago

Tortue Gallery, Santa Monica, California

1985 Drawings, Santa Barbara Museum of Art, California

1986 Beyond Observation, Schmidt Bingham Gallery, New York

Fairweather Hardin Gallery, Chicago

Tortue Gallery, Santa Monica, California

1988 Joyce Treiman: Friends and Strangers, a Retrospective, traveling exhibition: Fisher Gallery, University of Southern California, Los Angeles; Memorial Art Gallery of the University of Rochester, New York; Oregon Art Institute, Portland; with accompanying shows at Tortue Gallery, Santa Monica, California; Schmidt Bingham Gallery, New York; Fairweather Hardin Gallery, Chicago*

1989 Paintings and Related Drawings, Tortue Gallery, Santa Monica, California

1990 The Artists Series: Monotype Portraits of Eight American Painters, traveling exhibition: Davis Art Gallery, Columbia, Missouri; Santa Barbara Museum of Art, California; The Arkansas Arts Center, Little Rock; Fresno Art Museum, California

Schmidt Bingham Gallery, New York

1991 Fairweather Hardin Gallery, Chicago

1992 Joyce Treiman: Echoes, Recent Pastel Drawings, Schmidt Bingham Gallery, New York*

The Last Paintings and a Selection of Unexhibited Works from the 1980s, Tortue Gallery, Santa Monica, California

1993 Joyce Treiman: Drawings, Monotypes and Prints, 1962–1989, traveling exhibition: Schmidt Bingham Gallery, New York; John Almquist Gallery, North Shore Country Day School, Winnetka, Illinois; Davis Art Gallery, Stephens College, Columbia, Missouri

Eye Contact, Schmidt Bingham Gallery, New York

1994 A Survey of Works on Paper, 1960–1990, Tortue Gallery, Santa Monica, California

1996 Louis Stern Fine Arts, Los Angeles

GROUP EXHIBITIONS

(* denotes publication of an exhibition catalogue)

1943 **The Forty-ninth Western Annual**, Denver Art Museum

1945 **The Forty-ninth Annual Exhibition by Artists of Chicago and Vicinity**, The Art Institute of Chicago*

1946 **American Biennial**, Virginia Museum of Fine Arts, Richmond

The Fiftieth Annual Exhibition by Artists of Chicago and Vicinity, The Art Institute of Chicago*

Fifty-seventh Annual American Exhibition, Water Colors, and Drawings, The Art Institute of Chicago*

1947 **The Fifty-first Annual Exhibition by Artists of Chicago and Vicinity**, The Art Institute of Chicago*

Seventh Annual Exhibition by the Society of Contemporary American Art, The Art Institute of Chicago*

1948 **Contemporary American Paintings**, Virginia Museum of Fine Arts, Richmond*

The Fifty-fourth Western Annual, Denver Art Museum

The Fifty-second Annual Exhibition by Artists of Chicago and Vicinity, The Art Institute of Chicago*

Paintings by Chicago Artists, Chicago Galleries

Second Old Northwest Territory Art Exhibition, Illinois State Fair, Springfield*

1949 **The Fifty-third Annual Exhibition by Artists of Chicago and Vicinity**, The Art Institute of Chicago*

North Mississippi Valley Artists Fifth Annual, Illinois State Museum, Springfield*

Third Old Northwest Territory Art Exhibition, Illinois State Fair, Springfield

1950 **Contemporary American Painting and Sculpture**, Krannert Art Museum, University of Illinois, Urbana*

The Fifty-fourth Annual Exhibition by Artists of Chicago and Vicinity, The Art Institute of Chicago*

Young American Artists, The Metropolitan Museum of Art, New York*

1951 **Contemporary American Painting and Sculpture**, Krannert Art Museum, University of Illinois, Urbana*

Contemporary Art in the United States, Worcester Art Museum, Massachusetts

Contemporary Painting in the United States, 1951 Annual Exhibition, Los Angeles County Museum of Art*

Eleventh Annual Exhibition by the Society of Contemporary American Art, The Art Institute of Chicago

The Fifty-fifth Annual Exhibition by Artists of Chicago and Vicinity, The Art Institute of Chicago*

1951 Annual Exhibition, Milwaukee Art Institute

1951 Annual Exhibition of Contemporary American Painting, Whitney Museum of American Art, New York*

One-Hundred-Twenty-sixth American Exhibition, National Academy of Design, New York*

Sixtieth Annual American Exhibition, Painting and Sculpture, The Art Institute of Chicago*

Texas Wildcat, Fort Worth Art Museum*

Watkins Gallery, Washington, D.C.

Young Painters, U.S.A., circulated by the American Federation of Arts: College of Wooster, Wooster, Ohio; Art Alliance of Altoona, Pennsylvania; University of Mississippi, University; Jacksonville Arts Club, Florida; Tulane University, Newcomb College, New Orleans; Bates College, Lewiston, Maine; Carleton College, Northfield, Minnesota; University of North Carolina, Chapel Hill

1952 **American Abstract Art**, The Detroit Institute of Arts

Contemporary American Painting and Sculpture, Krannert Art Museum, University of Illinois, Urbana*

The Fifty-sixth Annual Exhibition by Artists of Chicago and Vicinity, The Art Institute of Chicago*

1952 Annual Exhibition of Contemporary American Painting, Whitney Museum of American Art, New York*

1953 **Contemporary American Painting**, John Herron Art Museum, Indianapolis

Contemporary Drawings, Wisconsin Union Gallery, University of Wisconsin, Madison*

The Fifty-seventh Annual Exhibition by Artists of Chicago and Vicinity, The Art Institute of Chicago*

1953 Annual Exhibition of Contemporary American Painting, Whitney Museum of American Art, New York*

North Mississippi Valley Artists Fifth Annual, Illinois State Museum, Springfield

Recent Accessions, Colorado Springs Fine Arts Center

1954 **Artists of Chicago**, Downtown Gallery, New York*

The Fifty-eighth Annual Exhibition by Artists of Chicago and Vicinity, The Art Institute of Chicago*

Midwest Painters, Wisconsin Union Gallery, University of Wisconsin, Madison

Religious Art, University of Chicago

Sixty-first Annual American Exhibition, Painting and Sculpture, The Art Institute of Chicago*

Twelfth National Exhibition of Prints, Library of Congress, Washington, D.C.*

Young Collectors, Dallas Museum of Art

1955 **The Fifty-ninth Annual Exhibition by Artists of Chicago and Vicinity**, The Art Institute of Chicago*

1955 Pittsburgh International Exhibition of Contemporary Art, Carnegie Institute*

Purchase Award Show, Stanford University, Stanford, California

The Sixty-first Western Annual, Denver Art Museum

1956 **The Sixty-second Annual American Exhibition, Painting and Sculpture**, The Art Institute of Chicago*

Contemporary American Painting and Sculpture, Krannert Art Museum, University of Illinois, Urbana*

Painter's Panorama, traveling exhibition: Dayton Art Institute, Ohio; Tupperware Gallery, Orlando, Florida*

Sixteenth Annual Exhibition by the Society of Contemporary American Art, The Art Institute of Chicago

The Sixtieth Annual Exhibition by Artists of Chicago and Vicinity, The Art Institute of Chicago*

Young Painters U.S.A., Cornell University, Ithaca, New York

1957 **Carnegie International**, Carnegie Institute, Pittsburgh

Contemporary American Painting and Sculpture, Krannert Art Museum, University of Illinois, Urbana*

1957 Chicago Artists, sponsored by the Art Institute of Chicago, at the Chicago Navy Pier

The Sixty-first Annual Exhibition by Artists of Chicago and Vicinity, The Art Institute of Chicago*

The Sixty-second Annual American Exhibition, Paintings and Sculpture, The Art Institute of Chicago*

1958 **Fifty-three Paintings from Chicago**, organized by the Art Institute of Chicago for Musée d'Art, Limoges

The One-Hundred-Fifty-third Annual Exhibition of American Painting and Sculpture, traveling exhibition: Pennsylvania Academy of the Fine Arts, Philadelphia; The Detroit Institute of Arts*

The Sixty-fourth Western Annual, Denver Art Museum

The Sixty-second Annual Exhibition by Artists of Chicago and Vicinity, The Art Institute of Chicago*

Young America, traveling exhibition: Whitney Museum of American Art, New York; Institute of Contemporary Art, Boston*

1959 **Annual National Exhibition of Painting and Sculpture**, Sarasota Art Association, Ringling Museum of Art, Sarasota, Florida*

California Art from American Museums, Lytton Center of the Visual Arts, Los Angeles

A Corporation Collects, circulated by the American Federation of Arts*

National Drawing Show, San Francisco Museum of Art

The New Chicago Decade, 1950–60: An Exhibition of Painting and Sculpture by Fourteen Artists Residing in Chicago and Vicinity, Lake Forest College, Illinois

Second Columbia Painting Biennial, Columbia Museum of Art, South Carolina

The Sixty-second Annual Exhibition by Artists of Chicago and Vicinity, The Art Institute of Chicago*

1960 **1960 Annual Exhibition of Contemporary American Painting**, Whitney Museum of American Art, New York

Ninth Annual Exhibition, Boston Arts Festival

The Sixty-sixth Western Annual, Denver Art Museum

The Sixty-third American Exhibition of Painting and Sculpture, The Art Institute of Chicago*

1961 **American Drawings**, Ball State College, Muncie, Indiana

Annual California Painting and Sculpture Exhibition, Art Center, La Jolla, California*

Contemporary American Painting and Sculpture, Krannert Art Museum, University of Illinois, Urbana*

1961 Annual Exhibition of Contemporary American Painting, Whitney Museum of American Art, New York*

1962 **Fifty California Artists**, traveling exhibition organized by the San Francisco Museum of Art for the Whitney Museum of American Art, New York; Walker Art Center, Minneapolis; Albright-Knox Art Gallery, Buffalo, New York; Des Moines Art Center, Iowa*

Fourth National Exhibition of Contemporary American Art, Oklahoma Art Center, Oklahoma City*

Lithographs from the Tamarind Workshop, traveling exhibition: The Grunwald Center for the Graphic Arts, University of California, Los Angeles; The Art Institute of Chicago*

Pasadena Third Biennial National Print Exhibition, Pasadena Art Museum, California*

Recent Painting U.S.A.: The Figure, traveling exhibition: The Museum of Modern Art, New York; Columbus Gallery of Fine Arts, Ohio; Colorado Springs Fine Arts Center; Baltimore Museum of Art; City Art Museum of St. Louis; San Francisco Museum of Art; Walker Art Center, Minneapolis*

Third National Exhibition: Ultimate Concerns, Prints and Drawings, Ohio University Gallery, Athens

1963 **Contemporary American Painting and Sculpture**, Krannert Art Museum, University of Illinois, Urbana*

Eight, Gallery One, Fine Arts Building, San Fernando Valley State College, Northridge, California

First California Small Images Exhibition, California State College, Los Angeles

1963 Eleventh Annual All-City Outdoor Art Festival, Barnsdall Park, Los Angeles

1964 **American Art**, The Art Institute of Chicago

Twelfth Annual All-City Outdoor Art Festival, Barnsdall Park, Los Angeles

Twenty-fourth Annual Exhibition by the Society of Contemporary American Art, The Art Institute of Chicago

1965 **Above and Below**, Terrain Gallery, New York

Artists' Artists, Lytton Center of the Visual Arts, Los Angeles

Contemporary American Painting and Sculpture, Krannert Art Museum, University of Illinois, Urbana*

Drawing Show, California State College, Northridge

Far West Regional Exhibition of Art across America, San Francisco Museum of Art*

First Annual Exhibition of Lithography, Florida State University, Tallahassee*

Inaugural Exhibition, University Art Gallery, San Jose State University, California

International Art Festival, Westwood Art Association, Century City, Los Angeles*

The Janus Impulse, 1965 Fine Arts Festival Exhibition, California State College, Los Angeles

National Exhibit of Small Paintings, Purdue University, Purdue, Indiana

New York World's Fair, Forum Gallery exhibition at the Transportation and Travel Pavilion, New York*

Nuovarte, Penelope Galleria d'Arte Contemporanea, Rome*

Selections, Felix Landau Gallery, Los Angeles

The Seventieth Western Annual, Denver Art Museum*

Some Aspects of California Painting and Sculpture, La Jolla Museum of Art, California*

Three-Man Drawing Show, Forum Gallery, New York

1966 **Art in Chicago Business**, Fairweather Hardin Gallery, Chicago*

Contemporary Art: The Human Image, Lang Art Gallery, Scripps College, Claremont, California*

First California Small Images Exhibition, California State College, Los Angeles

Seven California Figurative Artists, Palm Springs Desert Museum, California*

1967 **Artists' Artists**, Lytton Center of the Visual Arts, Los Angeles

Art Symposium and National Lithography Exhibition, Florida State University Art Gallery, Tallahassee

California Art from American Museums, Lytton Center of the Visual Arts, Los Angeles

Contemporary American Painting and Sculpture, Krannert Art Museum, University of Illinois, Urbana*

Fourth Annual Selected Paintings Exhibition, Washburn University, Topeka, Kansas

New Acquisitions, University of California, Los Angeles

Ten California Painters, Felix Landau Gallery, Los Angeles

1968 **Mainstreams '68: The First Annual Marietta College International Competitive Exhibition for Painting and Sculpture**, Grover M. Hermann Fine Arts Center, Marietta College, Marietta, Ohio*

Many Mini Things, Lytton Center of the Visual Arts, Los Angeles

Twenty-five California Women of Art, Lytton Center of the Visual Arts, Los Angeles

1969 **Contemporary American Painting and Sculpture**, Krannert Art Museum, University of Illinois, Urbana*

National Drawing Exhibition, San Francisco Museum of Art

Second Biennial Exhibition of Painting and Drawing, Mt. San Antonio College, Walnut, California*

Tamarind: Homage to Lithography, The Museum of Modern Art, New York*

1970 **Art on Paper**, Adele Bednarz Galleries, Los Angeles

National Exhibition of Small Paintings, Purdue University, Purdue, Indiana*

San Diego—South, San Diego Museum, California

1971 **American Portraits—Old and New**, Long Beach Museum of Art, California*

Contemporary American Painting and Sculpture, Krannert Art Museum, University of Illinois, Urbana*

Continuing Surrealism, La Jolla Museum of Art, California*

1971 Annual Exhibition of Contemporary Painting and Sculpture, Whitney Museum of American Art, New York*

Primera Bienal Americana de Artes Graficas, Museo La Tertulia Cartonde, Cali, Colombia*

1972 **Annual Exhibition**, Long Beach Museum of Art, California

One-Hundred-Forty-seventh Annual Exhibition, National Academy of Design, New York*

1973 Los Angeles Municipal Art Gallery, Barnsdall Park

The Lyric View, Lang Art Gallery, Scripps College, Claremont, California

One-Hundred-Forty-eighth Annual Exhibition, National Academy of Design, New York*

1974 **Contemporary American Painting and Sculpture, 1948–1974**, Krannert Art Museum, University of Illinois, Urbana*

Exhibition of Paintings Eligible for the Childe Hassam Fund Purchase, American Academy and Institute of Arts and Letters, New York

1975 **Exhibition of Paintings Eligible for the Childe Hassam Fund Purchase**, American Academy and Institute of Arts and Letters, New York

Impetus: The Creative Process, Los Angeles Municipal Art Gallery, Barnsdall Park*

Selections from the Collection of Rachel and Allen Weller, Krannert Art Museum, University of Illinois, Urbana*

1976 **Contemporary Monotypes**, Contemporary Graphics Center, Santa Barbara Museum of Art, California*

Exhibition of Paintings Eligible for the Childe Hassam Fund Purchase, American Academy and Institute of Arts and Letters, New York

Visions: Painting and Sculpture by Distinguished Alumni, 1945 to the Present: The School of the Art Institute of Chicago*

1977 **California Figurative Artists**, traveling exhibition: American Academy and Institute of Arts and Letters, New York; Krannert Art Museum, University of Illinois, Urbana; Tortue Gallery, Santa Monica, California*

Contemporary Issues: Works on Paper by Women, The Women's Building, Los Angeles*

Invitational Annual, San Francisco Art Institute*

1978 **Déjà Vu: Masterpiece Updated**, Downey Museum of Art, Downey, California

New American Monotypes, circulated by Smithsonian Institution Traveling Exhibitions Service, Washington, D.C.: Art Gallery, Towson State University, Baltimore, Maryland; John Mariani Gallery Fine Arts Center, University of Northern Colorado, Greeley; Anchorage Historical and Fine Arts Museum, Alaska; The Phillips Collection, Washington, D.C.; Mendel Art Gallery, Saskatoon, Saskatchewan, Canada; University Art Museum, University of Texas at Austin; University of Southern Mississippi, Hattiesburg; Art Gallery, Santa Fe Community College, Gainesville, Florida; Frederick S. Wight Gallery, University of California, Los Angeles*

1979 **American Watercolorists**, Mitchell Museum, Mount Vernon, Illinois*

Newport Harbor Art Museum, Newport Beach, California

One Hundred Artists One Hundred Years: Alumni of the School of The Art Institute of Chicago, The Art Institute of Chicago*

Portraits/1979, Los Angeles Municipal Art Gallery, Barnsdall Park

1980 **American Portrait Drawings**, National Portrait Gallery, Smithsonian Institution, Washington, D.C.*

Master Prints from the Gilkey Collection, Portland Art Museum, Oregon*

1981 **Alternative Realities in Contemporary American Painting**, Katherine Nash Gallery, University of Minnesota, Minneapolis*

Coastal Currents: A California/New York Exhibition, South Texas Art Mobile*

Decade: Los Angeles Painting in the Seventies, Art Center College of Design, Pasadena, California*

Forty Famous Californians, Judith Christian Gallery, New York

Portraits in Miniature, University of Southern California, Los Angeles*

Southern California Artists, 1940–1980, Laguna Beach Museum of Art, California*

Staying Visible, Helen Euphrat Gallery, De Anza College, Cupertino, California

1982 **The Artist as Subject**, Santa Monica College Art Gallery, California

Contemporary Triptychs, Montgomery Gallery, Pomona College, Pomona, California

Drawings by Painters, Long Beach Museum, California*

Los Angeles Art in Nagoya, Nagoya City Museum, Japan

Unique Impressions: The Monotype and Beyond, Malone Art Gallery, Loyola Marymount University, Los Angeles*

1983 **Twentieth-Century Drawings Acquired since 1958**, The Art Institute of Chicago

1984 **Ceci n'est pas le surréalisme: California—Idioms of Surrealism**, Fisher Gallery, University of Southern California, Los Angeles

Professor's Choice, Montgomery Gallery, Pomona College, Pomona, California

Selected Monotypes, traveling exhibition: Smith Andersen Gallery, Palo Alto, California; Santa Cruz Museum, Santa Cruz, California; Sheldon Memorial Art Gallery, Lincoln, Nebraska; Honolulu Academy of Arts; Arizona State University, Tempe*

Ten Los Angeles Artists, Jack Rutberg Fine Arts, Los Angeles

1985 **Black-and-White Drawings from the David Nellis Collection**, traveling exhibition: California State University, Los Angeles; Fine Arts Gallery, Loma Linda University, Loma Linda, California*

The Collector's Show, Arkansas Arts Center, Little Rock

Contemporary Monotypes, Gallery at the Plaza, Security Pacific National Bank, Los Angeles

The Figure in Twentieth-Century American Art: Selections from the Metropolitan Museum of Art, circulated by the American Federation of Arts: Jacksonville Art Museum, Florida; Oklahoma Museum of Art, Oklahoma City; Terra Museum of American Art, Evanston, Illinois; Arkansas Arts Center, Little Rock; Colorado Springs Fine Arts Center; Minnesota Museum of Art, St. Paul*

Sixth Annual Exhibition, Helen Lindhurst Fine Arts Gallery, University of Southern California, Los Angeles

31986 **Drawing: A Classical Continuum**, Los Angeles Municipal Art Gallery, Barnsdall Park

In the Advent of Change, The Fresno Arts Center, California

Kindred Spirits, Los Angeles Municipal Art Gallery, Barnsdall Park

Landscape, Seascape, Cityscape, 1960–1985, traveling exhibition: Contemporary Arts Center, New Orleans; The New York Academy of Art, New York

Looking In Looking Out: Contemporary Portraits by Women Artists, Montgomery Gallery, Pomona College, California

One-Hundred-Sixty-first Annual Exhibition, National Academy of Design, New York*

Through the Eyes of an Artist, Laband Art Gallery, Loyola Marymount University, Los Angeles

1987 **Contemporary Art of Southern California in Taipei**, Taipei Fine Arts Museum, Taiwan

Relationships, Long Beach Museum of Art, California*

A View of Her Own: Images of Women by Women Artists, Print and Drawing Study Room, Grinnell College, Grinnell, Iowa*

1988 **Art of Our Time**, Hadassah, Woodcliff Lake, New Jersey

The Face, Arkansas Arts Center, Little Rock

The Face of the Land, South Alleghenies Museum of Art, Loretto, Pennsylvania

Figuration, General Electric Corporation, Fairfield, Connecticut

Focus on Art, National Council of Jewish Women, Livingston, New Jersey

Oxymorons in Art, Schmidt Bingham Gallery, New York

Twentieth-Century Watercolors: Yesterday and Today, Long Beach Museum of Art, California

1989 **Artists' Artists**, Schmidt Bingham Gallery, New York

Positive I.D., Southern Alleghenies Museum, Loretto, Pennsylvania

1990 **Artists' Artists**, Long Beach Museum of Art, California*

Contemporary Monotypes, Sewall Art Gallery, Rice University, Houston

Twenty-one Years in Santa Monica: Contemporary Landscapes, Tortue Gallery, Santa Monica, California

1991 **The Art of the Print: Rembrandt to Warhol**, Portland Art Museum, Oregon*

California Monoprints, Sewall Art Gallery, Rice University, Houston

Her Story: Narrative Art by Contemporary California Arts, The Oakland Museum, California*

Individual Realists, Sezon Museum, Tokyo National Academy of Design Annual Exhibition, Japan

National Academy of Design One-Hundred-Sixty-sixth Annual Exhibition, National Academy of Design, New York

1992 **Drawings**, Louis Newman Galleries, Beverly Hills, California

Transforming the Western Image, traveling exhibition: Palm Springs Desert Museum, California; Boise Art Museum, Idaho; Tucson Museum of Art, Arizona; The Rockwell Museum, Corning, New York

1993 **The Collector's Show**, Arkansas Arts Center, Little Rock

Intersections: Art and Play, Armory Center for the Arts, Pasadena, California

Persistence of the Human Image, Fresno City College, California

1994 **The Collector's Show**, Arkansas Arts Center, Little Rock

Generations of Mentors, traveling exhibition: The National Museum of Women in the Arts, Washington, D.C.; Fresno Metropolitan Museum, California; Mount St. Mary's College Gallery, Los Angeles

1996 **Are You Blue? Epiphany in a Primary Color**, Schmidt Bingham Gallery, New York

1997 **Singular Impressions: The Monotype in America**, National Museum of American Art, Smithsonian Institution, Washington, D.C.

MUSEUM COLLECTIONS

Allen Memorial Art Museum, Oberlin College, Oberlin, Ohio

Arkansas Arts Center, Little Rock

The Art Institute of Chicago

Ball State College, Muncie, Indiana

Art Galleries, California State University, Northridge

Denver Art Museum

The Grunwald Center of the Graphic Arts, University of California, Los Angeles

Nora Eccles Harrison Museum of Art, Utah State University, Logan

Hirshhorn Museum and Sculpture Garden, Smithsonian Institution, Washington, D.C.

Illinois State Museum, Springfield

Long Beach Museum of Art, California

Los Angeles County Museum of Art

Memorial Art Gallery of the University of Rochester, New York

The Metropolitan Museum of Art, New York

Museum of Contemporary Art, Chicago

The Museum of Modern Art, New York

National Gallery of Art, Washington, D.C.

Pasadena Art Museum, California

Philbrook Art Center, Tulsa, Oklahoma

Portland Art Museum, Oregon

Santa Barbara Museum of Art, California

State University of Iowa, Iowa City

Tupperware Art Museum, Orlando, Florida

University of California, Santa Cruz

University of Oregon, Eugene

Whitney Museum of American Art, New York

Wichita Art Museum, Kansas

Ruth Chandler Williamson Gallery, Scripps College, Claremont, California

World Heritage Museum, University of Illinois at Urbana-Champaign

CORPORATE COLLECTIONS

Abbott Laboratories, North Chicago, Illinois

ABC Television, New York

ARAMARK, Philadelphia

Atlantic Richfield (ARCO), Los Angeles

BankAmerica Corporation (formerly Security Pacific Collection), San Francisco

The Chou Trust and Banking Company, Ltd., New York

City of Los Angeles

City of Santa Monica, California

Four Seasons Hotel, corporate offices, Alberta, Canada

Gardner, Carton, Douglas, Chicago

International Minerals and Chemical Corporation, Northbrook, Illinois

Kemper National Insurance Companies, Long Grove, Illinois

MBNA America, Newark, Delaware

MBNA America, New York

Memphis Cancer Center, Tennessee

Price, Raffel, Browne, Soil and Rowe, Los Angeles

Shearson American Express, Los Angeles

Stephens, Inc., Little Rock, Arkansas

Tudor/Bellweather, Chicago

BIBLIOGRAPHY

BOOKS AND CATALOGUES

Adrian, Dennis. **Visions: Painting and Sculpture: Distinguished Alumni, 1945 to the Present: The School of The Art Institute of Chicago.** Exh. cat. Chicago: The Art Institute of Chicago, 1976.

Apuleo, Vito. **Aspetti della pittura americana oggi.** Exh. cat. Rome: Penelope Galleria d'Arte Contemporanea, 1964.

Askin, Walter. **The Janus Impulse.** Exh. cat. Los Angeles: California State College, 1965.

Ball, Maudette W. **Southern California Artists, 1940–1980.** Exh. cat. Laguna Beach, Calif.: Laguna Beach Museum of Art, 1981.

Barton, Bruce Waller, and April Kingsley. **Alternative Realities in Contemporary American Painting.** Exh. cat. Minneapolis: University of Minnesota, 1981.

Bloch, Maurice. **Joyce Treiman: Friends and Strangers.** Exh. cat. Los Angeles: Fisher Gallery, 1988.

______. **Joyce Treiman: The Model in the Studio.** Exh. cat. Rancho Palos Verdes, Calif.: Palos Verdes Art Center, 1977.

Bosch, Gulnar K. **First Annual Exhibition of Lithography.** Exh. brochure. Tallahassee: Florida State University, 1964.

Brewer, Donald J. **Some Aspects of California Painting and Sculpture.** Exh. cat. La Jolla, Calif.: La Jolla Museum of Art, 1965.

Brodsky, Judith K. **Contemporary Issues: Works on Paper by Women.** Exh. cat. Los Angeles: The Women's Building, 1977.

Byrnes, James B. **Contemporary Painting in the United States.** Exh. cat. Los Angeles: Los Angeles County Museum of Art, 1951.

Chiego, William J. **Master Prints from the Gilkey Collection.** Exh. cat. Portland, Oreg.: Portland Art Museum, 1980.

Clapp, Verner W. **Twelfth National Exhibition of Prints.** Exh. cat. Washington, D.C.: Library of Congress, 1954.

Collins, J. L. **Women Artists in America.** Chattanooga: University of Tennessee, 1973.

Colt, Thomas L., Jr. **Contemporary American Paintings.** Exh. cat. Richmond: Virginia Museum of Fine Arts, 1948.

Culler, George D. **Far West Regional Exhibition of Art across America.** Exh. cat. San Francisco: San Francisco Museum of Art, 1965.

Cummings, Paul. **Twentieth-Century American Drawings: The Figure in Context.** Exh. cat. Baltimore: Schneidereith and Sons, 1984.

Douke, Daniel. **Black-and-White Drawings from the David Nellis Collection.** Exh. cat. Los Angeles: California State University, 1985.

Dreibank, Laurence. **Decade: Los Angeles Painting in the Seventies.** Exh. cat. Pasadena, Calif.: Art Center College of Design, 1981.

Farmer, Jane M. **New American Monotypes.** Exh. cat. Washington, D.C.: Smithsonian Institution Press, 1978.

______. **Selected Monotypes.** Exh. cat. Palo Alto, Calif.: Smith Andersen Gallery, 1984.

Fishko, Bella. Introduction to **New York World's Fair Catalog.** New York: Forum Gallery, 1965.

Fraser, Joseph T., Jr. **The One-Hundred-Fifty-third Annual Exhibition of American Painting and Sculpture.** Exh. cat. Philadelphia: Pennsylvania Academy of the Fine Arts, 1958.

Fugitt, Patricia J. **Coastal Currents: A California/New York Exhibition.** Exh. cat. South Texas Art Mobile, 1981.

Genauer, Emily. **A Corporation Collects.** Exh. cat. New York: American Federation of Arts, 1959.

Gilkey, Gordon W. **Echoes: Recent Pastel Drawings.** Exh. brochure. New York: Schmidt Bingham Gallery, 1992.

Goodrich, Lloyd. **Young America 1957.** Exh. cat. New York: Whitney Museum of American Art, 1957.

Heyman, Therese. **Her Story: Narrative Art by Contemporary California Artists.** Exh. cat. Oakland, Calif.: The Oakland Museum, 1991.

Ianco-Starrels, Josine. **Artists' Artists.** Exh. cat. Long Beach, Calif.: Long Beach Museum of Art, 1990.

______. **Impetus: The Creative Process.** Los Angeles: Los Angeles Municipal Art Gallery, 1975.

______. **Kindred Spirits.** Exh. cat. Los Angeles: Los Angeles Municipal Art Gallery, 1986.

______. **Relationships.** Exh. cat. Long Beach, Calif.: Long Beach Museum of Art, 1987.

______. **Selections from the Collection of Security Pacific National Bank.** Los Angeles: Los Angeles Municipal Art Gallery, 1982.

Joachim, Harold, and Esther Sparks. **Drawings by Joyce Treiman.** Exh. cat. Chicago: The Art Institute of Chicago, 1979.

Kemper, James S., and Joan E. Robertson. **Kemper Art Collection.** Long Grove, Ill.: Kemper Art Collection, 1978.

Klausner, Betty. **Contemporary Monotypes.** Exh. cat. Santa Barbara, Calif.: Santa Barbara Museum of Art, 1976.

Kuang-Nan, Huang. **Contemporary Southern California Art.** Exh. cat. Taipei, Taiwan: Taipei Fine Arts Museum, 1987.

Kuh, Katherine. **One Hundred Artists One Hundred Years.** Exh. cat. Chicago: The Art Institute of Chicago, 1980.

Leavitt, Thomas W., Jr. **Pasadena Third Biennial National Print Exhibition.** Exh. cat. Pasadena, Calif.: Pasadena Art Museum, 1962.

Leslie, Alfred. **National Exhibition of Small Paintings.** Exh. brochure. Purdue, Ind.: Purdue University, 1970.

Lieberman, William S. **Tamarind: Homage to Lithography.** Exh. cat. New York: The Museum of Modern Art, 1969.

Longman, Lester D., and Maurice Bloch. **Joyce Treiman Retrospective, 1947–1977.** Exh. cat. Los Angeles: Hennesey and Ingalls, 1978.

Marrow, Marva. **Inside the Los Angeles Artist.** Salt Lake City: Gibbs M. Smith, 1988.

McCullagh, Suzanne Folds. **Joyce Treiman: Drawings, Monotypes, and Prints, 1962–1989.** Winnetka, Ill.: John Almquist Gallery, 1993.

Miller, Richard McDermott. **National Academy of Design, One-Hundred-Sixty-first Annual Exhibition.** Exh. cat. New York: National Academy of Design, 1986.

______. **National Academy of Design, One-Hundred-Sixty-sixth Annual Exhibition.** Exh. cat. New York: National Academy of Design, 1991.

Morrisey, Ann. **Portraits in Miniature.** Exh. cat. Los Angeles: University of Southern California, 1981.

Neal, Reginald. **Second Old Northwest Territory Art Exhibition.** Exh. cat. Springfield: Illinois State Museum, 1948.

Opitz, Glenn B. **Mantle Fielding's Dictionary of American Painters, Sculptors, and Engravers.** Poughkeepsie, N.Y.: Apollo, 1986.

Plagens, Peter. **Sunshine Muse: Contemporary Art on the West Coast.** New York: Praeger, 1974.

Pomeroy, Jim. **Invitational Annual.** Exh. cat. San Francisco: San Francisco Art Institute, 1977.

Pomeroy, Ralph. **Joyce Treiman.** Exh. brochure. New York: Forum Gallery, 1981.

Rich, Daniel Catton. **Joyce Treiman and Dante.** Exh. brochure. Chicago: Charles Feingarten Gallery, 1955.

Robinson, Susan. **Unique Impressions: The Monotype and Beyond.** Exh. cat. Los Angeles: Loyola Marymount University, 1982.

Robinson, Wahneta T. **American Portraits—Old and New.** Exh. cat. Long Beach, Calif.: Long Beach Museum of Art, 1971.

Rubinstein, Charlotte. **American Women Artists.** New York: Avon, 1982.

Sadik, Marvin, and Harold Francis Pfister. **American Portrait Drawings.** Exh. cat. Washington, D.C.: Smithsonian Institution Press, 1980.

Schwartz, Barry. **The New Humanism.** New York: Praeger, 1974.

Shipley, James R., and Allen S. Weller. **Contemporary American Painting and Sculpture, 1948–1974.** Exh. cat. Urbana: University of Illinois Press, 1974.

Sims, Lowery Stokes. **The Figure in Twentieth-Century Art.** Exh. cat. New York: American Federation of Arts, 1984.

Sparks, Esther. **Joyce Treiman Drawings.** Exh. cat. Chicago: Fairweather Hardin Gallery, 1984.

Steen, Ronald E. **Déjà Vu: Masterpieces Updated.** Exh. cat. Downey, Calif.: Downey Museum of Art, 1978.

Story, Lewis Wingfield. **The Seventieth Western Annual.** Exh. cat. Denver: Denver Art Museum, 1964.

Strauber, Susan. **A View of Her Own: Images of Women by Women Artists.** Exh. cat. Grinnell, Iowa: Grinnell College, 1987.

Sweet, Frederick A. **The Sixty-second American Exhibition, Paintings, Sculpture.** Exh. cat. Chicago: The Art Institute of Chicago, 1957.

Urrutia, Lawrence. **Continuing Surrealism.** Exh. cat. La Jolla, Calif.: La Jolla Museum of Art, 1971.

Washburn, Gordon Bailey. **1955 Pittsburgh International Exhibition of Contemporary Art.** Exh. cat. Pittsburgh: Carnegie Institute, 1955.

Wayne, June. **New Dimensions in Lithography.** Exh. cat. Los Angeles: University of Southern California, 1962.

Weller, Allen S. **Contemporary American Painting and Sculpture.** Exh. cat. Urbana: University of Illinois Press, 1956.

______. **Contemporary American Painting and Sculpture.** Exh. cat. Urbana: University of Illinois Press, 1965.

______. **Contemporary American Painting and Sculpture: The Measure of Modern Art.** Exh. cat. Urbana: University of Illinois Press, 1961.

______. **Contemporary American Painting and Sculpture: Subject Matter in Contemporary Art.** Exh. cat. Urbana: University of Illinois Press, 1950.

______. **Contemporary American Painting and Sculpture: Subject, Object and Content.** Exh. cat. Urbana: University of Illinois Press, 1963.

______. **Contemporary American Painting and Sculpture: Truth and Vision in Contemporary Art.** Exh. cat. Urbana: University of Illinois Press, 1952.

______. **Contemporary American Painting and Sculpture: What Are We Looking For?** Exh. cat. Urbana: University of Illinois Press, 1957.

______. **Contemporary American Painting and Sculpture: What the Painter Thinks.** Exh. cat. Urbana: University of Illinois Press, 1951.

______. **Joyce Treiman.** Exh. cat. New York: Forum Gallery, 1963.

Weller, W. A. **Selections from the Collection of Rachel and Allen Weller.** Exh. cat. Urbana: University of Illinois Press, 1975.

White, Lawrence Grant. **One-Hundred-Twenty-sixth Annual Exhibition.** Exh. cat. New York: National Academy of Design, 1951.

Wight, Frederick S. **Tamarind and the Art of the Lithograph.** Exh. cat. Los Angeles: University of California, 1962.

Wilson, William. **Joyce Treiman: Paintings, 1961–1972.** Exh. cat. La Jolla, Calif.: La Jolla Museum of Contemporary Art, 1972.

ARTICLES AND REVIEWS

Adlow, Dorothy. "Denver's Annual Exhibition." **Christian Science Monitor,** July 24, 1948, p. 4.

______. "'Young America' Show." **Christian Science Monitor,** October 26, 1957, p. 10.

Alf, Martha. "Big Prints, Little Paintings." **Artweek** 7, no. 26 (July 31, 1976): 7.

______. "The Psychological World of Joyce Treiman." **Artweek** 7, no. 10 (March 6, 1976): 6–7.

Allen, Jane, and Derek Guthrie. "Identity: In the Nineteenth Century and in the Eye of a Camera." **Chicago Tribune,** February 4, 1973, p. 13.

Allman, Paul. "Art Who? A Great Artist and Wit." (Los Angeles) **Weekend Vistas,** March 24, 1978, p. 6.

Anderson, Isabel. "Expressionism: Joyce Treiman." **Images & Issues** (March–April 1984): 26.

Armstrong, Lois. "Exhibition in Los Angeles." **Art News** 68 (December 1969): 73.

"Art of the State: California." **New West Magazine** 6, no. 1 (January 1981): 54.

"Art: Spreading Business." **Time,** January 26, 1959, p. 93.

"Art: The Customary Is Bizarre." **San Diego Union,** December 10, 1972.

Artner, Alan G. "Art Notes." **Chicago Tribune,** May 30, 1991, p. 11A.

______. "A Double Loss: Joyce Treiman Dies during Exhibit at Soon-to-Close Gallery." **Chicago Tribune,** June 6, 1991, p. 13G.

______. "Joyce Treiman." **Chicago Tribune,** October 16, 1986, p. 9E.

Ashton, Dore. "Art: Oskar Moll Exhibited." **New York Times,** March 4, 1960, p. 20.

Aubin, B. "Drawings: Art Institute of Chicago Exhibition." **Visual Dialog,** no. 3 (April 1979): 18–19.

Barry, Edward. "If You Want to See Today's Art, This Exhibit Has It!" **Chicago Tribune,** May 24, 1964, sec. 5, p. 2.

______. "Much of Value Found in Art of Chicagoans." **Chicago Tribune,** May 30, 1952, part 2, p. 2.

Berges, Marshall. "Joyce and Kenneth Treiman." **Los Angeles Times,** June 10, 1979, Home sec., pp. 46–49.

Blum, June. "Palihi, PTA Offers Glimpses of 'How They Live.'" (Pacific Palisades, Calif.) **Palisadian-Post,** March 13, 1967.

Breuning, Margaret. "National Academy Stages One Hundred Twenty-sixth Annual Exhibition." **Art Digest** 25, no. 13 (April 1, 1951): 7.

Brian, Doris. "Americans under Thirty-six: Is the Middle of the Road on the Way to the Future?" **Art Digest** (April 1, 1959): 8.

Bridaham, Lester. "Burbank Youngsters Take Top Honors in Second Northwest Territory Annual." **Art Digest** 22, no. 19 (August 1, 1948): 9.

______. "Third Old Northwest Territory Annual." **Art Digest** 23, no. 9 (August 1, 1949): 6.

Brown, Betty. "Autobiographical Imagery in the Art of L.A. Women," pp. 123–24, and "Leading Ladies," pp. 164–66. In **Yesterday and Tomorrow: California Women Artists,** edited by Sylvia Moore. New York: Midmarch Arts Press, 1989.

______. "Believing in the Human Spirit." **Artweek** 14, no. 43 (December 17, 1983): 6.

Bulliet, C. J. "Art in Chicago: Primitives and Prizewinners." **Art Digest** 25, no. 2 (October 15, 1950): 25.

______. "Chicago Artists Miss Their Own Mark in Their 1950 Annual." **Art Digest** (June 1, 1959): 12.

______. "Prize Winners." **Chicago Daily News,** June 2, 1951, Home & Life sec., p. 2.

______. "Student Takes Highest Chicago Honors." **Art Digest** (June 1, 1951): 12.

Bulmer, Marge. "Critic's Choice: Kindred Spirits." (Los Angeles) **Reader,** May 9, 1986, sec. 2.

Burg, Copeland. "Best of Modern Art in Women's Exhibit." **Chicago Herald-American**, March 29, 1953.

______. "U of I Annual Art Festival to Open Sunday at Urbana." **Chicago Herald-American**, February 25, 1951, p. 2.

Burkhart, Dorothy. "Joyce Treiman Puts Herself into Her Work." **San Jose** (Calif.) **Mercury News**, October 7, 1982, p. 2d.

Burrows, Carlyle. "Many Exhibitions around New York of Established Artists and Newcomers." **New York Herald Tribune**, November 12, 1950, sec. 5, p. 10.

Canaday, John. "Art: New Talent in Printmaking Show." **New York Times**, May 22, 1971, p. 27.

______. "Whitney Again: The Annual Shows Regulars along with Twenty-two Newcomers." **New York Times**, December 17, 1961, sec. 2, p. 21.

"Cantos and California: Paintings Inspired by Dante's Divine Comedy at the Charles Feingarten Gallery, Chicago." **Art News** 54 (April 1955): 15.

Chattopadhyay, Collette. "Representations." **Artweek** 23 (March 12, 1992): 13.

______. "Three Perspectives on Drawing and Paper." **Artweek** 26 (October 1995): 16–17.

"Chicago Notes." **Women Artists News**, Winter 1985, p. 28.

"Concerts and Canvases at Ravinia." **Chicago Tribune Magazine**, June 14, 1964, p. 42.

Curtis, Cathy. "Art Notes: 'Paint-In' to Protest Canyon Development." **Los Angeles Times**, October 21, 1989, Home sec., p. 3.

______. "A Little Show on the Draw." **Los Angeles Times**, April 16, 1996, p. F2.

______. "Tasty Tape; at 'Choice Encounter,' the Videos Steal the Show." **Los Angeles Times**, December 31, 1992, p. 4.

Danieli, Fidel A. "Figurative." **Artforum** 11, no. 12 (Summer 1964): 53.

Daniels, Mary. "Four-Legged Art Form Gets a Gallery Showing." **Chicago Tribune**, June 16, 1985, Home sec., p. 8.

Davenport, Seoniadh. "Obituary." **Art News** 90 (November 1991): 31.

Davis, Charles E., Jr. "Joyce Treiman: Art to Make You Think." **Los Angeles Times**, December 30, 1965, part 4, p. 1.

"Denver Annual." **Art Digest** 22, no. 20 (September 15, 1948): 34.

Devree, Howard. "Art: Talent under Thirty-five." **New York Times**, February 27, 1957, p. 24.

______. "Group Exhibitions of Work by Artists European and American." **New York Times**, September 19, 1954, p. 12.

______. "A Talent Forecast: Thirty Young Artists in a New Survey." **New York Times**, March 3, 1957, p. 16.

______. "Whitney Round-Up." **New York Times**, November 23, 1958, p. 13.

"'Divine Comedy' Inspires Winnetka Artist." **Winnetka** (Ill.) **Talk**, August 25, 1955.

Donohue, Marlena. "The Galleries: Santa Monica." **Los Angeles Times**, July 31, 1987, Home sec., p. 21.

______. "The Galleries: Santa Monica." **Los Angeles Times**, November 24, 1989, Home sec., p. 19.

"Downtown Gallery Show." **New York Times**, September 26, 1954, p. 12.

Dubin, Zan. "Art News: 'Silent-Bid Auction' to Benefit AIDS Victims." **Los Angeles Times**, September 6, 1987, p. 96.

______. "Art News: Winogrand Looks at the U.S.A." **Los Angeles Times**, June 4, 1989, Calendar sec., p. 84.

______. "Eyeing the Gallery Scene: The Looking Is Free—and Often Wall-to-Wall Stimulating." **Los Angeles Times**, April 4, 1987, p. 1.

______. "'Relationships': Four Artists as People Watchers." **Los Angeles Times**, May 6, 1987, Calendar sec., p. 1.

Duemling, Hertha Stein. "Winner of Chicago's Annual Exhibit Displays Wide Range." (Chicago) **News-Sentinel**, November 12, 1953, p. 15.

Dunham, Judith. "Seventy-five Years of California Art." **Artweek** 7, no. 31 (September 18, 1976): 1.

"Exhibition at Forum Gallery." **Art News** 61 (September 1962): 13.

"Exhibition at Forum Gallery." **Art News** 65 (December 1966): 59.

"Exhibition at Hewitt Gallery." **Art News** 49 (November 1950): 68.

"Exhibition at Hewitt Gallery." **Art Digest** 25, no. 4 (November 15, 1950): 21.

"Exhibition at Nelson Gallery, Chicago." **Art News** 52 (March 1953): 45.

"Exhibition at Willard Gallery." **Arts** 34 (March 1960): 63.

"Exhibition at Willard Gallery." **Art News** 59 (April 1960): 57.

Faison, S. Lane, Jr. "Joyce Treiman." **Nation**, December 31, 1955, p. 33.

"The Fine California Art: A Wonderful Local Exhibit." **Berkeley Gazette**, January 27, 1968, p. 16.

Folkart, Burt A. "Joyce Treiman: Eclectic Painter and Sculptor." **Los Angeles Times**, June 4, 1991, p. 26.

"Forum Gallery Exhibition." **Art News** 70 (Summer 1971): 62.

"Four North Artists Display Works at U of I Show." **Chicago Tribune**, March 6, 1957.

Friedlander, Alberta R. "Three Artists—Three Unique Styles." **Chicago Tribune**, February 23, 1964, sec. 5, p. 2.

Geer, Susan. "Jorge Pardo Gets Honest 'Bout Hype." **Los Angeles Times**, August 2, 1991, sec. F, p. 18.

______. "Moses Experiences Emotional Force." **Los Angeles Times**, July 4, 1991, Home sec., p. 4.

Genauer, Emily. "Art: Viewing 'Young America.'" **New York Herald Tribune**, March 3, 1957, p. 10.

Goodman, Calvin. "Monotype: A Singular Form." **American Artist** 45 (January 1981): 58.

Gould, Charles. "Gordon Gilkey and His Art: How He Collected It." **Northwest**, December 3, 1978, pp. 4–9.

Gregory, Jane. "Joyce Treiman: Hewitt Exhibition." **Art News** 49 (November 1950): 68.

______. "Treiman Brings Her 'Journal' to Chicago." **Chicago Sun-Times**, May 30, 1982, p. 10.

Hagsberg, Marilyn. "Treiman's Disturbing Narratives." **Artweek** 3, no. 42 (December 9, 1972): 1.

Hale, David. "Art in Review." **Fresno (Calif.) Bee**, October 16, 1994, p. 13.

Hammond, Pamela. "Joyce Treiman." **Art News** 91 (April 1992): 130.

Hancock, Marianne. "Review: Forum Gallery, New York Exhibition." **Arts Magazine** 45 (Summer 1971): 57–58.

Haydon, Harold. "Art: The Deftly Controlled Style of Joyce Treiman." **Chicago Sun-Times**, February 4, 1973, sec. 3, p. 12.

______. "Galleries." **Chicago Sun-Times**, May 28, 1982, p. 68.

______. "Review: Joyce Treiman." **Chicago Sun-Times**, February 16, 1964, sec. 3, p. 3.

Hazlitt, Gordon J. "Do California Artists Have More Fun?" **Art News** 77 (February 1978): 64.

Hemmerdinger, William. "'Joyce Treiman' Tortue Show." **ArtScene**, December 1983, p. 9.

Hentoff, Nat. "Whom Are We Talking To? Certainly Not to Artists." **Humanist Alternative** 10, no. 1 (Spring–Summer 1973): 84.

Holland, Frank. "Big Exhibit Marks Closing of North Side Gallery." **Chicago Sun-Times**, August 22, 1954, sec. 2, p. 6.

______. "Brush, Camera Make Fine Show." **Chicago Sun-Times**, July 9, 1950, p. 17.

______. "Chicago Artists Win Seven of Twelve Awards at Illinois State Fair." **Chicago Sun-Times**, August 15, 1948, sec. 2, p. 5.

______. "Chicagoans Exhibit Ranges from Abstract to Realism." **Chicago Sun-Times**, January 31, 1954, sec. 2, p. 6.

______. "Chicago Exhibits a Cross Section." **Chicago Sun-Times**, June 4, 1950, p. 17.

______."Conservative Show at Chicago Galleries." **Chicago Sun-Times**, January 27, 1952, sec. 2, p.10.

______. "Contemporary Art Show Best to Date." **Chicago Sun-Times**, April 29, 1951, sec. 2, p. 19.

______. "Contemporary Show Is Interesting." **Chicago Sun-Times**, June 21, 1953, Features sec., p. 8.

______. "Fifty-five Thousand See Institute Exhibit of Religious Masterpieces." **Chicago Sun-Times**, September 5, 1954, p. 5.

______. "Magnificent Mile Show a Success." **Chicago Sun-Times**, May 31, 1953, sec. 2, p. 8.

______. "Palmer House Showing Superb." **Chicago Sun-Times**, August 5, 1951, sec. 2, p. 16.

______. "Three South Side Shows Display Interesting Works." **Chicago Sun-Times**, November 25, 1945, p. 34.

______. "Two Chicago Women Stage Outstanding Solo Shows." **Chicago Sun-Times**, April 6, 1958, sec. 3.

______. "Woelffer, Weiner Win Top Awards at Institute 'Best Chicago Art Show.'" **Chicago Sun-Times**, 1949.

Howell, Betje. "Grand Manner Portraits." **Los Angeles Herald Examiner**, August 29, 1971, p. D8.

______. "Imagery, Fantasy in Joyce Treiman's Show at Tortue." (Santa Monica, Calif.) **Evening Outlook**, December 1, 1979, p. 6D.

______. "Joyce Treiman: Figurative Painter." **Art Forum Newsletter** 7, no. 1 (September–October 1987): 4.

______. "Painted Riddles Give Challenge." **Los Angeles Herald Examiner**, February 22, 1976.

______. "Treiman: Ambiguity Is Her Art Trademark." (Santa Monica, Calif.) **Evening Outlook**, September 19, 1981, p. 6d.

______. "Treiman: Artistic Insight into Human Personality." **Los Angeles Herald Examiner**, December 5, 1976.

Hutchinson, Louise. "A Timid Soul's Ego Gets Badly Bruised by Prize Art Works." **Chicago Art Tribune**, December 6, 1959, p. 15.

Ianco-Starrels, Josine. "Art News: A Show of Just Plain Folks." **Los Angeles Times**, March 16, 1986, p. 86.

______. "Art News: Cameron Photography Leads Three Fall Shows." **Los Angeles Times**, August 31, 1986, p. 80.

______. "Art News: Drawings by Painters Due." **Los Angeles Times**, January 17, 1982, p. 9.

______. "Art News: Mary Jane Jacob Named Chief Curator of MOCA." **Los Angeles Times**, October 19, 1986, p. 89.

______. "Art News: Robert Morris Works Focus on Environment." **Los Angeles Times**, April 27, 1986, Calendar sec., p. 95.

______. "Joyce Treiman." **Arts Magazine** 55, no. 7 (March 1981): 20.

______. "Joyce Treiman in Conversation with Josine Starrels." **Visual Dialog** 3, no. 2 (Winter 1977–78): 4.

"Illinois Annual Surveys State of Nation's Art for Midwest." **Art Digest** 25, no. 12 (March 15, 1951): 7.

Ives, Dorothy. "Contemporary Figurative Realism at Its Best." **Chicago Post-Tribune**, February 9, 1973.

Jacobs, Jody. "Fashion Show to Benefit Tracy Clinic." **Los Angeles Times**, May 25, 1982, p. 4.

Jennings, Bunny. "Joyce Treiman Exhibit." **Santa Barbara** (Calif.) **Chronicles** (April 1980): 14.

Jennings, Jan. "Treiman Exhibit Is Readied." **San Diego** (Calif.) **Evening Tribune**, November 17, 1972.

Johnson, Barry. "Sweet Passages and Passions." **Sunday** (Portland) **Oregonian**, July 17, 1988, p. C1.

"Joyce Treiman Art on Display Feb. 5–29." **Chicago Tribune**, February 3, 1964, sec. 2, p. 8.

"Joyce Treiman: Friends and Strangers." **Drawing** (November–December 1988): 89.

"Joyce Treiman: Friends and Strangers Review." **Front Row** (Summer 1988): 50.

Kandel, Susan. "'Mentors' Champions Twelve Local Women in Art." **Los Angeles Times**, February 23, 1995, p. 1.

Kapitanoff, Nancy. "Retrospective Hand Picks Positive Images of Women in Art." **Los Angeles Times**, July 19, 1992, p. 84.

Kind, Joshua. "Ravinia's Paintings and Sculpture Rate Less than a Rave from Critic." **Chicago Tribune**, June 28, 1964, sec. 5, p. 2.

Kozloff, Max. "Faith amid Violence: Show Gives Disquieting View of Modern Man." **Chicago Maroon**, January 11, 1957, p. 11.

Krasner, Belle. "Expressionism, Abstraction, Surrealism Predominate at the Whitney." **Art Digest** 25, no. 4 (November 15, 1950): 13.

Kurcfeld, Michael. "Making Faces." **California Magazine** 8, no. 4 (April 1983): 100.

K. L. " Forum Gallery Show." **Art News** 65 (December 1966): 59.

Langsner, Jules. "Poet as Hero at the Landau Gallery." **Art News** 60 (Summer 1961): 46.

Loper, Mary Lou. "On View." **Los Angeles Times**, January 17, 1988, p. 6.

Luban, Frances. "Joyce Treiman: Painting from Within." **American Artist** 39 (September 1975): 44–49.

Marks, Ben. "Knowing Oneself." **Artweek** 20 (November 30, 1989): 11–12.

Martin, Fred. "Point of View: End of Decade I." **Artweek** 10, no. 33 (October 13, 1979): 3.

McKenna, Kristine. "Artists' Artists a Surprise Package at Long Beach Museum." **Los Angeles Times**, February 16, 1990, Home sec., p. 28.

"Memorial to Be Held for Joyce Treiman." **Los Angeles Times**, June 26, 1991, p. 3.

"Modern Artist Who Defied Modernism." **Oakland (Calif.) Tribune**, April 2, 1978.

Muchnic, Suzanne. "Architecture and British to Invade in 1988." **Los Angeles Times**, January 3, 1988, Calendar sec., p. 70.

______. "The Art Galleries: Santa Monica." **Los Angeles Times**, January 17, 1986, Calendar sec., p. 6.

______. "Art Review: Exploring Emotional Connections in 'Spirits.'" **Los Angeles Times**, May 5, 1986, Calendar sec., p. 1.

______. "Art Review: The Great Divide between Two Shows." **Los Angeles Times**, March 26, 1986, Calendar sec., p. 1.

______. "Art Review: The Variegated Visions in Watercolor." **Los Angeles Times**, October 8, 1988, Calendar sec., p. 1.

______. "Book Review: The L.A. Art Scene Gets the Brush-off—and Its Due." **Los Angeles Times**, January 1, 1987, Calendar sec., p. 10.

______. "City Spirit: N.Y. Comes to Loyola." **Los Angeles Times**, March 10, 1986, Calendar sec., p. 1.

______. "Exploring Emotional Connection in Spirits." **Los Angeles Times**, May 5, 1986, Calendar sec., p. 1.

______. "An Identity Issue in Women's Images." **Los Angeles Times**, October 5, 1986, Calendar sec., p. 5.

______. "Joyce Treiman Ventures through Another Terrain with Landscapes." **Los Angeles Times**, January 3, 1985, p. 1.

______. "A Network of Artists in L.A." **Los Angeles Times**, February 14, 1985, Calendar sec., p. 1.

______. "These Artists' Figurative Concerns." **Los Angeles Times**, January 21, 1978, p. 7.

______. "Two Exhibits Hum along with Chorus." **Los Angeles Times**, August 16, 1981, Calendar sec., p. 97.

Normile, James. "Contemporary Portraiture." **Architectural Digest** 32, no. 1 (July–August 1975): 64.

Olten, Carol. "Joyce Treiman, Seven San Diegans in La Jolla Shows." **San Diego** (Calif.) **Union**, November 11, 1972.

Owyans, Judy. "The Art Scene." (Santa Monica, Calif.) **Evening Outlook**, September 12, 1970.

S. P. "New Modes in Art Mark Local Shows." **New York Times**, November 10, 1950, p. 25.

Pousette-Dart, Nathaniel, ed. "American Painting Today." In **A Cross-Section of Our Contemporary Art**. New York: Hastings House Publishing, 1956.

"Prize Winners." **Winnetka** (Ill.) **Talk**, November 12, 1953, p. 42.

"Recalling the Year's Lost Artists." **Chicago Tribune**, December 29, 1991, p. 20.

"Review." **Chicago Sun-Times**, May 7, 1950, sec. 2, p. 19.

"Review." **Pictures on Exhibit** (April 1975): 13.

Reynolds, Judith. "MAG and Visual Studies Blaze in Human Light." (Rochester, N.Y.) **City Newspaper**, May 26, 1988, p. 9.

Rickey, Carrie. "Joyce Treiman's Art Show." **La Jolla** (Calif.) **Light**, December 21, 1972.

Ridgeley, Frances S. "Art Gallery in Summer." (Springfield, Ill.) **Living Museum** 11, no. 3 (July 1949): 21.

Rivas, Paul. "The Palette." **Beverly Hills** (Calif.) **Courier**, September 3, 1965, p. 7.

______. "Review: Felix Landau." **Beverly Hills** (Calif.) **Courier**, August 21, 1964, p. 7.

Robb, Marilyn. "This Summer in Chicago." **Art News** 50 (Summer 1951): 40.

Rosenthal, A. "New Directions for Joyce Treiman: Tortue Gallery Exhibition." **Artweek** 10, no. 42 (December 15, 1979): 2.

Rubin, David S. "Seven Artists Who Are Women." **Visual Arts Magazine** (Summer 1984): 26.

Rush, David. "Review: Contemporary Monotypes by Eight Artists." **Artweek** 7, no. 35 (October 16, 1976): 6.

"Salute to the Singular." **Time**, February 28, 1964, pp. 72–73.

Schipper, Merle. "Independent Artist Treiman Stays in Touch with Times." (Los Angeles) **Westwood Villager** 1, no. 14 (September 18, 1981): 6.

Schoen, Juliet P. "Paintings Mirror Treiman's Image." (Pacific Palisades, Calif.) **Palisadian-Post**, January 19, 1978, p. 13.

Schulze, Franz. "Contemporary Art Show a Mixture of Many Styles." **Chicago Daily News Panorama**, May 16, 1964, p. 13.

______. "The Human Figure According to Four Artists." **Chicago Daily News Panorama**, February 22, 1964, p. 13.

______. "Straightforward Portraits." **Chicago Daily News**, April 21, 1962.

______. "Two Bright Spots in a Dull Ravinia Art Exhibition." **Chicago Daily News**, June 28, 1964.

Schwartz, Barry. "Humanism in Modern Art." **Humanist** (July–August 1973): 28–31.

Seldis, Henry J. "Art Free-for-All—a Memorable All-City Festival." **Los Angeles Times**, June 28, 1964.

______. "Art: The Creative Process in Words and Pictures." **Los Angeles Times**, November 16, 1975, Calendar sec., p. 70.

______. "Art Walk: A Critical Guide to the Galleries." **Los Angeles Times**, February 10, 1978, p. 10.

______. "Feast of Another Sort." **Los Angeles Times**, February 12, 1961, p. 16.

______. "In the Galleries: 'Poet' a Wordless Wonder." **Los Angeles Times**, April 28, 1961, sec. 11, p. 4.

______. "Joyce Treiman Achieves Blend of Sculpture, Painting." **Los Angeles Times**, August 24, 1964.

______. "The La Jolla Show: A Majority of One." **Los Angeles Times**, November 5, 1961, p. 28.

______. "Making Business at All-City Show." **Los Angeles Times**, July 18, 1966, sec. 4.

______. "Many Mini Things at Lytton Center." **Los Angeles Times**, January 15, 1968, sec. 4, p. 6.

______. "MoMA Show Worth Seeing in Spite of Its Lacunae." **Los Angeles Times**, June 27, 1976, p. 26.

______. "Museum Show Verdict Is No Contest." **Los Angeles Times**, September 24, 1961, p. 22.

______. "New York's Grudging Tribute to Tamarind." **Los Angeles Times**, May 4, 1969, Calendar sec., p. 44.

______. "'Surrealism' a Scintillating Assembly." **Los Angeles Times**, March 14, 1971, p. 62.

______. "A Treiman Tour de Force at La Jolla Museum." **Los Angeles Times**, December 17, 1972, Calendar sec., p. 90.

Seldis, Henry J., and William Wilson. "Art Walk." **Los Angeles Times**, October 10, 1969, sec. 4, p. 9.

______. "Art Walk: La Cienega." **Los Angeles Times**, November 12, 1971, sec. 4, p. 6.

______. "Art Walk: La Cienega." **Los Angeles Times**, November 19, 1971, sec. 4, p. 12.

______. "Art Walk: La Cienega." **Los Angeles Times**, February 15, 1974, sec. 4, p. 12.

______. "Art Walk: La Cienega." **Los Angeles Times**, February 20, 1976, sec. 4, p. 10.

Shere, Charles. "When a Painter Assembles Exhibition, Expect the Unusual." **Oakland** (Calif.) **Tribune**, August 7, 1977, pp. 22–25.

Shopen, Kenneth. "This is Prize-Winning Art." **Chicago Daily News**, November 11, 1953, p. 52.

Smith, Adrienne. "Joyce Treiman: Drawings." **New Art Examiner** (January 1985): 57.

Snow, Shauna. "Art World: The History of Battle Is Mere Putty in His Hands." **Los Angeles Times**, September 2, 1990, p. 76.

Speyer, James A. "Art News from Chicago." **Art News** 55 (April 1956): 18.

Stang, Fred. "Review: Monotypes—Colored Poems Enclosed in Mystery." **Santa Barbara** (Calif.) **News and Review**, October 1, 1976.

Tannenbaum, Barbara. "Painting in Chicago: 1945–1965." In **Chicago: The City and Its Artists, 1945–1978**. Ann Arbor: The University of Michigan Museum of Art, 1978.

"Three Area Artists Win State Fair Exhibition Prizes." **Chicago Sunday Tribune**, August 15, 1948, p. 12N.

Tillim, S. "Exhibition at Forum Gallery." **Art News** 37 (May 1963): 110.

"Times Honors Women of the Year." **Los Angeles Times**, December 14, 1965.

Treiman, Joyce. "Joyce Treiman." In **California Painters: New Work**. San Francisco: Chronicle Books, 1989.

"Treiman Art Wins Rave." (Pacific Palisades, Calif.) **Palisadian-Post**, October 10, 1985, p. 12.

Turner, Nancy Kay. "A Grand Odyssey." **Artweek** 19, no. 6 (February 13, 1988): 6.

"Twenty Treiman Paintings on Display at Gallery." **New York Times**, May 2, 1986, sec. C, p. 25.

Vils, Ursula. "Hailed for Achievement, Times Honors Women of the Year." **Los Angeles Times**, December 14, 1964, part 5, p. 11.

Weigle, Edith. "There Are Readable Books in Modern Art." **Chicago Sunday Tribune**, June 27, 1957, sec. 7, p. 5.

______. "What a Contrast! Squares and People." **Chicago Sunday Tribune**, April 1, 1962, part 5, p. 5.

Weisberg, Ruth. "An Appetite for Life." **Artweek** 16 (February 9, 1985): 7.

______. "Divergent Realities." **Artweek** 12 (October 3, 1981): 16.

______. "Southern California: A Figurative Report." **Artists' Choice Museum Newsletter,** January–February 1981, pp. 4–5.

Weiss, Susan Zelvin. "Arts of Work: Corporate Culture Makes Quite a Showing." **Chicago Tribune,** September 27, 1992, p. 18.

Weller, Allen S. "Chicago." **Art Digest** 27, no. 14 (April 15, 1953): 13.

______. "Chicago: Exhibition of Thirty Large Drawings Draws on Themes from Dante's Inferno at the Feingarten Gallery." **Art Digest** 29 (May 15, 1955): 10.

______. "Coast-to-Coast." **Art Digest** 38 (November 5, 1963): 14.

______. "Six Artists from the Great Lakes States." **Art in America** 43 (February 1955): 39.

Welles, Elenore. "Profile: Joyce Treiman." **ArtScene,** January 1988, p. 13.

"What about Modern Art?" **Where Magazine** (July 8, 1950): 5.

Willis, Thomas. "Art Institute Observes Sesquicentennial Tribute." **Chicago Tribune,** June 19, 1968.

Wilson, William. "Art: Aw-Shucks Funk in a Stew at Long Beach." **Los Angeles Times,** May 28, 1972, p. 50.

______. "The Art Galleries: Santa Monica." **Los Angeles Times,** November 28, 1986, p. 14.

______. "The Blossoming of L.A. Artist in '88." **Los Angeles Times,** January 1, 1989, Calendar sec., p. 72.

______. "A Curator's Declaration of Independence: Josine Ianco-Starrels Works to Give a Unified Vision to the Visual Arts." **Los Angeles Times,** September 2, 1990, Calendar sec., p. 75.

______. "Exhibition of Figure Treatment." **Los Angeles Times,** March 13, 1972, p. 3.

______. "The Galleries: Santa Monica." **Los Angeles Times,** November 25, 1983, sec. 4, p. 2.

______. "The Galleries: Santa Monica." **Los Angeles Times,** January 11, 1985, sec. 4, p. 14.

______. "1979 End of the Year Memorials." **Los Angeles Times,** December 23, 1979, Calendar sec., p. 110.

______. "One Festival That Ought to Be Two." **Los Angeles Times,** June 22, 1973, p. 1.

______. "'One Hundred' Exhibition in LAICA's New Setting." **Los Angeles Times,** March 28, 1977, p. 3.

______. "Opening a Window on the West." **Los Angeles Times,** February 26, 1992, Home sec., p. 1.

______. "Patronage and the Corporate Patriarchy." **Los Angeles Times,** March 20, 1977, p. 70.

______. "'People' Links Up with Real World." **Los Angeles Times,** March 3, 1992, p. 6.

______. "Portrait Show at Museum." **Los Angeles Times,** August 30, 1971, p. 8.

______. "Retrospective of Festival Winners." **Los Angeles Times,** May 5, 1975, p. 14.

______. "Something for Everyone at Barnsdall." **Los Angeles Times,** May 25, 1969, part 4, p. 1.

______. "Treiman Retrospective: Career of a Maverick." **Los Angeles Times,** February 5, 1978, p. 86.

______. "Treiman's Memories of Familiar Faces." **Los Angeles Times,** February 14, 1988, pp. 81–83.

______. "Wide Awake in a Dream World." **Los Angeles Times,** April 26, 1976, sec. 4, p. 1.

______. "Women's Exhibition Nicely Balances Art, Femininity." **Los Angeles Times,** March 18, 1968, part 4, p. 14.

Wolff, Theodore F. "Art Galleries Present Summer Fare for All Tastes." **Christian Science Monitor,** July 7, 1986, p. 27.

______. "Be It Zany, 'Bookish,' or Surprising, It's Art of Interest." **Christian Science Monitor,** March 12, 1981, p. 18.

______. "George Bellows: A World of Passionate Coloration in Black and White." **Christian Science Monitor,** April 22, 1985, p. 25.

______. "Joyce Treiman." **Christian Science Monitor,** March 12, 1981, p. 18.

______. "Many of Today's Best Artists Are Women, but Recognition Lags." **Christian Science Monitor,** December 22, 1986, p. 21.

______. "More than Superb—Alive." **Christian Science Monitor,** September 5, 1975, p. 38.

______. "Profound or Provincial, American Realism Searches for Meaning." **Christian Science Monitor,** December 12, 1985, p. 22.

______. "Swimming against the Contemporary Tide." **Christian Science Monitor,** May 31, 1988, p. 21.

______. "Those Summer Art Shows." **Christian Science Monitor,** June 29, 1987, p. 25.

______. "Treiman's Art—Engagingly Enigmatic." **Christian Science Monitor,** April 28, 1986, p. 27.

______. "Twentieth-Century American Drawings." **Christian Science Monitor,** April 22, 1985, p. 26.

______. "Undoing Stereotypes." **Christian Science Monitor,** June 3, 1987, p. 30.

______. "Westward-Ho! The Art Capital of America." **Christian Science Monitor,** December 14, 1989, p. 13.

______. "Where Have All the Painterly Painters Gone?" **Christian Science Monitor,** December 21, 1982, p. 18.

______. "Women on the Frontiers of Art." **Christian Science Monitor,** January 11, 1989, p. 16.

"Worcester Elects a U.S. Survey." **Art Digest** 25, no. 9 (February 1, 1951): 15.

Wortz, Melinda. "Art Review." **Los Angeles Times,** March 21, 1977, sec. 4, p. 5.

Wright, Elizabeth J. "A Painter's Painter: Joyce Treiman." **Santa Barbara** (Calif.) **Chronicles,** April 1, 1980, p. 3.

Zimmerer, Kathy. "Joyce Treiman." **Visions Magazine** 2, no. 3 (Summer 1988).

INDEX

Page numbers in **boldface** refer to illustrations.

PHOTOGRAPH CREDITS

Arkansas Art Center: page 34 left

© 1996, The Art Institute of Chicago, All Rights Reserved: page 53

John Berens: page 83

Will Brown: pages 142, 151

Glenn Castellano © National Academy of Design: page 93

Michael Christmas: page 91

Geoffrey Clements, © Whitney Museum of American Art, New York: page 77

Michael Culpepper Studio, Columbus, Georgia: page 148

© Illinois State Museum: page 52

Robert Mates: pages 16, 19

Wayne McCall: page 67

Scott McClaine: pages 54, 125

Jay McNally: pages 26, 27, 111, 141

Memorial Art Gallery of the University of Rochester: pages 116, 117

The Metropolitan Museum of Art, New York: page 143

Cindy Momchilov: page 121

Kevin Montague: page 101

Musée de la Ville de Paris/P. Pierrain: page 45

© The Museum of Modern Art, New York: pages 10, 11

© National Gallery of Art: pages 12, 15

© 1996 Douglas M. Parker Studio, Los Angeles: pages 28, 29, 32, 33, 34 right, 35, 36, 38–40, 42, 49, 55, 59, 60, 62, 69, 70, 73, 75, 78, 80, 81, 85, 88, 92, 95, 98, 104–8, 114, 115, 118–20, 123, 129, 133, 135, 137, 138, 155, 157, 159, 164

© Portland [Oregon] Art Museum: page 63

Adam Reich: pages 100, 126–28, 130–34, 139, 153

Murray Riss: page 161

Lee Stalsworth: page 109

Eric Stephenson © Denver Art Museum: page 51

Carl Thome: page 163

Michael Tropea: pages 23, 25, 30, 61, 65, 87, 110, 113, 145, 149

Thomas P. Vinetz: page 89

John Wilson White: pages 50, 79, 99, 147

Graydon Wood: pages 43, 71, 97, 103, 131

Joe Ziolkowski, © MCA, Chicago: page 57

759.13 TRE
10/98
Duncan, Michael,
Joyce Treiman

WITHDRAWN

LOWER MERION LIBRARY SYSTEM
30043000469704

LUDINGTON PUBLIC LIBRARY
BRYN MAWR & LANCASTER AVES.
BRYN MAWR, PA 19010-3471